ITALIAN POLITICS

The Istituto Cattaneo, founded in 1965, is a private, nonprofit organization. It aims to promote, finance, and conduct research, studies, and other activities that contribute to the knowledge of contemporary Italian society and, especially, of the Italian political system.

ITALIAN POLITICS
The Return of Politics

Edited by

David Hine and Salvatore Vassallo

A Publication of the Istituto Cattaneo

Berghahn Books
New York • Oxford

Italian Politics: A Review, Volume 14

First published in 2000 by
Berghahn Books

Editorial Offices:
604 West 115th Street, New York, NY 10025 USA
3, NewTec Place, Magdalen Road, Oxford OX4 1RE, UK

© 2000 Berghahn Books

A CIP catalog for this book is available from the Library of
Congress and the British Library

ISBN 1-57181-798-0 (hardback)
ISSN 1086-4946

CONTENTS

Party acronyms used in the text

Listed below are the main party acronyms used in this text. The extreme fluidity of the Italian party spectrum in the 1990s makes it difficult to provide a up-to-date list of acronyms. Some labels have been used only in some areas, and for some elections. Some acronyms which have come into widespread use do not accurately capture the official party name. Some parties are referred to by more than one acronym. On occasion two groups have been in dispute over the use of a name.

AN = Alleanza nazionale
CCD = Centro cristiano democratico
CDL = Cristiani democratici per le libertà
CDR = Centro democratico per la repubblica
CDU = Cristiani Democratici Uniti
DC = Democrazia cristiana
DS = Democratici di sinistra
FI = Forza italia
LN = Lega nord
MS-FT = Movimento sociale – fiamma tricolore
MSI = Movimento sociale italiano
PCI = Partito comunista italiano
PDCI = Partito dei comunisti italiani
PDS = Partito democratico della sinistra
PDS-DS = Partito democratico della sinistra – Democratici di sinistra
PLI = Partito liberale italiano
Polo = Polo delle libertà
PPE = Partito popolare europeo

PPI = Partito popolare italiano
PR = Partito radicale
PRI = Partito repubblicano italiano
PS = Partito socialista
PSDI = Partito socialista democratico italiano
PSI = Partito socialista italiano
RI = Rinnovamento italiano
SDI = Socialisti democratici italiani
SI = Socialisti italiani
PPST/SVP = Partito popolare sud tirolese – Südtiroler Volkspartei
UDR = Unione democratica per la Repubblica
UPE = Unione popolare europea
PRC *or* RC = Partito della rifondazione comunista; Rifondazione
    comunista

The Istituto Cattaneo's Internet

http://www.cattaneo.org

At this web address one may visit the Istituto Cattaneo's Internet site. It consists of many pages, two of which deserve special attention:

Archives

In this page the Istituto Cattaneo provides free access to documentary archives regarding various characteristics of the Italian social and political system: a chronology of the main political and social events from 1990; book reviews of studies and empirical research published over the last three years; background data on Italian society; election results; party membership (since 1945); government and institutional posts of the republican era.

Data

Through this web page citizen and the scientific community may access data which reflect the Istituto Cattaneo's statutory pledge to promote empirical knowledge on Italian society. The data are located in two distinct archives which are periodically updated: the first contains detailed Italian election results (ADELE: 'Archivo dati elettorali'), the second offers sample survey data (DICA: 'Dati inchieste campionarie').

The 'Archivio dati elettorali' (ADELE) contains data concerning the national elections for the Chamber of Deputies from 1948 to 1966; the data is organized at the municipal level (over 8000 ecological units). For each national election (1948, 1953, 1958, 1963, 1968, 1972, 1976, 1979, 1983, 1987, 1992, 1994, and 1996) one may access the number of those having the right to vote, actual voters, valid votes and party list votes. The archive also contains the results of the elections held June 2nd, 1946, which gave birth to the Italian Republic (institutional referendum and election of the Constitutional Assembly).

The 'Dati inchieste campionarie' (DICA) archive currently offers data regarding two major research programs: itanes (Italian National Election Studies: 1990–1996); political participation and social situation in Bologna (1984–1994). The user who accesses this archive can engage in interactive statistical analysis of the results of any single survey, generating, for example, frequency distributions, contingency tables, and selected statistics.

CHRONOLOGY OF ITALIAN POLITICAL EVENTS, 1998

January

1   Criticisms in the President of the Republic's end-of-year speech against the tendency of certain members of the judiciary to use the power of arrest too lightly evoke mixed reactions. In a public letter Di Pietro openly criticises the Head of State and defends the judiciary.

Treasury Minister Carlo Azeglio Ciampi announces officially that the budget deficit in 1997 was 2.7 percent: i.e., comfortably within the parameters established by the Maastricht Treaty. The stock exchange puts on 2.38 percent.

The law on privacy comes into full operation.

The Ambrosiano Veneto Bank buys Cariplo bank group for L.8,619 billion, thereby creating the Banca Intesa financial group.

5   A new all-time high in the stock exchange with the Mibtel at 17,762 (+ 3.23 percent).

9   Against the background of the controversy of the Di Bella case, the government declares its readiness to set up commissions to test the Di Bella treatment in eight Italian cancer research institutes. In the meanwhile, the regions of Puglia and Lombardy agree to supply the treatment free of charge to patients, thereby coming into conflict with the Health Minister.

11   In a unanimous vote, the 'Padanian Parliament' of the Northern League sets up the so-called 'Padanian National Guard' and approves the establishment of 'Padanian' elementary schools.

12   The parliamentary commission empowered to authorise legal proceedings against members of parliament rejects the request by Milan investigating magistrates for authorisation to arrest Cesare Previti (*Forza Italia*) by ten votes (some of which from People's Party members) to eight.

The 'Northeast Movement', promoted by the Mayor of Venice, Massimo Cacciari and the former president of Veneto industrialists, Mario Carraro, is launched with the aim of stimulating a strongly federalist reform of the state, in a direct challenge on the Northern League's own political ground.

The Minister for Health, Rosy Bindi reaches agreement with the regions on the Di Bella treatment. The trial is to be rapid and widespread but not to be used by the USL (local health authorities) until the experiment is complete.

Gian Mario Rossignolo becomes the new president of Telecom Italia replacing Guido Rossi.

15   The Senate approves the decree which allocates L.1,140 billion to manage the administration of milk-quotas. COBAS opposes the measure claiming it is inadequate and sets up road blocks in several parts of the country.

The Mayor of Rome Rutelli receives the Pope on an official visit to the Campidoglio (the offices of the Rome city council), thirty-one years after the visit of Paul VI.

16   Mino Fuccillo, senior member of the *La Repubblica* editorial team, becomes the new editor of *Unità* replacing Giuseppe Cardarola.

20   The lower house of Parliament rejects the application to arrest Cesare Previti (*Forza Italia*) by 341 votes against to 248 in favour with 21 abstentions. The League and the votes of half of the People's Party are crucial to the outcome.

The association of municipalities and the Conference of Presidents of the Regions submits a joint packet of amendments to the constitutional reform proposal to the Bicameral Commission.

21   Enzo Siciliano resigns as President of RAI (state-owned television company). This is followed by resignation of all other members of the Council of Administration.

The government and *Rifondazione Comunista* (RC) reach an initial agreement on the thirty-five-hour working week. It will enter into force in 2001, but there are immediate incentives for firms to reduce working hours. There are cautious reactions from trade unions; Confindustria opposes the agreement.

22   It is announced that Cesare Romiti will leave the presidency of FIAT as from the 30 January and will be replaced by Paolo Fresco.

Cossiga launches his project to bring together that part of the political centre that is 'outside the Pole, distinct and distant from the right and for now, alternative to the left'.
Testing of the Di Bella treatment begins on 2,600 patients, in twenty-one centres and with nine protocols.

26 The Chamber's examination of the constitutional reform project drafted by the Bicameral Commission begins.

29 The Presidents of both houses of Parliament nominate the new members of the RAI Council of Administration. Robert Zaccaria becomes the new President. The new Director-General is Pierluigi Celli.

31 The National Association of Magistrates criticises the Bicameral Commission's plans for reform of the legal system, in particular the proposal to divide the CSM (Supreme Council of the Judiciary) into two, and introduce separate career structures. President Scalfaro shares the judicial worries, and Fini surprisingly announces that AN is willing to discuss further the part relating to the CSM, thus provoking tensions in the *Polo*.

February

2 Berlusconi indicates a preference for a return to a proportional electoral system.
A commuter train crashes in Milan leaving twenty-three injured. Criticisms of managing director Giancarlo Cimoli, and of Transport Minister Claudio Burlando's management of the State rail company ensue.

6 The Board of Directors of the S. Paolo and IMI companies approve the merger of the two institutes. A credit conglomerate worth L.350,000 billion is created.

8 The Italian Democratic Socialist Party (SDI) is created out of a merger of Enrico Boselli and Ottaviano Del Turco's SI (Italian Socialists), Ugo Intini's PS (Socialist Party) and Gianfranco Schietroma's PSDI (Italian Socialist Democratic Party).

9 Giuseppe Soffiantini (kidnap victim) is freed after 237 days in captivity. His family pay a ransom of L.5 billion under the supervision of the Brescia Public Prosecutor's Office. An investigation of the management of the kidnapping is initiated and leads to the arrest of Carabinieri general Francesco Delfino.

11 The lower house of Parliament begins voting on the section of the Bicameral Commission reform project dealing with federalism.

12 Cossiga and Berlusconi meet to discuss reforms. Cossiga (former President of the Republic) advises Berlusconi to oppose

more vigorously what he defines as a completely unacceptable reform project.

14 After three days of work, the new 'States General of the Left' ends in Florence. D'Alema proposes that the party adopt a new symbol (with the rose used as the symbol of European social democracy replacing the hammer and sickle at the foot of the oak tree) along with a new name: *Democratici di Sinistra* (DS).

16 Cossiga's new party, the Democratic Union for the Republic (UDR) is launched. Mastella breaks with the CCD (Christian Democrats of the Centre), Buttiglione and other individual MPs leave the *Polo* to join the UDR.

18 The monopoly on fixed-line telephones ends. The Ministry of Communications concede licences to Infostrada (Olivetti and Mannesmann) and Wind (ENEL, Deutsche Telekom and France Telecom).

 After weeks of accidents, investigations and heated controversies, the senior management of FS (Italian state railways) is sacked. The new president is Claudio Demattè, who replaces Giorgio Crisci, though managing director Giancarlo Cimoli retains his post.

19 The new immigration law is approved by the Senate.

 The senior management of Telecom Italia is changed. Tomaso Tommasi da Vignano leaves his job as managing director. The post of president (Gian Mario Rossignolo) is reinforced by two directors-general: Vito Gamberale and Francesco De Leo.

21 Milan's Public Prosecutor, Gherardo Colombo rejects the Bicameral Commission's recommendations on the legal system defining them as an agreement born out of blackmail. All political parties protest. Minister Flick initiates disciplinary action Colombo.

25 The PDS criticises Flick's actions, branding them inadequate in relation to the thorny justice questions. Other government parties also express criticisms. Once Prodi's support is assured, the Minister refuses to resign.

 The ministerial circular that gives tax relief of up to 41 percent to renovate houses is issued.

26 Meeting in joint session, the Supreme Court establishes the right of convicted criminals to appeal on the grounds of inadequate prosecutorial justification in cases heard before the new article 513 of the penal procedural code comes into force. This article provides for the admissability at trial of statements made before a Public Prosecutor only if they are reconfirmed in the hearing.

March

1 AN's first policy conference concludes.
3 The leadership of the CDU approves the formation of a federal relationship with the UDR. But the conflict between Buttiglione and Formigoni intensifies with the latter's unwilling to break with the *Polo*.
4 The government approves the so-called 'Economic status measure' (*indicatore della situazione economica*, or ISE), otherwise known as the *riccometro* or 'wealth-meter' – a system to assess the right to access social assistance. Parliament makes modifications to the project while retaining the overall framework.
  Cossiga threatens to abandon the UDR because of internal conflicts over the distribution of posts among the Union's leaders. Mastella establishes the CDR (the Democratic Centre for the Republic). After a few days Cossiga's threat is withdrawn and the UDR forms a unitary parliamentary group.
5 The referendum request concerning the abolition of the proportional quota of seats in the electoral system for the lower house of Parliament, proposed by a cross-party group led by Segni and Occhetto, along with Di Pietro, is deposited with the Supreme Court. Various members of the *Polo*, and Francesco Cossiga, add their names.
6 The former president of FS (Italian state railways), Giorgio Crisci is investigated in the context of inquiries into the high-speed rail project; his offices are searched. He is alleged to have received bribes in January 1997 to rig tenders. Meanwhile, FS's difficulties continue with further labour conflicts and more accidents.
  At the national council of the CDU, Buttiglione's proposed party strategy review defeats Formigoni's by just two votes.
9 Ciampi presents the contents of the annual DPEF (Economic and Financial Planning Document) for 1999 in Brussels, winning approval for Italy's proposals for debt and deficit reduction.
  Member states of the Kosovo Contact Group send a warning to Serb Leader Slobodan Milošević to stop his offensive against the Albanian population. They also request sanctions including halting all financial aid to Serbia.
  Lazio's Regional Administrative Court orders the free distribution of somatostatina, the medication at the heart of 'Di Bella's multi-therapy' to all terminal cancer patients, and the nomination of an *ad acta* Commissioner to apply the measure. Minister Bindi defines the order as 'subversive'.
13 After a week of investigation into his presumed contacts with Mafia circles, the government unanimously removes under-

secretary for Home Affairs Angelo Giorgianni's from his post. None of the conclusions are transformed into penal cases.

The government approves the legislative decree reforming the retail trade proposed by Industry Minister Bersani. The decree provides for the liberalisation of licensing and opening hours and the reduction of fourteen product categories to just two: foodstuffs and non-foodstuffs. Retailer representatives, Confcommercio and Confesercenti protest vigorously.

16 Demonstrations against unemployment are held in various southern cities. Trade unions accuse the government of inertia on southern unemployment and threaten a general strike.

18 Berlusconi asks D'Alema to turn the 'Casa Letta' deal (on electoral reform) into a bill as a condition for calling off the referendum initiative and relaunching the entire reform process.

21 Di Pietro forms the new political reform movement calling for higher standards in public life – 'L'Italia dei valori' ('Values for Italy').

23 President Scalfaro sends the law on party financing back to the Parliament claiming it lacks adequate financial cover.

24 The government approves a bill on the thirty-five-hour working week. Confindustria reasserts its opposition and threatens to halt business-labour cooperation.

The government approves a statutory instrument on public employment that including several innovations, such as the possibility of redundancy, flexible use of labour, transfers, production bonuses and reform of public examinations.

25 Italy is officially included in the group eleven countries that will adopt the single currency from 1 January 1999.

Assuming the role of godfather to the UDR's parliamentary groups, Cossiga states that, if necessary, he will vote on the government's side in the vote on the DPEF.

The Council of State accepts the appeal presented by Minister Bindi and suspends the Lazio Regional Administrative Court's order on the free distribution of the Di Bella medication. It then passes to the Supreme court.

27 In a special session, Confindustria's executive committee gives a mandate to its President, Giorgio Fossa, to negotiate with the government. Confindustria's threat to repudiate the 1993 labour agreement is revived, and the government is asked to initiate negotiations on a new more transparent and solid basis.

29 Closing the League Convention, Bossi denies the League is an extremist movement and deliberately avoids use of the word 'secession'.

31 Reacting to UDR overtures, the DS reiterates the need to maintain the existing majority as it was elected in 1996. It asks RC to agree to stay in the majority for the remainder of the legislature. Bertinotti responds cautiously, proposing a commitment of one year. Cossuta opposes any fixed time limit.

April

1 The dialogue between government and business associations reopens. Prodi visits Confindustria to discuss the South and policies of social partnership with Giorgio Fossa.
   D'Alema's proposal to speed up reforms through a rationing of parliamentary time unleashes protests from *Forza Italia* and the RC, and the latter threatens to break away from the majority.
   Di Pietro and DS parliamentarians publish a draft bill to be presented through 'popular initiative' proposing a second-ballot electoral system.

3 The government passes the so-called 'health-ometer', which sets out the rules for access to free health-care on lines closely following the principle contained in the so-called 'wealth-ometer'.
   There are sharp exchanges between Milan's Public Prosecutor, Ilda Boccassini and Interior Minister Giorgio Napolitano (with whom the President of the Republic sides) over a Home Affairs Ministry directive that decentralises control over the special police corps.

6 New record for the Stock Exchange, bringing the Mibtel to 26,337 points (+ 3.16 percent).

8 After the law on party financing is sent back to the Parliament by Scalfaro (because of a lack of financial cover), the Senate approves a new text by 206 votes to 9, with 4 abstentions and the open dissent of Antonio Di Pietro.

14 After having received a formal judicial warning of investigation in relation to the Soffiantini kidnapping, Carabinieri General Francesco Delfino is arrested on a charge of extortion for allegedly receiving L.1 billion from Soffiantini's family, after promising his release.

15 The government presents the 1999 DPEF to the parliamentary majority and the social partners. It entails a narrowing of the deficit by L.13,500 billion lire over that otherwise likely (with L.9,500 billion in cutbacks and L.4,000 billion in additional revenue). Public investment, focused on the south, amounts to L.26,000 billion over three years, while the tax burden for the same period is projected to fall by 2 percent. It is confirmed

that tax-payers will get back 60 percent of the 'Euro-tax' they have paid.

On the eve of *Forza Italia*'s Convention, Berlusconi criticises the Bicameral Commission's recommendations and proposes a proportional electoral system linked to a strong chief executive modelled on German lines. There are negative reactions even within the *Polo*, and subsequently Berlusconi returns to his former proposal for a majoritarian semi-presidential system.

Credit and Unicredit merge and create a financial group with the largest number of retail outlets in Italy and a turnover of over L.300,000 billion per annum.

18 *Forza Italia*'s first national convention ends with a mass rally in Milan. Opening the convention, Berlusconi restates his reservations about the recommendations of the Bicameral Commission, warning that *Forza Italia* is not willing to vote for reforms that lack incisiveness. Other convention themes include: overture to the *Lega* on some issues and a bitter attack on the government and judiciary for seeking to circumvent democracy. Also a bitter attack on Prodi, who, at the simultaneously-held convention of the Greens, attacks FI for its complete lack of policy proposals.

20 People's Party leader Franco Marini, expresses concern for the prospects of institutional reform in the wake of FI's convention, and presses D'Alema to take strong measures to save the reform process. Even Fini sees difficulties ahead, but blames Prodi's attacks on Berlusconi for the proposal to eliminate the justice dossier from the reform plan.

21 D'Alema threatens to resign from the presidency of the Bicameral Commission if progress on reforms are held up. The *Polo* and *Ulivo* return to negotiation and a first deal is reached on federalism.

The Governor of the Bank of Italy reduces the discount rate to 5 percent, the lowest level since 1973.

The *Ulivo* National Committee, which Prodi aims to make the organisational expression of a future unified party representing the coalition (a plan greeted sceptically by coalition leaders) meets for the first time.

22 General Francesco Delfino attempts suicide in prison where he is detained in the Soffiantini case. Subsequently, his conditions improve.

24 After various meetings with Prodi, D'Alema and the National Association of the Judiciary, President Scalfaro attempts to mediate on the question of judicial reform. His suggestion is to include only general principles of the new judicial order in the Constitution itself leaving other aspects to ordinary legislation.

27 The Stock Exchange sheds 6.42 percent.

28 Cossiga announces the UDR's willingness to vote in favour of the DPEF, which wins the support of the entire parliamentary majority including the RC, though the latter expresses concern about the *rapprochement* of Cossiga and the government, and the emerging possibility of a new parliamentary majority.

29 Following Cossiga's decision, Prodi and Veltroni declare they have no intention of changing the composition of the majority: any votes additional to the existing parties will be additions not substitutions.

Definitive approval of the law on party financing in the lower house of Parliament. Three hundred and sixty-four votes for and thiry-one against (the latter consisting of Di Pietro's group, the Patto Segni group, and Mastella's CDR).

30 First-reading approval in the Senate for the regulation that abolishes sentences of life-imprisonment, by a large majority, though with the opposition of RI (Dini's *Rinnovamento Italiano*) and Minister Flick.

The European Parliament approves the entry into force of a single currency in the eleven countries, including Italy, which the European Commission judges to have satisfied the Maastricht convergence criteria.

May

2 The Euro is launched. Negotiation on the presidency of the European Central Bank is difficult, though Wim Duisemberg is eventually nominated, for an eight-year term, but with talk of an informal agreement for a hand-over after four years to a French representative. The new president however, denies any such commitment. In the Executive Committee, Italy is represented by Tommaso Padoa-Schioppa, former president of CONSOB.

4 The Euro is greeted enthusiastically by financial markets and European stock exchanges record significant gains. The MIB rises by 4.38 percent.

5 Admiral Guido Venturoni, Chief of the Defence Staff, is nominated President of the NATO Military Committee: the first time that an Italian official has occupied such a senior role.

6 A large landslide brought on by heavy rains hits the towns of Quindici, Sarno, Bracigliano and Siano in Campania, leading to dozens of deaths and leaving thousands homeless. There are arguments inside and outside the government about the adequacy of land-protection measures.

It emerges that Licio Gelli has escaped from house arrest at his Arezzo villa. The Supreme Court had earlier definitively sentenced him to 12 years imprisonment for the bankruptcy of Banco Ambrosiano. Arguments within the majority.

8 In the Milan investigation of the Mondadori award and the SME affair, Berlusconi and Previti are suspected of having bribed the judges responsible for managing the sale negotiation.

11 The *Polo* makes approval of the Bicameral Commission recommendations on increased powers for the President of the Republic a condition for its approval.

13 On the enlargement of NATO to central Europe, RC senators vote against the government while the *Polo* and the UDR vote in favour.

14 With the League and RC's voting against, the lower house of Parliament approves the articles of the constitutional reform proposal in relation to the direct election of the President of the Republic.

After various meetings, the European People's Party (EPP) leader Wilfried Martens opens negotiations with FI for its entry into the People's Party group of the European Parliament. Both the PPI and Prodi intervene to try to block this possibility.

15 Luigi Spaventa, President of the Monte dei Paschi di Siena Bank, becomes the new president of CONSOB, in the wake of Tommaso Padoa-Schioppa's ECB appointment.

Senate President Mancino expresses concern about the Bicameral Commission's recommendation on semi-presidentialism.

18 Partly thanks to Italian mediation, the U.S.A. and EU reach agreement on sanctions against European countries having trade relations with Iran, Libya and Cuba. At the same time, the U.S. embargo on these countries is relaxed.

19 The escape of Mafia boss Pasquale Cuntrera, accused of international drug trafficking, becomes public knowledge. There are arguments about the frequency of prison breakouts.

20 Justice Minister Flick offers his resignation over the Gelli and Cuntrera cases. Following consultation with the parliamentary majority, which confirms its confidence in the Minister, Prodi rejects the resignation.

21 Trade unions break with the government over the employment issue. Relations with Confindustria improve after entry into the Euro but business representatives seek a significant reduction in the tax burden.

22 The government approves the bill raising the school-leaving age to sixteen, to come into force in 1999. The PPI expresses concern about divisions on education reform.

Twenty years after the approval of law 194 on the availability of abortion, the Pope urges a revision of the law and binds Catholic politicians to show responsibility on this issue.

23 Through its President Cardinal Camillo Ruini, the Italian Bishop's Conference openly asks the government for public funding for non-state schools. Marini declares that he agrees and hopes for a generalised school reform programme that includes this issue.

D'Antoni proposes the setting up of the so-called 'Greater CISL', a plan which aims to involve all Christian organisations involved in the social sector under the flag of a unitary Forum. Some interpret this idea as a first step towards the reunification of the Catholics at a political level.

24 Mafia boss Pasquale Cuntrera is arrested in Spain. The government is delighted by the speed with which he was identified and captured.

Local elections in various municipalities and provinces. The first round sees the immediate election of four *Polo* mayors and six *Polo* provincial presidents compared with three *Ulivo* mayors and three *Ulivo* Provincial Presidents. The League reaches the second ballot only in Treviso. Support grows for the centre parties of the two political divisions and the UDR achieves a satisfactory result – especially in the south – in its first electoral test.

27 After a week's delay, the Chamber debate on constitutional reform re-opens and Berlusconi announces FI will vote against if substantial modifications are not made to the powers of the President of the Republic.

Asian stock exchanges collapse again with negative effects in Europe also. Milan loses 3.03 percent.

30 In his annual report, Central Bank Governor Fazio praises the financial policies of the government which led to the entry into the Euro but asks for more to be done on jobs, through more labour-market flexibility and a rapid decrease in the tax burden.

Open confrontation between Berlusconi and D'Alema on the Bicameral Commission recommendations. D'Alema accuses Berlusconi of having succumbed to neo-centrist temptations, following a strategy deliberately designed to inflict short-term damage on himself (i.e., D'Alema).

June

1 In view of imminent regional elections in Friuli-Venezia Giulia a single list of candidates is agreed for candidates of the polit-

ical centre. Marini, Dini, Buttiglione and Mastella are present at the launch, with Cossiga's blessing despite his absence.

2 All efforts at mediation on reform fail and the Chamber of Deputies suspends its examination of the Bicameral Commission's recommendations.

   Cesare Romiti, former FIAT president, is nominated president of RCS Editori and becomes a Gemina shareholder (with 18.8 percent of its shares).

   The first session of the European Central Bank Council is held in Brussels; responsibilities are assigned to individual members. Tommaso Padoa-Schioppa is given international relations, payment systems and bank supervision.

3 After Milan's Public Prosecutor Francesco Greco's request of a five-and-a-half-year sentence for Berlusconi in the All-Iberian case, FI launches a vigorous attack on the Milan prosecuting team and walks out of the Senate in protest.

4 Berlusconi and Cossiga meet. After congratulating Berlusconi on his decision to block reform, the former President of the Republic re-launches his scheme for a broad alliance of the centre which would mark the demise of the *Polo* as an organic alliance between FI and AN. Fini seeks clarification from Berlusconi.

   Definitive internal break in the CDU between Buttiglione and Formigoni who accuses the former of having abandoned the *Polo* and founds the CDL (*Cristiani democratici per le libertà*).

   The RAI board of directors nominates the new heads of division, network and journalism. Giulio Borrelli is the new director of RAIUNO news, Nuccio Fava of RAITRE news and Clemente Mimun is confirmed in office as head of RAIDUE news.

   After seven months of negotiations, the proposed merger of COMIT and the Banca di Roma falls through. Many commentators see this as a defeat for Mediobanca and Enrico Cuccia, who directed the operation and who a few days earlier met with Prodi.

5 PPI leader Marini severely criticises the newspaper of the Italian Bishops' Conference, *Avvenire*, which he claims has been adopting an unjustifiably harsh line vis-à-vis the party for its stance on artificial insemination, education and the family. A tense period between the PPI and the Catholic press begins, with interventions even from Cardinal Camillo Ruini and the Pope in the *Osservatore Romano*.

6 At the young industrialists' conference, Berlusconi attacks the judiciary, accusing it of issuing sentences that are motivated by persecutory political designs against him; he threatens to block all progress on reform in retaliation.

7 Second round of local elections. The *Polo* increases its vote against the *Ulivo*, which loses the municipalities of Piacenza and Parma.

9 The president of the lower house of Parliament, Violante, removes the constitutional reform text from the agenda after having received notification from D'Alema on the political impossibility of continuing the discussion in the Bicameral Commission. The move marks the formal winding-up of the Bicameral Commission for Constitutional Reform.

With the agreement of Helmut Kohl and Josè Maria Aznar and by a large majority, the EPP parliamentary group in Brussels votes for the entry of FI's European parliamentary representatives. Subsequently, Prodi announces that he will not participate in the next EPP summit if Berlusconi is invited and will send a formal letter of protest to the Group's President and other People's Party leaders.

Agostino Casaroli dies. Casaroli was a key figure in Vatican foreign policy especially vis-à-vis the socialist regimes in eastern European countries, who signed the new Concordat with the Italian State in 1984.

Wind, the company born from an agreement among ENEL, Deutsche Telekom and France Telecom, wins the tender for the third mobile telephone licence, competing with TIM and OMNITEL.

10 The UDR is officially set up as a political party. Cossiga explains its identity and programme. After having contributed to blocking the Bicameral Commission, the UDR commits itself to initiate relations with centre parties on both sides of the political spectrum. It applies to join the PPE parliamentary group in Strasbourg, and aims to generate a unitary list of all parties that belong to the EPP in the European elections.

12 DS Senator Passigli proposes a referendum providing for the abolition of the '*scorporo*' procedure in lower house elections. D'Alema offers DS help to collect signatures.

15 Elections in the region of Friuli-Venezia Giulia, where the proportional representation system operates. The results show a high percentage of abstentions (36 percent), the defeat of the League (down 6 percent since the general election of 1996), 11 percent for the centre unitary lists (PPI, Dini, UDR), a good increase for the DS, while AN and FI show a slight fall. The result does produce a ruling majority in the region. The centre list is divided on future alliances.

FI membership of the PPE group blocked as a result of resistance from the Prime Ministers of Belgium and Luxembourg.

FI's European MEPs will join the group as individuals. Prodi expresses satisfaction.

16 The new law on conscientious objection is definitively approved by the Senate.

17 During the meeting of the majority on the launching of a new phase of government action after entry to the Euro area, Prodi expresses concern about the next vote on NATO enlargement where the opposition of the RC is promised. The *Polo* declares that it will vote in favour as long as the government acknowledges it lacks a majority and resigns.

22 Paolo Fresco is nominated FIAT president

23 The lower house of Parliament definitively ratifies the NATO treaty of enlargement to Poland, Hungary and the Czech Republic. Given the opposition of RC, the votes of the UDR (consulted in advance by the Premier) turns out to be crucial.After the vote the President of the Republic receives Prodi and asks for a clarification of the majority with a parliamentary debate and vote of confidence. Critical of Prodi's attitude vis-à-vis the UDR, D'Alema fears the consequences of the vote for the future of the government. Bertinotti threatens a political crisis on education and employment.

24 In the face of DS criticism, Prodi restates the need for a clarification and asserts that he is not willing to govern with unstable and variable majorities but only with the majority elected in 1996. He asks Bertinotti to reach a solid and stable agreement or there will be a split. The UDR declares that its willingness to rescue the government cannot be relied on, in other difficult situations.

25 Welcoming Formigoni to FI, Berlusconi re-launches the idea of setting up of a Commission of Inquiry into Tangentopoli. The governing majority is not in favour.

26 The first meeting is held between Prodi and Bertinotti over controversial policy issues including Kosovo, education, employment and the south, bio-ethics and the family. In the end, Bertinotti says he is disappointed; the *Ulivo* threatens a split if the RC refuses an agreement.

27 Welcoming the Forum of Family Associations, the Pope criticises the work of the government in relation to abortion and family policies, which he condemns as weak, imprecise and inadequate.

29 Bertinotti floats the possibility of the RC leaving the majority, and confirms his differences with Prodi and clashes with party colleague Cossuta, who is pushing for an agreement retaining RC's place in the majority.

The *Washington Post* outlines the plans of Blair, Clinton and Prodi to form a new 'Centre-left' or 'Democratic' International.

July

1   Official visit of the prime minister to Iran.
The threat of clandestine immigration returns to the Italian coasts; in a single night there are over four hundred landings. The phenomenon continues daily, leading to some deaths and diplomatic difficulties with the countries from which the boats leave, especially North Africa, during this period.

2   The UDR holds its constituent convention. Honorary President Cossiga nominates Mastella as party leader, Buttiglione as President of the Executive and Scognamiglio as President of the National Assembly. He also launches an appeal to centrists on both sides of the main political divide to join a united centre list at the European elections.

3   After blunt correspondence with Ciampi in which he laments his marginalisation from the management of the privatisation process, Billionl President Mario Sarcinelli, pressed by Ciampi, resigns. Subsequently, the former president of Confindustria, Luigi Abete, is nominated to replace him.

4   Internal clash in the RC between Bertinotti and Cossuta on the possibility of a break with the government. *Ulivo* parties present their programmatic proposals to Prodi in view of the vote of confidence in the majority.

7   Berlusconi is condemned in the first degree to two years and nine months imprisonment for bribes paid by Fininvest to the financial guard (Guardia di Finanza).

8   The majority offers the *Polo* a compromise in relation to the Commission of Inquiry into Tangentopoli, allowing its establishment as long as it does not interfere with the work of judges, and has only investigative powers in relation to corruption.

9   Majority summit. Prodi declares that the government has embarked on a new drive for reform. While noting progress, Bertinotti fails to see the changes he demanded. Final decisions are postponed to the leadership of the RC and the parliamentary confidence debate.

10   Trade unions criticise the government's proposal that the task of direct hiring of labour be allocated to the Agency for the South.

13   All Iberian trial: Berlusconi is condemned in the first degree to two years and four months imprisonment and Craxi to four years for illegal financing of parties. Street protests are organised by FI to support its leader.

14   The Commission of Inquiry into poverty at the Premier's office reveals that in 1997 family nuclei living in destitution increased to 166,000 (11.2 percent of the population). More young cou-

ples rather than pensioners are hit. Bertinotti uses the occasion to distance himself from government social policies.

15 Opposition from many DS and PPI parliamentarians blocks negotiations on the Commission of Inquiry into Tangentopoli.

17 Speaking at the opening of the Senate debate, Prodi asks for full and not only provisional trust in the government. He presents government policy on unemployment (tax relief for firms hiring in the south, infrastructure plan, commitment of the government for a reduction in duties and the approval of the law on the thirty-five-hour working week before the end of the year). He attacks Berlusconi confirming full support for the work of judges.

18 Supported by Veltroni, Antonio Bassolino launches the idea of a Constituent Assembly of the *Ulivo* which would held consolidate its structure and capacity for co-ordinated action. Prodi is pleased with the idea, but the PPI and D'Alema are openly critical.

19 At the session devoted to the judicial system at the General Assembly of the Left, D'Alema launches a final offer to the *Polo* for the Commission on Tangentopoli: five 'wise men' nominated by the Presidents of the two houses of Parliament will draft a report on corruption to present in Parliament. The *Polo* controversially declines the offer.

The RC's Political Committee approve Bertinotti's proposal for a critical vote of confidence in the government, thus postponing the final clash until the debate on the financial bill after the summer.

20 Palermo's Public Prosecutor confiscates documents belonging to the twenty-two Fininvest holdings, in the context of investigations into money-laundering.

22 After the Senate, the lower house of Parliament votes confidence in the government with the votes of the *Ulivo* and the RC.

23 The vote on the Commission on Tangentopoli is delayed until September because of the lack of agreement between and within the two political divisions.

The Committee promoting the electoral referendum which proposes the abolition of the proportional quota, deposits 687,000 signatures with the Supreme Court.

The Parliament elects nine lay members of the CSM: six proposed by the *Ulivo*, three by the *Polo*. One place remains to be allocated but agreement fails to be reached.

27 The CDU dissolves itself into the UDR and transforms itself into political-cultural association.

During the meeting of the leadership of DS, D'Alema laments having been too often left alone by parties during a difficult

period and defines the proposal for a Constituen
as not being shared.
Split between Massimo Cacciari and Mario Ca.
founders of the Northeast movement. After an exchan,
ters, Carraro communicates his disengagement.

28 The Di Bella methods are rejected by the Expert Comn
which defined four of the nine protocols of the multi-therapy
inefficient in the absence of improvement in the patients
undergoing treatment.

29 The Chamber rejected the bill on the vote of Italians abroad
because of the lack of the necessary quorum. Controversy of
AN and FI because of the absence of many blue parliamentarians during the vote.

31 Clandestine landings on the Adriatic coast and in Sicily continue. The three-year programme for immigration policy which
provides for pre-fixed quotas and measures to favour the integration of regular immigrants are approved.

August

1 At the end of the investigation into the Ustica massacre Roman
public prosecutors responsible for the case assert that the
tragedy was provoked by an explosion. They seek to commit
the four generals of the Aeronautica to trial for having misled
investigations.
Definitively closing the work of the 'Padanian Parliament',
Bossi sanctions the abandonment of the 'secession' policy,
indicating a federal reform obtained through democratic pressure as an objective of the League movement.

4 The PPI leader says he is in favour of accepting UDR votes in
support of the government's budget. Prodi reiterates that both
the majority and the budget must not be changed. Bertinotti
considers this reaction to Marini's proposal insufficient and
asks once again for a 'change' in government economic policy.
Giovanni Verde, university lecturer in trial law and lay member
of the PPI, is elected with twenty-nine votes out of thirty-two
as CSM vice president.

7 In the region of Friuli-Venezia Giulia, a minority centre-right
executive is established and led by Roberto Antonione (FI)
thanks to the abstention of the DS.
In a meeting with the Premier, Cossiga reiterates the UDR's
willingness to vote for the budget, clarifying that UDR votes
could not substitute for those of the RC. Prodi affirms that he

intends to carry out every useful attempt to maintain the support of the RC.

10 Various meetings reveal the attempt to build an agreement between the UDR and the League to resist possible temptations to reform the electoral law into a majority system.

11 Luigi Lombardini, head of the Cagliari district Public Prosecutor's office, who is being investigated in relation to the payment of a ransom for the release of Silvia Melis, commits suicide. Heated side-taking by *Polo* members against the investigation done by Palermo judges follows. Subsequently various elements emerge confirming the existence of an illegal network set up by Lombardini to intermediate payment of ransoms for kidnapping done by Sardinian organised crime.

13 Nerio Nesi's proposal for an 'additional note' to the DPEF which takes into account the RC's requests outside the document leads to a harsh polemic between Bertinotti and Cossuta on the party's stance in relation to the government.

14 Chigi Palace confirms the rumours about the meeting planned for 21 September among Prodi, Blair and Clinton to define the project of a Permanent Conference of the Centre-Left (the so-called World *Ulivo*).

17 First rejection of the government decree on the new Milan stopover at Malpensa 2000 by the European Commission. A conflict begins and lasts for months.

18 The International Monetary Fund rejects Italian employment plans, defining the thirty-five-hour working week useless and underlining the need for increased flexibility in the labour market.

20 The brother of Cardinal of Naples, Mario Lucio Giordano, is arrested for usury. Judicial procedures are initiated which see the involvement of the cardinal.
Minister Ciampi launches the idea of a new social pact to include businesses and trade unions in order to promote employment according to the concertation methods used for financial recovery.

22 A judicial note for usury, recycling and extortion is sent to the Cardinal of Naples, Michele Giordano, by Lagonegro's Public Prosecutor's office, and the bishop's curia is searched. The Cardinal's reactions are harsh and he holds that the sovereignty of the Church and the Concordat agreements had been violated. CEI and Vatican express concern.

24 The Vatican intervenes in the Giordano case with a prudent declaration that expresses necessary closeness to the prelate. It underlines a possible violation of the Concordat as well as the

excessive spectacularisation of the financial guard intervention in the curia.

25 D'Antoni continues the controversy with the government and from the meeting of the CL in Rimini he relaunches a general strike proposal against that which he defines as government immobilism vis-à-vis work, employment and development.

27 The Vatican formalises its opinion on the Giordano investigation in a document that examines four possible violations of the Concordat.

30 From the national feast of friendship, Prodi launches a challenge to Bertinotti on the Budget asking him to decide if he wishes to support the government or provoke a crisis.

31 The Russian parliament rejects the hypothesis of a government led by Viktor Chernomyrdin, recalled by Yeltsin after the previous government crisis. Wall Street falls by 6.37 percent and drags the stock exchanges of the world with it. They continue to be uncertain and volatile.

Bertinotti replies to Prodi threatening a crisis if the government does not accept the RC's conditions.

Interviewed by Radio Vatican, Cossiga declares the willingness of the UDR to vote the budget substituting the RC's votes if they decide to vote against it.

September

1 In an article in *Liberazione*, Cossuta makes the RC's internal conflicts explicit and defines the leadership of Bertinotti as 'exclusivist' and 'leaderistic'.

3 At the end of a meeting of the leadership of the RC, Bertinotti and Cossutta confirm their disagreement on political strategy.

At the UDR party in Telese, D'Alema urges Cossiga's party to choose a political alliance and declares his interest in an enlargement of the centre-left.

4 After 266 days of capture, Alessandra Sgarella, Brescian businesswoman kidnapped by Anonima Sarda, is released.

At the National Coordination of the *Ulivo*, Prodi reiterates his intention not to accept changes in the majority. Marini and D'Alema are more willing to think of a tentative alliance with the UDR. A working group to formulate proposals on justice is set up.

6 In Telese Cossiga responds to D'Alema's invitation, and refuses the hypothesis of joining the centre-left. The UDR will vote for the budget if Prodi sets off the crisis.

On a visit to London, D'Alema denies there are real plans for a 'world *Ulivo* federation'.

9   Prodi declares that the government, hitherto uncommitted on the issue of constitutional reform, will engage on the side of specific reform proposals. He hopes for very broad inter-party agreement but does not exclude reforms being pushed through by a more limited alliance. An earthquake in Calabria and Basilicata, measuring seven degrees on the Mercalli scale, leads to two deaths and many injuries.

10   After being on the run for 141 days, Licio Gelli, is arrested in Cannes.

Minister Flick presents a complex proposal on reform of the legal system that provides for an amnesty for minor crimes, and special concessions for those accused of illegal financing of parties and budget forgery. It also provides for special treatment of those condemned for terrorist crimes. In a meeting of the majority, party leaders reject Flick's proposals though they are supported by Prodi.

13   Albania in chaos once again. An opposition deputy is assassinated and opposition leader Sali Berisha organises street protests. Numerous violent clashes between protesters and the police. Prodi convenes an emergency meeting. Specially trained agents go to Albania to support the local police force. The government passes a decree on immigration in which a maximum of 35,000 residency permits are made available for those who can document their presence in Italy before 27 March 1998.

15   After weeks of controversies, the clash intensifies between the European Commission and the Italian government on Burlando's decree. This decree fixes the date of the opening of the new Milan hub airport, Malpensa 2000, for 25 October. The Commission rejects the decree, while the government suspects interference by some foreign companies interested in the failure of the project.

16   After a meeting of the majority in which the budget bill is presented and discussed, Bertinotti declares that he sees no concessions to RC in the government's economic policy and rejects the law, though leaving some room for dialogue.

17   The government meets trade union confederations and secures what is on balance a positive judgement on the budget.

After some internal conflicts, an agreement in the majority is reached on the legal system and an appeal from the *Polo* to open dialogue on this theme follows.

Fabrizio Comencini leaves the leadership of the Liga Veneta in open conflict with Bossi.

18 Marcello Sorgi, former director of Tg1, is nominated director of *La Stampa* replacing Carlo Rossella.

The UDR decides to set up its headquarters in Piazza del Gesù, historical headquarters of the Christian Democrats, sharing rooms with the CDU and sharing the building with the PPI.

20 Closing the national *Festa dell'Unità*, Massimo D'Alema appeals to Bertinotti not to provoke a political crisis and accuses Berlusconi of pursuing personal interests through politics. Berlusconi responds that D'Alema is a Stalinist.

The Pope concludes the celebration of the centenary of the birth of Paul VI and beatifies Giuseppe Tovini the founder of the Banco Ambrosiano in Brescia.

21 The majority of the leadership of the RC (thirty out of forty-six) supports the Bertinotti line on the budget. Cossuta's stance, that is to maintain critical dialogue, with the government, is defeated.

Romano Prodi, Tony Blair and Bill Clinton meet during a seminar organised in the University of New York to discuss relations at an international level between centre-left (Third Way) governments.

22 The government outlines the budget proposals, tempting Bertinotti with the promise of a measure on the thirty-five-hour working week. Prodi reiterates that he seeks approval of the budget by the majority that emerged from the election and not on the basis of any new alliance of parties. Marini repeats that he is willing to accept UDR votes, since the group had already voted for the DPEF.

24 After conflict and controversy in the Chamber, and a meeting with the Chamber presiding committee, the President, Luciano Violante, decides to postpone voting on the Tangentopoli commission until 20 October. The majority and the UDR agree. The *Polo is* against.

The government approves the budget and its related provisions. Measures worth L.14,700billion are announced: L.1,200billion more than previously agreed, to be spent on the poorer sections of society. The measures include reimbursement of 60 percent of the Euro-tax, an increase in social pensions, tax incentives for jobs in the south, reduction of duty on first-time house buying, and vouchers for chronically ill people.

The CSM's disciplinary section commits former councillor Italo Chitti to trial for an episode dating back to when he was GIP in Milan with the charge of collusion with public prosecutors during investigations.

26 Cossiga commits the UDR to approving the Budget but only if Prodi resigns.

Francesco Rutelli and Enzo Bianco announce the formation of a political movement that aims to build on the experience of the directly-elected mayors, and to mount a challenge to the *Ulivo*.

27 Helmut Kohl defeated in German election. New coalition formed by the SPD and the Greens. The Chancellorship goes to Gerhardt Schröder. Thirteen out of fifteen European countries are now led by centre-left coalitions.

29 After having congratulated the new German chancellor, Prodi launches a proposal to invest the excess reserves of European Central Banks (a total of L.200 thousand billion) to combat unemployment on a continental level and relaunch development projects.

   Following the major political crisis in Albania, a new prime minister is nominated: thirty-year-old Pandeli Majko, leader of the Albanian Socialist Party. He replaces Fatos Nano who rose to power after the violent protests against the Berisha government in 1997.

30 Change in the management of TG3. Ennio Chiodi is nominated to replace Nuccio Fava who gets the post of editorial manager.

October

1 The government approves a package of measures for employment and the south connected with the budget. It provides for the setting-up of the Agency for Italian Development with the task of coordinating and restructuring public firms in the south and different proxies for the government, such as incentives, social welfare support provisions and liquidations.

   In the face of the reaffirmed hostility of Bertinotti, Prodi admits that the risk of crisis has increased. President Scalfaro declares in the meantime that the legislature must not be allowed to collapse.

   On the back of IMF reports on the economic situation, of financial crashes of speculative funds, world stock exchanges suffer heavy falls. Milan loses 4.9 percent, partly the consequence of additional internal factors.

2 D'Alema writes to Bertinotti asking him not to bring down the government and underlines the risks posed by early elections.

3 At the start of the political committee of the RC, Bertinotti proposes the party vote against the budget and withdraw its support from the government's parliamentary majority. Cossuta in contrast argues for remaining in the majority to avoid a general drift of political life to the right. Gulf inside the party widens.

Veltroni predicts that the RC will withdraw its confidence, the government will seek a vote of confidence from Parliament and affirms what that has been circulating for some time: namely that a handover of the prime minister's office from Prodi to D'Alema can only happen after a fresh general election.

4 The RC's political committee approves the position of Bertinotti over Cossutta by 188 over 332.

The Liga Veneta Repubblica led by Fabrizio Comencini is born, and the separation from Bossi's League is approved.

5 After the RC's Political Committee, Prodi goes to the Head of State to report. He confirms that the government will seek a vote of confidence in Parliament.

Cossutta resigns from the presidency of the RC.

In Florence, the Franco-Italian summit takes place. Prodi, Chirac and Jospin discuss an organic partnership between the two countries and Germany. The Italian political situation also discussed. The news that Prodi is counting on 312-313 votes out of the 316 necessary for the majority is leaked.

6 The majority of the RC's two parliamentary groups align with Cossuta against the decision to bring the government down.

At the centre of attention, the UDR continues to declare itself ready to vote for the Budget but not for a vote of confidence in the government and consider the *Ulivo* experience to be at an end.

The UN Security Council passes a resolution to condemn Serb operations in Kosovo. NATO is ready to intervene militarily but some countries of the Alliance, including Italy, continue to press for a negotiated solution.

The Spanish Central Bank lowers interest rates and gave respite to stock exchanges (Milan +4.5 percent). A season of lowering of the cost of money in Europe begins in view of the adjustment to the Euro and re-launching development.

7 The government presents itself to the lower house of Parliament for a vote of confidence. After having recalled government action, Prodi appeals to Bertinotti, reconfirming the request for confidence from the majority that emerged from the 1996 elections.

During the debate, the head of the RC's parliamentary party, Oliviero Diliberto, announces a vote in favour of the majority, thus definitively sanctioning the party split. To differing extents, Marini and D'Alema open up to the UDR position in particular, in relation to doing without the majority of 21 April 1996. The UDR, however, announces a vote against.

9 The government does not win the confidence vote: 312 votes in favour and 313 against. *Ulivo* parties except Silvio Liotta of

RI who is immediately expelled from the party and the parliamentary group of RC voted in favour. The *Polo*, League and the rest of the RC faithful to Bertinotti and the UDR vote against. Prodi goes to the Quirinale to hand in his resignation, which is accepted without hesitation. For the first time in the history of the republic, a government resigns after being formally voted out of confidence by Parliament. Different hypotheses emerge: Prodi mark II, technical government, institutional government or large accord. The elections appear the most unlikely outlet.

10 After lunch with D'Alema in Bologna, Prodi clearly refuses to accept a limited reappointment to approve the Budget with the vote of confidence of the UDR.

    Cossiga announces that the hypothesis of a Prodi mark II government would not have his support while if D'Alema were to lead the government, the UDR would be interested.

11 In Bologna during a protest organised by the *Ulivo*, Prodi gives a heated defence of the experience of the government and the *Ulivo* project, reiterating his unwillingness to accept solutions that undermine the path of the bipolarisation of the party system. The Partito dei comunisti italiani (PDCI) is born and founded by those who left the RC. Cossuta excludes any agreement with Cossiga's UDR.

12 A meeting is held between the delegations of the DS led by D'Alema and the UDR with Cossiga. Agreement is reached in principle on the possibility of avoiding elections and the need to give the country a government that went beyond the approval of the budget.

    While consultations continue, Scalfaro invites Prodi to dinner. They discuss the hypothesis of a reappointment supported by the *Ulivo* but Prodi repeats his unwillingness to accept UDR votes. He timidly advances the hypothesis of a technical government led by Ciampi.

    In Kosovo, diplomatic pressure on the Serb leader Slobodan Milošević continues under the threat of armed intervention. Italy decides to concede its military bases but Cossuta is against this, this time agreeing with Bertinotti.

13 Once the consultations conclude, Scalfaro gives a limited appointment to Prodi supported by the *Ulivo* and, according to the President also by other political forces, including the UDR. Prodi accepts the mandate but reiterates his conditions: faithfulness to the *Ulivo* project and the existence of a solid majority to support him.

    Cossiga considers Prodi's words not very encouraging and nies having supported his nomination to Scalfaro. He lays down three conditions: an admission that the 21 April majority no longer exists, a new government to be built expressly seeking UDR support, and the government to take account of the opinion and indications of the UDR.

In Kosovo, Milošević accepts the conditions laid down by the UN mediator for the withdrawal of troops and the arrival of two thousand observers. NATO suspends the air-raid plan.

14 The UDR declares its unwillingness to support a second Prodi government.

15 After the rejection, Prodi and the *Ulivo* political forces launch D'Alema as a candidate.

16 President Scalfaro gives D'Alema the appointment. From the *Polo*, criticisms emerge in relation to unconstitutionality as well as the threat of dramatic initiatives.

Giuseppe Drago (UDR) resigns as President of the Sicilian Region and opened the crisis of the majority of centre-left. A period of turbulence begins in some southern regions governed by the *Polo* (Calabria, Puglia, Campania).

The Italian Bishop Conference newspaper, *Avvenire*, the SIR agency and *Osservatore romano* criticise the solution hypotheses to the crisis and the President of the Republic.

17 D'Alema meets the UDR and Cossuta's followers and gets the go-ahead for the formation of a government.

18 Dini, Cossiga and Marini meet to evaluate the new political prospective and the hypothesis of forming unitary lists for the next European elections.

19 After having agreed six pages of a programme with the new majority and presented it to Scalfaro, D'Alema receives a full mandate to form a government.

Polo criticisms of the Head of State over the management of the crisis continue. The presidents of both houses express their solidarity with Scalfaro. While defining the government 'clandestine', Berlusconi is willing to open dialogue on electoral reform after a meeting with D'Alema.

20 On an official visit to the Quirinale, the Pope reiterates the Church's position on the family and education. After controversies with Catholic newspapers, Scalfaro underlines the lay character of the State and the autonomy of Catholics in their political choices. D'Alema and Prodi are present.

21 Massimo D'Alema's government takes office.

The European Commission presents economic forecasts for the Autumn which see Italy with a growth rate of 1.7 percent against an average of 3 percent of countries of the single currency.

22   Massimo D'Alema presents the government programme to the lower house for a vote of confidence,. Two points are qualifying: taking on of all the financial commitments of the previous government (reimbursement of Euro-tax, development pact, thirty-five-hour working week) and the direct commitment of the government to begin dialogue between the majority and opposition on reforms.

23   The D'Alema government wins the vote of confidence in the lower house: 333 votes in favour, 281 against and 3 abstentions. Scalfaro responds to criticisms from the *Polo* defining those who judge his behaviour incorrect as constitutional illiterates.

24   The *Polo* holds a protest in Milan against the management of the crisis and the formation of a new government. Harsh criticisms especially of Cossiga and UDR parliamentarians.

25   At the extraordinary convention of the League, Bossi confirms the new 'moderate' stance of the party.

After long controversies between the European Commission and the Italian government, the new Malpensa 2000 airport opens and there is immediate chaos because of the defects in the computer system. Discomfort for passengers continues for some days.

Numerous clandestine landings on the Puglia coasts coming from Albania. Clashes between two rubber dinghies and the explosion of one of these leads to several victims including a six-month-old baby.

26   The Bank of Italy governor Antonio Fazio cuts the discount rate by one point bringing it to 4 percent.

27   D'Alema obtains the confidence of the Senate: 188 in favour, 116 against and 1 abstention.

28   Prodi intervenes in the political debate after a period of silence allying with the electoral referendum and proposing a unitary list of the *Ulivo* in the European elections to combat what he calls the prejudicial anti-*Ulivo*ism of some members of the majority. Some political exponents including Di Pietro and Occhetto agree. D'Alema and Marini are sceptical.

During a meeting of the leadership of the party, D'Alema designates Veltroni to succeed him at the leadership of the DS.

30   The government approves a law by decree which provides for the reimbursement of 60 percent of the Euro-tax. The adjournment of eviction, the recruitment of five thousand public employees, and an amendment to the Budget which provides for a maternity check of L.300,000 to 400,000 to unemployed persons or atypical workers, are also approved. D'Alema holds that there was a risk of recession and invokes a new develop-

ment pact. He asks the opposition not to obstruct the speedy approval of the measure. Berlusconi declares that the *Polo* must demonstrate a sense of responsibility.

The Telecommunications Authority passes the new measures covering broadcasting frequencies: seventeen networks with national coverage (eleven for national transmission and six regional ones). The maximum ownership ceiling is two networks. Digital TV will have four experimental channels: definitive take-off for digital is planned for 2010.

31 In a letter to *Corriere della Sera*, Berlusconi seeks to relaunch a dialogue on reform, with the declared aim of testing out the real willingness of the majority to reach a broad cross-party deal.

November

2 The Constitutional Court declares the new article 513 CPP as reformed by the Parliament in 1997 unconstitutional. Most of the political class accuses the Court of an improper invasion into its domain.

3 After a series of postponements, the lower house rejects by a margin of six votes the establishment of a commission of inquiry into Tangentopoli. There is vigorous protest from the opposition *Polo*. The Greens and the Socialists vote in favour of the proposal, alongside the *Polo*. The abstention of the League and centre parties is crucial.

The D'Alema government presents its budget. The three-year allocation for the right to study is increased to L.1,200 billion. Support is to be provided for mothers without insurance cover. The carbon tax is set up and tax relief for self-employed workers under thirty-two years that start up a business in the south is also provided for. Positive reaction from Confindustria which asks for a reduction of taxes, while Trade unions are more cautious.

Francesco Rutelli, Massimo Cacciari and Enzo Bianco, together with other mayors present the political movement *Centocittà* ('one hundred cities') and *Legambiente* also become members.

5 Procedures for the regularisation of immigrants open. Tens of thousands of immigrants throng to police stations to benefit from the amnesty. Difficulties and accidents occur for many days. In the mean time, on the Puglia coasts clandestine landings continue.

6 Walter Veltroni is elected as new leader of the DS with 89 percent of votes. D'Alema becomes president of the party. Due to

the absence of an agreement on a two-round run-off electoral system, for Veltroni the DS will support the Segni-Di Pietro referendum.

7 After having threatened a crisis, the UDR carries out the threat in the Campania region sneaking away from the centre-right majority.

As the first acts of his leadership, Veltroni visits Norberto Bobbio and then to the grave of Fr. Giuseppe Dossetti. The PPI criticises the movement of the new leader on terrain not traditionally his.

9 During the vote on the budget in the budget commission, the majority is divided on the financing of non-state schools with the Greens and Socialists against.

Lawyers proclaim a week of strike against the sentence of the Constitutional Court on article 513. Scalfaro takes a harsh stance against the strike.

10 The government approves a legislative decree proposed by the Minister of Industry Bersani which heralds the end of ENEL's monopoly in the production of electrical energy.

12 At the end of the work of the General Assembly of the Italian Bishop Conference, its president, Cardinal Camillo Ruini, asks the new government to deal with the question of school equality by allocating a financial contribution to Catholic schools.

Abdullah Öcalan the leader of the PKK is arrested in Rome. There are two international warrants for his arrest, Turkish and German. He enters Italy thanks to the help of a PRC parliamentarian. A delicate diplomatic controversy begins on one hand, with the Turkish government and Öcalan's extradition to Turkey is denied, and on the other hand, with the German government which decides not to request extradition.

13 At the end of a series of experiments carried out on 386 patients, the Superior Institute of Health definitively rules the therapy to treat tumours adopted by Professor Luigi Di Bella ineffective.

Veltroni announces the composition of the leadership of DS. Franco Passuello, who resigned from his job at the ACLI the day before, becomes responsible for the organisation. This is not welcomed by the PPI.

After having convened the coordination of the *Ulivo* to relaunch the coalition and propose a unitary list for the European elections, Prodi cancels the meeting because of profound distance and dissent in relation to his proposals, especially by the Popular party.

17 Angelo Capodicasa (DS) becomes the new president of the Sicilian executive. Even if with difficulty, the first regional executive of the new 'centre-left' is passed.

19 The Movement for Popular Europe is launched by Pellegrino Capaldo, former president of the Banca di Roma. In line with Cossiga's political plans, its stated aim is a fundamental reconstruction of Italian political alignments.

22 The vote in Trentino Alto Adige for the renewal of the autonomous provinces signals a victory of the centre-left and a record for the SVP which reached 56 percent of votes in Bolzano. In Trento, the Margherita list promoted by the mayor of Trento, Lorenzo Dellai, which groups the PPI and the Movement for the *Ulivo* is successful (22 percent).

23 The firm News Corp Europe is presented in London and signalled the axis between the magnate of telecommunications, Rupert Murdoch, and the former president of the RAI, Letizia Moratti. Murdoch is negotiating with Telecom to enter into the management of the cable TV Stream.

25 After controversies and internal divisions, the majority reaches an initial agreement on school equality, which provides contributions and tax relief to the families of students enrolled in state and non-state schools for costs incurred for canteens, transport and foreign language. There are no contributions for the payment of fees.

26 The president of the Italian Bishops' Conference, Cardinal Camillo Ruini, intervenes in the debate on schools asking for more financing for non-state schools – up to four million lire per annum for every enrolled student.

27 In Milan a march of students protesting against school equality clashes with police for having tried to occupy a Catholic private school. In Rome, a delegation of parents, teachers and Catholic school students gives the President of the Senate, Nicolo Mancino, a petition for school equality signed by over one million four hundred thousand people.

29 First electoral round of various local government elections. Striking fall in turnout. Modest progress for the centre-left which wins three provincial presidencies and one city mayor in the first round.

December

1 The lower house of Parliament approves a reform of housing rent legislation. The new law ends controlled rent and intro-

duces two new forms of contract. First, a free-style one between the tenant and owner and second, a fixed one, which is the result of an agreement between tenant trade unions and owner associations.

2 After the administrative vote in Campania the crisis of the regional executive comes to a head and the President Antonio Rastrelli (AN) resigns.

Taking up the proposal contained in the *Ulivo*'s electoral programme, a group of parliamentarians close to Prodi presents an electoral reform proposal based on a two-round run-off system with a second ballot and an indication of the candidate for premier. Positive reaction of Veltroni and criticisms from the PPI.

3 The Central Banks of the eleven Euro countries cut the cost of money to 3 percent in view of the entry into force of the Euro. Bankitalia stays at 3.5 percent leading to some criticisms from other countries.

7 The DS announces that it will runs candidates jointly under both its own symbol, and that of the *Ulivo,* at the next election. Prodi approves, but the PPI does not, claiming that it has not been agreed between coalition partners in the alliance.

9 Repudiating prior declarations of Buttiglione, for the first time Cossiga declares that the formula on which the D'Alema government is based has a strategic respite for the UDR.

12 Minister Amato presents some elements of a proposal for mediation on the electoral law.

13 The second round of administrative elections confirms the high percentage of abstentions which increase by 9 percent vis-à-vis the first round. The province of Rome is won by the *Polo*, while in the municipality of Brescia, the *Ulivo* candidate wins out.

The fourth National Conference of Volunteers concludes in the presence of D'Alema, who welcomes almost all requests presented to him: more funding, tax allowances and a commitment to redefine the juridical statute of volunteer work.

While the negotiations between Telecom and Rupert Murdoch are still ongoing, the RAI agrees on a digital platform with the French Canal Plus.

16 The lower house definitively approves a new law on banking foundations.

In the absence of a precautionary agreement with the UN and their European allies, the U.S.A. and Britain militarily attack Iraq.

17 D'Alema calls for an end to the Anglo-American offensive in Iraq.

18 After a meeting of the Movement for the *Ulivo,* Prodi lays out his conditions for the European elections: no common list with

the UDR, a unitary *Ulivo* list or party lists with a common *Ulivo* symbol and a unitary programme.

20 The lower house of Parliament definitively approves the 1999 budget.

After new searches in the office of the bishop, the Cardinal of Naples, Michele Giordano openly attacks the investigating magistrates of Lagonegro, accusing them of ideological hostility to the Catholic Church.

21 A 'referendum-front' rally is held in Rome: Fini, Casini, Veltroni and Prodi participate.

22 The government signs the new development pact with thirty-two trade unions and business representatives. The pact covers tax relief on labour costs for firms (3 percent) and IRPEF discounts for workers (1-2 percent), activation of investments worth L.20,000 billion in 1999, and L.1,600 billion earmarked for training over three years.

The first meeting of the government majority on electoral reform is held. Minister for Institutional Reform Giuliano Amato presents four separate sets of proposals for examination.

23 Governor Fazio lowers the cost of borrowing to 3 percent, the level reached by the European Central Bank for Euro countries.

Confederal trade unions and sectoral organisations sign an agreement that fixes new rules for strikes.

26 It is revealed that Telecom has reached an agreement with Rupert Murdoch providing for the transfer of 80 percent of the cable TV Stream in preparation for the launch of a second digital platform.

28 The stock exchange recovers all the losses caused by the Asian crisis and puts on 2.84 percent, bringing the Mibtel to 23,720 points. While remaining some way short of the overall record, in a year the Stock Exchange has put on 41percent.

31 The definitive value of the Euro is fixed with respect to national currencies. One Euro is worth L.1936.27.

Translated by Claire Marie O'Neil

INTRODUCTION:
ONE STEP TOWARDS EUROPE; TWO STEPS BACK FROM INSTITUTIONAL REFORM[1]

David Hine and Salvatore Vassallo

1998 should have been the year in which Italian political life entered the realm of 'European normality'. The Prodi government's success in securing participation in European Monetary Union was expected by many to consolidate Italy's standing as a reliable and respected partner among the major states of the Union. At the same time, the government should have been strengthened by the credibility this achievement gave it in the eyes of public opinion, and this in turn ought to have underwritten the political stability necessary to push forward the process of institutional reform. Convergence with European standards at the institutional level was the declared aim of the *Bicamerale* (the Bicameral Commission on Institutional Reform). Under the chairmanship of Massimo D'Alema, the *Bicamerale* was expected to exploit Italy's renewed international credibility and governmental stability to secure the long-elusive goal of wide-ranging constitutional reform.

On 25 March 1998, both the European Commission and the European Monetary Institute reported that Italy had made sufficient progress towards fulfilment of the criteria for economic and monetary convergence laid down in the Maastricht Treaty to qualify her for first-wave membership of monetary union. However, neither this, nor other achievements credited to the Prodi government, were enough to secure the political and institutional developments that had been hoped for. Less than two months later, on 2 June, the *Bicamerale* was definitively and deliberately blocked by the leader of *Forza Italia*, Silvio Berlusconi. The third attempt in fifteen years to reform the institutional framework through a parliamentary commission thus ended in the same manner as its predecesors. On 9 October, moreover, Romano Prodi was forced to acknowledge the irretrievable breakdown of his parliamentary majority. He failed, albeit by just one vote, to secure a vote of confidence in the Chamber of Deputies. The thirteenth Republican legislature therefore went the same way as its predecessor. The coalition which had fought the election with a preselected prime-ministerial candidate, and which had been given a majority by the electorate, fell apart in mid-legislature, to be substituted by a new, post-electoral coalition agreement. On this occasion, moreover, the short-term solution of a non-party technocratic government was not adopted, but rather the potentially more lasting one of a government directly built from the parties which supported it. As the principal political actors themselves acknowledged, therefore, the collapse of the *Bicamerale*, and of the Prodi government, rudely interrupted the political and institutional developments set in train by the 1996 election result, and any prospect it seemed to herald of a consolidation of party-system bipolarity around the two coalitions of the *Ulivo* and the *Polo delle Libertà*.

The most immediate and visible causes of this turn of events were the changing interests and motives of the main political actors. However, it is increasingly clear that the Italian political transformation cannot be properly understood without taking into account the linkage between the internal dynamics of the national political system and changes in the European political context. Pressures for European convergence, both within and beyond the Maastricht economic and monetary convergence criteria, were responsible for some of main institutional modifications and sectoral reforms introduced by the Prodi government. It was, moreover, precisely the climate generated by the absolute necessity of the convergence criteria, and the dominance of the doctrines of stability laid down so vigorously by the Bundesbank, along with the need, in that context, to restore Italian credibility, that underwrote the hold exercised by Prodi and Ciampi over the government.

Berlusconi's sudden decision to block the *Bicamerale* appeared in part to be motivated by his personal and legal situation, but he also seems to have perceived that Italy's qualification for monetary union was not bringing any special electoral benefit for the Prodi government, given the unchanged, indeed growing, level of unemployment, and given the possibility that the imbalance between the

Italian party system and its European counterparts could create significant problems for the survival of the *Ulivo* coalition. Similarly, behind the decision by Fausto Bertinotti, leader of *Rifondazione Comunista*, to break with the Prodi government lay not only short-term intra-party calculations, but also the explicit intention of escaping from the policy straight-jacket imposed by Maastricht.

Finally, international developments quickly had an impact on the newborn government of Massimo D'Alema, and especially on the inter-party balance on which it was based. The unexpected climate of recession generated by the Asian financial crisis, and by the simultaneous election of a large number of left-wing governments across the EU, opened up the possibility of a relaxation of the EMU Stability Pact and a softening of the monetary rigour which had been imposed unremittingly since the exchange-rate crisis of 1992. Instead, there at last appeared some possibility of policies oriented more towards increasing employment, if necessary through extensive public investment. While such a policy might leave D'Alema feeling more at home among his European colleagues, and more comfortable in managing the internal conflicts of his own coaltion, it also provided possible excuses for postponing highly necessary reforms in the social, economic, and institutional fields.

The Politics of Convergence

The Prodi government undoubtedly had a number of creditable achievements to its name. The most significant was the reduction of the budget deficit, confirmed by the EU's confirmation in May 1998 that Italy was ready to participate in monetary union. Admittedly, much of the credit is attributable to decisions taken before the Centre-Left came to power, and to falling interest rates and debt-servicing costs. Nevertheless, the last two budget cycles – those of 1996 and 1997 – also made a major contribution to the process. As late as September 1996 there had still been a fairly widespread assumption that Italy would join monetary union with a delay of at least a couple of years compared with France and Germany. However, when it became clear that even Spain was determined to meet the 1999 deadline, the Prodi government had to respond with additional budgetary measures to ensure it qualified.

Certainly, the political circumstances the government enjoyed on coming to power were favourable. Ensuring Italian participation in EMU had been the *Ulivo*'s key campaign issue. Its election could be seen symbolically as an endorsement of that policy – albeit with less conviction in the light of detailed examination of the election results themselves. The likelihood of a full five-year term for the government made it possible to present the restrictiveness of the 1997 budget as the prelude to a more expansive phase of policy in advance of the next general election, and hence to synchronise the electoral cycle with the economic one.

With a reasonable level of internal cohesion, and the prospect of a long run ahead of it, the government embarked on a series of initiatives which came to legislative fruit during 1998. Several were long-awaited improvements which, albeit without any formal constitutional change, made significant contributions to structural and institutional reform. Indeed, the way in which they were achieved was something of a reform in its own right, for the centre of gravity in policy formulation seemed to shift significantly towards the executive. The intervention of party secretaries was limited, and the role of Parliament much reduced. The government operated through delegated authority, enjoying a freedom of manoeuvre circumscribed, as regards both principles and substantive contents, in the loosest possible way, and often bordering on the limits of constitutionality.

Thus, by use of delegated legislation, 1998 brought the completion of the rationalisation, begun in earlier years, by which the budget, the budgetary process, and the Ministry of the Budget were all significantly overhauled (see the chapter in this volume by David Felsen), and power was concentrated in the hands of the Treasury Minister (currently Carlo Azeglio Ciampi) and the Director-General of the Treasury (currently Mario Draghi). The year also brought a further round of legislative reform in pursuit of the Bassanini decentralisation initiatives contained in law 59/97. During the year more than a dozen legislative decrees were issued in pursuit of the authority granted to the government by this law, including a significant reform of the law on public employment and the higher civil service (on which issues see the chapter by Mark Gilbert).[2] Significant innovations through delegated legislation were also effected to health-service financing, with the removal of the special *'tassa per la salute'*, and the establishment if *Irap* (a tax on regional productive output), which gave the regional authorities a limited degree of fiscal autonomy, with the removal of a series of small tax charges on business, and with a redesign of the structure of personal income-tax.

Beyond these specific legislative achievements, the general performance of the Prodi government could also, without undue charity, be judged as quite creditable, particularly in view of the unexpected pressures that developed on a number of fronts: the Constitutional Court's ban on the reiteration of decree-laws; the earthquakes in Umbria and the Marches; and the emergency security situation that arose in Albania. In some sectors (transport, education) the legacy of a long period of inadequate infrastructure investment was beginning to show alarming problems. In the transport sector there was a wave of industrial action and an unprecedented number of railway accidents that put a question mark against the credibility, security and effectiveness of the entire rail system. Strikes and other travel problems were not absent in the air-transport sector either, with the government having for the first time to face a bitter conflict with the European Commission (on the Malpensa affair see the chapter by David Hine).

The government also faced its fair share of minor accidents and difficulties, including the extraordinary incident provoked by the popular clamour for Professor Di Bella's quite unproven (and in early trials ineffective) cancer treatment, amplified in its effects by the opposition, and by some dubious intervention by the administrative courts. In other areas where the cohesion of the majority was under threat (expansion of NATO, assistance to private schools, artificial fertilisation, the thirty-five-hour working week), the government did its best to play down the divisions in its majority. Its biggest difficulty was the limited nature of the resources it could devote to the south, and this provided one of the main issues on which Fausto Bertinotti justified the decision of *Rifondazione Comunista* to break with the majority. The government's greatest weakness was perhaps an inability to show, even symbolically, that it was concerned and engaged by the issue, focused as it was on its European objectives, and hampered by the unwillingness of the main social and political actors to support the possibility of launching – even at the level of public utterances – the so-called 'phase two' of its programme.

The life of the Prodi government was certainly never completely smooth, therefore, particularly during the passage of its three autumn budget cycles, but, in relation to most of its predecessors in the 1990s, the government generated an impression of legislative activism, of reasonable – though by no means complete – administrative cohesion and coordination, and (RC apart), of a relatively stable parliamentary majority built on an identifiable, electorally endorsed, coalition.

The Failure of the 'Strategy of the 21 April'

The survival of the government was nevertheless strictly linked to the pursuit and overall reinforcement of what can be called the 'strategy of the 21 April' (the date of the *Ulivo's* 1996 election victory). The term 'strategy' is clearly elusive, since behind the apparent solidarity of the prime minister and the leaders of the various parties of his coalition there lurked a good deal of serious mutual suspicion. Moreover, whether it grew out of any real collective purpose, or simply short-term coincidence of interest, the 'strategy' was built on two distinct pillars: European policies, pursued by the Prodi government, and institutional reform, where the main protagonist was the PDS leader, Massimo D'Alema.

The government's survival in office, and with it the strengthening of bipolarity, would also benefit even in the short term from the continuation of the work of the *Bicamerale*. In the short term it facilitated a satisfactory division of labour between the *Ulivo* as a coalition, the leadership of which was not called into question, and the leaders of the individual parties, who were preoccupied with negotiations over institutional reform. In particular, Massimo D'Alema could be satisfied with the credibility he would generate for himself as the statesman-like architect of reform, and with the possibility that through this he would eventually be a fully legitimised candidate for the prime minister's office.

There was also a prospect that the reforms being advanced in the *Bicamerale* – technically imperfect, but clearly designed to freeze in place the *Ulivo/Polo* bipolarity and strengthen the stability of the government – could at least reduce, though not eliminate, the disproportionate bargaining power of the smaller parties. It was striking that after the 1996 election, and in contrast to what had happened in the past, such a goal could be in the interests of all the main political actors (AN, FI, and the PDS), and as long as it was accompanied by some residual element of proportionality, seemed acceptable to the PPI as well. In short, a window of opportunity might be presenting itself to overcome the usual barriers to reform, since in the course of the transformation of the political system, the partisan interests of the main actors had changed – albeit not irrevocably – towards a more majoritarian and competitive party democracy.

Analytically, however, it remains unclear quite what the failure of the *Bicamerale* demonstrates about the possibility of a consensual, broad-based party agreement on constitutional reform. It may show that it is *radically impossible* – either because the interests of the parties, and their political strategies are in unavoidable conflict, as Gianfranco Pasquino shows in his chapter, or because what Italians call *un potere costituito* (a political class elected to hold office) cannot transform itself into *un potere costituente*[3] (a group of representatives mandated to define the rules of office-holding). Or it may show simply that failure on this occasion has arisen from the fact that the key actors in the rule-drafting exercise were not all focused exclusively on the rational pursuit of political objectives.[4]

In particular, the moment chosen by Silvio Berlusconi to torpedo the *Bicamerale*, and the justification he gave for doing so, suggest that the decision was taken impulsively, and for short-term reasons, principal among which was that constitutional reform was not going to lead to the sort of change in the judicial-political balance of power he had hoped for, and that if his own judicial difficulties were to get worse, no-one amongst those he was negotiating with intended to offer him any assistance. Hence the judgement that it was better to face the court proceedings pending against him (some of which were about to come to a conclusion) by raising the stakes through heightened confrontation with the parties of the majority. Such considerations were certainly mixed in with those of a strictly political character.

It had become clear, already in the first round of local elections, that there was political space for Francesco Cossiga's new centrist political group, and that the latter's aims could serve Berlusconi's interests as well. At the same moment, the leaders of the European People's Party announced their willingness to make *Forza Italia* a part of the EPP in the European Parliament, a development which underlined the extent to which the domestic political alliances of the PPI in Italy were out of line with those elsewhere in the EU.

Both factors, the former in the short term and the latter in the longer term, suggested that, with Cossiga's help, *Forza Italia* could gain from a general shift of the political centre of gravity inside the *Polo* which would help it take centrist votes away from the PPI. This became all the more likely as it grew clear that the government was drawing no electoral premium from Italy's ability to satisfy the EMU convergence criteria. Indeed there was a growing backlog of issues (NATO enlargement, private schools, IVF, the thirty-five-hour week) on which moderates in the coalition were electorally vulnerable. Such a strategy would also clip the wings of *Alleanza Nazionale*, whose leader was becoming a serious contender for the leadership of the *Polo*, and who, thanks to the institutional stabilisation of bipolarity, would be able to free himself from Berlusconi's patronage. But if the collapse of the *Bicamerale* allowed Berlusconi to intensify the tone of ideological conflict, softened the impact of his judicial difficulties, and even won him a degree of short-term popularity, it certainly did not – and could not – generate the expected effects in terms of inter-party relationships.

Thus it may have been that non-political considerations led Berlusconi to misjudge the impact of what seemed to him to be good political calculations driving his strategy. That strategy certainly brought him into conflict with AN, and also generated increasing discontent with FI's parliamentary ranks. Unable to express their views openly by the lack of internal party democracy, some of these dissidents in turn opted to leave the party (on which issue see the chapter by Marco Tarchi and Emanuela Poli). Most significantly of all, the subsequent tactics of Francesco Cossiga showed how little foundation there was to Berlusconi's calculations concerning a shift in the centre of gravity in the *Polo*. Cossiga too, wanted such a shift, but only as a means of displacing Berlusconi as the leader of the centre-right, and to achieve this it was indispensible to destroy the constitutional reform process.

At any event the collapse of the *Bicamerale* once more focused the attention of party leaders on the government, and with – for the government itself – some unfortunate consequences. Just as it was becoming clear to D'Alema that he had lost the chance to be the broker of constitutional reform slip, the fortunes of several of his peers in other EU states were on the rise, and the sight of colleagues assemble for meetings of the European Socialist group, and proceed straight on to Heads of Government summits, was clearly a certain humiliation. It was only natural, therefore, that D'Alema should start to ask why it was still necessary to give such unconditional PDS support to Prodi, while everywhere in Europe the left was putting its own leaders in power. Ironically a similar question was starting to arise in the ranks of the PPI. For Prodi had always insisted – in the interests of serving as a leader above the parties of his coalition – on maintaining an ambiguous relationship with the PPI. Thus it was that what had been Prodi's great strength while the Maastricht criteria continued to loom so large in the aftermath of the 1996 election – his origins in the moderate part of the coalition, without, however, being institutionally tied to any single party – began to become a serious element of weakness.

Unlike technocrat prime ministers like Ciampi and Dini, Prodi had secured the direct personal sanction of the voters, but what he shared with them was the need to rely on the support of parties which retained their loyalty to individual party leaders rather than to the 'leader of the coalition'. Things might have been different if Prodi had been able to give greater organisational cohesion to the *Ulivo* coalition as a political unit, or if the institutional context had been less hostile. But he appeared to show little awareness of the importance of either. His evident indifference to the fate of the *Bicamerale*, his unwillingness to push the parties of the *Ulivo* towards a deal on institutional reform, and his failure to accept Berlusconi as the legitimate leader of the opposition (a necessary condition for any overall *bipartisan* agreement on reform) suggest that Prodi supposed that Italy's institutional problems had already, thanks to the 1996 election result, his own installation in Palazzo Chigi and the securing of the monetary convergence criteria, been resolved. Without his own political resources, and in an institutional context that did nothing to sustain governmental stability, Prodi found he had few resources to deal with the open rebellion launched by *Rifondazione* or the more concealed efforts to the same end by other parts of his majority.

Against expectations, moreover, the achievement of the convergence criteria brought no significant benefits in terms of his personal popularity. The business class had been among his most ardent supporters, and gave him some credit for the results of his economic reform packages, and for policies that helped particular sectors (for example in relation to the motor industry, through incentives to new car purchase, and to the building industry through housing refurbishment programmes). But it continued to express doubts about him. It was no coincidence that a leading figure from the businesss world, Marco Tronchetti Provera, had alrady expressed the view in 1997, during a bitter confrontation between the government and *Confindustria*, that Massimo D'Alema should become prime minister. For their part, the unions, CISL no less than the others, remained extremely cool towards the prime minister.

Although these factors made the government an inherently fragile one, there were also unexpected contingent factors in its eventual downfall which were beyond the control of any of the coalition parties: Bertinotti's determination to leave the majority and escape the uncomfortable logic imposed by the identification of the government with the whole of the Italian left; Cossiga's desperate search for the political visibility and importance that he could not hope to derive from an opposition role shared with Berlusconi and Fini; Prodi's initial unwillingness, in a position of weakness, to do a deal with the UDR – an error itself arising from a miscalculation about the numbers of last-minute defections likely within his own majority. A crucial role was also played by the President of the Republic. This role was not as decisive as that played in the crisis of December 1994, when Scalfaro was the broker of a new coalition to replace the one that had collapsed. But it did involve presidential reiteration of what has become almost a constitutional convention concerning the obligation to make every effort to keep the existing legislature in being – even if this means the emergence of a coalition different from that endorsed by voters. And this in turn allowed all the actors in favour of a reworking of the structure of the coalition (Cossiga no less than Bertinotti) to exercise their potential for political blackmail without any immediate electoral risk.

Once (for reasons well-explained in the chapter by Sergio Fabbrini) a technocratic solution to the crisis had been excluded, the only solution left was a new *postelectoral* coalition agreement.

Without doubt the best-qualified individual for this operation –
given the open support he enjoyed from Cossiga's UDR, and from
Cossutta's faction which had broken away from *Rifondazione
Comunista* and even, though less explicitly, from the PPI secretary,
Franco Marini – was Massimo D'Alema.

The New Version of the Centre-Left

The D'Alema government undoubtedly opened a new chapter in
Italy's institutional transition, although in so far as it brought a
resumption of the practice of (postelectoral) coalition mediation
and bargaining it actually appeared in certain respects to mark the
end-stage of transition. The failure of the *Bicamerale* and the ensu-
ing Prodi crisis were generally interpreted as a significant brake on
the reform process of the 1990s, though as we shall see it would be
wrong to see the formation of a centre-left government led by the
leader of the DS as a straightforward step backwards towards the
First Republic.

The resumption of postelectoral coalition bargaining certainly
brought (or perhaps simply brought into the open) a strong sense
the former style of political life. In the first place, while the departure from the majority of *Rifondazione Comunista* could be interpreted as the defection of a group that never fully accepted the
Ulivo programme, the entry into the majority of a group elected
with the votes of the opposition parties undermined the credibility
of the institutional conventions inspired by majoritarian competitive democracy that all the candidates elected on the lists of the
Polo and the *Ulivo* in 1996 claimed to adhere to. The creation of the
UDR and its entry into the governing majority was moreover only
one part of the heady series of changes of party group that have
been practised by MPs in the current legislature.[5]

The formation of the government through a process of postelectoral coalition bargaining brought a clear cost in terms of the size of
the governmental team, and put in office, albeit in limited numbers,
individuals of doubtful competence and credibility. Overall, however,
thanks to the retention of some key figures – most notably Ciampi at
the Treasury – it was difficult to argue that the quality of ministerial
personnel was clearly worse than in the preceding government.

The D'Alema government's freedom of manoeuvre was likely to
be circumscribed by the demands of its component parties, keen to
assert their individual bargaining power and to differentiate themselves from one another. It was certainly going to be difficult, for
example, for the D'Alema government to cope with the first seri-

ous, albeit little noticed, test of its capacity to take tough decisions: the reform of the stucture of the ministries of Italian central government, and their reduction in number, provided for in the so-called Bassanini Law (n. 59/1997) implementation of which had been repeatedly postponed.

However, it was at regional government level that the return of post-electoral politics offered very clear evidence of the sort of degeneration that could happen. Where the centre-right majorities had been especially fragile, once the second year of the legislature arrives, and with it the point at which the collapse of a ruling executive no longer leads automatically to fresh elections, coalition conspiracies and party bargaining returned. As has occurred before, the solution to the crisis in the largest southern regions (Calabria, Campania, Sicilia) was determined, in the wake of the government agreement at national level, by national party leaders acting on the basis of a 'fair' distribution of the presidencies of the ruling executives. Moreover, in a repeat of behaviour not unknown in the First Republic, there were even conflicts between factions of a single party, the PPI, even though the latter had only about one third as many votes as the former Christian Democrat Party.

This said, the allocation of the office of President of the Council of Ministers to the leader of the largest party – albeit without direct electoral sanction – did appear to overcome a damaging peculiarity of the Italian political system in the shape of the incomplete legitimacy of the PDS as a governing party. It made the two major coalition alignments, the context of party relationships, and operation of institutional rules, much more congruent. Naturally, though this eliminated certain ambiguities, it seemed to close the door for good on certain important institutional innovations.

The PDS was (and remains) numerically the dominant group on the centre-left, as well as its centre of gravity. It also serves to integrate the excessively fragmented components of the coalition. That the leader of the PDS was not thought of as the right candidate for the premiership in the 1996 elections was an anomoly generated by the fear that the PPI electorate was wary of an agreement with 'post-communists' and would not be willing as a result to vote for the *Ulivo*. In the absence of formal mechanisms of personal investiture either before the formation of the government – such as primary elections – or after it – for example, institutional rules strengthening the power of the chief executive – the candidacy of a nonpartisan leader for the coalition exposed the government to permanent ambiguity over the type of legitimacy the chief executive enjoyed: on the one hand the electoral legitimacy based on voter support for coalition and leader together, and on the other that based on party and parliamentary mediation (see, on this issue, the chapter in this volume by Sergio Fabbrini).[6]

With the formation of the D'Alema government, there has therefore been a return to the legitimation of the government through exclusively party and parliamentary mechanisms, making more difficult the transition to a new framework in which, as in competitive parliamentary systems, the two processes of legitimation tend to be superimposed on one another. The albeit narrow window of opportunity to introduce significant institutional reform which opened with the election of 21 April 1996 appears moreover to have been closed definitively.

If, at this point, that part of the electorate which voted in 1994 and 1996 for the centre-right shows itself unwilling to cross the polar divide (especially if the centre-left is dominated by the DS) Cossiga's ideas, to which the centrist catholics could have lent their support, would become impractical, and the boundaries of the present majority would be frozen (on the possibility of significant electoral shifts between the blocks, see the chapter by Renato Mannheimer and Giacomo Sani). If the institutional rules remain unchanged, however, the freezing of the boundaries between the centre-right and centre-left would not reduce party fragmentation. On the contrary, it is likely that the practices of *trasformismo* and parliamentary splintering that have marked the first half of the 1996 legislature will persist into the second half, and indeed that the tensions in the now highly overcrowded 'centre' of the coalition (RI, *l'Italia dei valori*, Prodi, UDR, PPI, *Centocittà*) will continue indefinitely rather than be resolved. Worse still, perhaps, hope of effective electoral reform, let alone of a resumption of the path of constitutional reform, now seems very thin. Once again, with the closure of the window of opportunity of the third *Bicamerale*, only pressures from outside the party system itself (such as the referendum procedure) can hope to overcome the mutual vetoes that block the parliamentary process.

In addition to the limits implicit in the way it was put together, this second version of the centre-left faced in the second half of the legislature a range of difficulties for inter-party relations not present in the first half, including, almost immediately, a referendum on electoral reform, European Parliament elections, and the election of a new President of the Republic, followed a year later, by regional elections. Faced with these electoral challenges, and with constitutional reform impractical, the best hope of the D'Alema government therefore lay in its capacity to develop those policy initiatives the foundations of which were laid down by the Prodi government, adding to them a more visible and stronger commitment to the problems of employment, and of the south.

Thanks to the measures of economic reform taken between 1992 and 1998, with interest rates already approximating to the European average and with debt-servicing costs falling, the credibility premium inherited by the new government thanks to the work of its predecessors gave some additional margin of manoeuvre on either expenditure or taxation. In the 'Social Compact' signed on 22 December, it was evident that there was both a clear style of approach (social concertation) and a detailed list of measures to which the government intended to give priority in exploiting this opportunity. Through it D'Alema won the apparently enthusiastic support of a social coalition even wider in scope than the party coalition on which he depended in Parliament. Here too, however, it was possible to foresee that the very broad range of representative groups which signed the agreement, like the parties that sanctioned the formation of the government, would not be backward in pressing their far from compatible interests.[7]

The govermental programme to which the contents of the social compact alluded must, moreover, be placed in an international context which contained numerous uncertainties. After several years of slow growth, the Italian economy might reasonably have been expected to be on the verge of a new period of more rapid expansion in 1998 and 1999. However, by the second half of 1998 the global financial crisis had started to have an impact on investment and business confidence in Europe. Expectations of growth were scaled back, especially for Italy. Europe's centre-left governments started to talk in neo-Keynesian terms of renegotiating the terms of the EMU Stability Pact, and of deficit spending and employment creation schemes to stimulate the economy. The impact of this new psychological climate in Italy was still, at the end of 1998, very uncertain, but the possibility remained that it would remove the pent-up inhibitions inside the Italian parties and the Italian Parliament that, since 1992, had placed the initiative in financial and economic management so firmly in the hands of the executive.

The challenge for the new D'Alema government, therefore, was to manage its EMU debt-servicing premium effectively, in a political atmosphere where the pressures from its broad parliamentary majority, from the even broader social coalition it has assembled, from the approach of elections, and from the changing European policy climate, all pushed in the direction of a more permissive attitude towards public expenditure, and of less coherent policy-making. It was a formidable challenge for the skills of the new President of the Council, who, following the failure of the *Bicamerale*, needed to show a capacity both to broker agreements that would get him into office, and, having done so, to ensure their implementation.

Notes

1. An earlier version of the introduction, along with the other chapters in this volume, was discussed at a seminar held on 19 December 1998 at the Mulino Association Library, Bologna. We wish to thank the participants of the seminar – and in particular apart from the authors of the book, Stefano Ceccanti, Carlo Guarnieri, Angelo Panebianco, Arturo Parisi and Paolo Segatti – for helpful observations and advice on this and other papers.

2. On the revision of *Decreto* n. 29/1993 on the '*dirigenza pubblica*' (*D.Lgs*. 80, 1998), by which, *inter alia*, the operational independence of the *Direttori Generali* is strengthened, as is the freedom of ministers to appoint them, see the articles published in the special issues of *Le istituzioni del federalismo*, n. 5, 1998.

3. See Angelo Panebianco, *Due opposte concezioni della democrazia. Un presidente non un arbitro*, *Corriere della Sera*, 3 gennaio 1999.

4. This view has been developed in: Salvatore Vassallo, *Il cambiamento delle istituzioni politiche (intra)visto dalla Bicamerale*, paper presented at the Annual Conference of the *Società Italiana di Scienza Politica*, Milano, 18-20 June 1998.

5. See in this connection the data in Table C3 and C4 of the appendix. This 'fluidity' in the partisan affiliations of MPs was both *permitted* by systemic factors which made defection from the group or coalition of election relatively costless, and it was *incentivised* by distributive and regulatory factors, such as the rules by which an individual MP could claim a share of public party financing, and by which as few as two MPs could claim access to the *Provvidenze per l'editoria di partito*.

6. It is no coincidence that the position of 'nonparty of a coalition' is unknown in multi-party parliamentary systems. See Laver, M. and Shepsle, K.A. (eds), *Cabinet Ministers and Parliamentary Government*, Cambridge: Cambridge University Press, 1994; Blondel, J. and Cotta, M. (eds), *Party and Government*, London: Macmillan, 1996.

7. It was in particular uncertain what would happen to the reform of the distribution sector launched by the Prodi government, and whether the D'Alema government would, as the Under-secretary at the Presidency of the Council of Ministers stated, ensure its full implementation, in spite of the rediscovered support for the government, manifested by the main associations representing the sector.

1

The Two Lefts:
Between Rupture and Recomposition

Oreste Massari and Simon Parker

For the two main strands of the Italian left, 1998 was an eventful and sometimes dramatic year. Under the leadership of Massimo D'Alema, the reformist mainstream left took on direct responsibility for government in a new centre-left coalition, untried in terms of stability and coherence. What might be described as the radical, or even 'combative', left, in contrast, definitively cut the ties that had insecurely bound it to the *Ulivo* coalition since the elections of 1996. Its choice was the radical one of 'opposition to the system'. In the process it suffered a lacerating schism which fundamentally compromised its electoral future and indeed its very existence as a political party. As the reformist left evolved, it assumed an ever more 'responsible' and governmental character, while the combative left showed in no uncertain terms that it wanted nothing to do with such responsibilities. Even more than in the past, therefore, the two strands of the Italian left opted for political directions quite independent of one another. Given where each ended up, in fact, the distance between them was probably as great as it had ever been.

From the PDS to the DS

For the PDS the year began with the so-called *Cosa 2* initiative.[1] The aim was to bring together the various components of the left in a 'social democratic party' of a European stamp. It ended with

the transfer of the post of PDS party secretary from Massimo
D'Alema to Walter Veltroni, who more than any other figure within
the party embodied the values of the *Ulivo*. The tension within the
PDS between the idea of a 'social democratic party' and that of a
'party of the *Ulivo*' was unexpectedly eased by the fall of the Prodi
government and the subsequent reshuffle that installed D'Alema in
Palazzo Chigi and Veltroni as party secretary. The construction of
a European-style social democratic movement was supposed not
only to refine the PDS's post-communist identity, but also and
more importantly to incorporate within the *Ulivo* project various
other groups that had been left without direct party representation
after the restructuring of the political system that occurred between
1992 and 1994. These included reformist Catholicism (the Social-
Christians), the secular centre (the Republicans and some ex-Lib-
erals), Socialists, and the 'United Communists' who had broken
with *Rifondazione Comunista* during the Dini premiership.

The *Stati Generali della Sinistra* (General Assembly of the Left)
which took place in Florence from 12-14 February 1998 was the
most significant meeting in a process which had begun with the
launch of the *Forum della Sinistra* (Left Forum) in January 1996.
This convention had generated a new political formation known as
Democratici della Sinistra (Left Democrats) to which the afore-
mentioned groups were affiliated in a federal model allowing for
different levels of membership. At the same time, it opened the
transitional constituent phase of the new party, which was scheduled to conclude in a national congress to be held in advance of the
European elections in the spring of 1999.[2]

The key policies were to be those that had initially been developed
by the Left Forum, which were said to represent the most innovative
strands in European socialist thought. It was stressed, however, that
there remained a central role for parties and party organisation.
D'Alema's ideas on politico-institutional modernisation and innovation were rooted in the belief that Italian democracy was best reconstructed through parties, albeit parties which were renovated and
differentiated from their predecessors.[3] On this point, D'Alema, along
with the leadership of the party, drew a distinction between his position and that strongly advocated by both his predecessor as party secretary Achille Occhetto, and the '*Ulivista*' tendency both inside and
outside the PDS. According to the latter view, the Italian crisis that
developed as a result of '*partitocrazia*' (the perjorative 'party-ocracy')
could be overcome only if the traditional forms of party representation were superseded by 'direct' institutional and political forms, and
if, as a consequence, the centre-left coalition became a unified political entity. D'Alema's view, in contrast, was that the degeneration of

the party system was due to Italy's so-called 'blocked democracy', and to the absence of alternative governments. It followed therefore that the goal should not be to move beyond party democracy but to rebuild it within an institutional system capable of stabilising the existing bipolarity. The different analyses of the issues at stake – the interpretation of the Italian crisis and the prospects of emerging from the already protracted transition – were to reverberate around the interpretation of the *Ulivo* alliance and of the Prodi government itself for most of the year.

For the '*Ulivisti*' inside and outside the party, the electoral and policy-making alliance that won the elections of 21 April 1996 (albeit with the external support of Communist Refoundation) should have produced a qualitative change, transforming it from a loose alliance of convenience into a real political actor capable of imposing its political sovereignty on its component parts and thus eventually of absorbing them. For the *Ulivisti*, therefore, the Prodi government was the optimal way to achieve majoritarian democracy, and indeed Prodi himself was always lukewarm towards the work of the of the Bicameral Commission on Constitutional Reform (*Bicamerale*) which he saw as a less satisfactory route to this objective. D'Alema, in contrast, while continuing to give the government full and loyal support, saw institutional reform as vitally necessary, because without it both the DS and the wider coalition would continue to be vulnerable to the continuing power of veto of *Rifondazione Comunista*.

If the *Cosa 2* project placed the new formation fully and legitimately in the mainstream of European social democracy, its *modus operandi* and its outcomes did not live up to this ambition. What should have been a fundamental stage in the process of combining the various elements of the reformist left into a single organisation, in reality produced only limited support and little interest. The *Cosa 2* operation was managed in a highly bureaucratic way[4] which failed fully to involve the rank-and-file of the party, especially at local level. In addition, the PDS secretary often failed take a personal stake in the development of *Cosa 2* in the way that he had during the deliberations of the *Bicamerale*. The major limiting factor was the absence of important elements of the socialist area, including the key figure of Giuliano Amato. Although it succeeded in signing up some significant groups from the traditional spectrum of Italian politics, *Cosa 2* could not, in the end, be described as much more than an enlarged PDS. It was therefore inadequate for launching itself on the electoral marketplace as a potential reservoir for left votes, particularly given the fact that the constituency of *Rifondazione Comunista* had remained unaffected by the reformist initiative of the PDS.

From Prodi to D'Alema

After the successful entry of the lira into the single European currency in May and the failure of the *Bicamerale* in June, relations between the largest party of the coalition and the government became more difficult as the DS began to exert more active pressure on government policy-making. With the entry into the Euro and the end of the *Bicamerale* a cycle of government and party-government relations appeared to draw to an end. Paradoxically, having reached the European finishing post – an objective around which the majority had found a strong motive for cohesion – the absence of a government programme, or at least some motivating or legitimizing goal, was exposed. By early summer, D'Alema was already criticizing the government's performance and announcing a 'second phase' of policy for the coalition, which would be particularly concerned with the problems of unemployment and the south.[5]

From May onwards, relations between Prodi and D'Alema clearly became more complex. It is true that when *Rifondazione* seemed to put the government's majority at risk – on NATO enlargement, and later on the Finance Bill – the official position of the party was full support for the majority which had voted it in, in 1996. 'If Fausto Bertinotti pulls out' – declared D'Alema on 6 May 1998 – 'the UDR will not come in [to government], instead we'll go to the polls.' And on the eve of the fall of the Prodi government on 5 October, D'Alema could still declare there would be 'no messengers sent to Palazzo Chigi', while Walter Veltroni, as Deputy Prime Minister, party number two, and a convinced *'Ulivisti'*, declared that D'Alema could only become Prime Minister following new elections in which he would explicitly be a candidate for such a post and after primary elections had been held among the party membership.[6] For his part Armando Cossutta, as leader of the *Rifondazione* dissidents, who eventually seceeded from the party and joined the coalition, declared that the votes of his deputies would never be combined with those of the UDR in order to form an alternative to the Prodi government.

The reality was more complex. D'Alema had already earlier in the summer been quoted as being in favour of early elections in order to reap the electoral dividend of the government's European success, when in September relations between himself and Prodi reached a new low point. In the middle of a crisis instigated by *Rifondazione Comunista* over the Finance Bill, D'Alema embarked on a long visit to Latin America, seemingly in order to distance himself from the very problems that were overtaking the governing majority. Despite the various proclamations of unity – each of which was subsequently undermined by events – what prevailed was the precariousness of political groupings and of their relationships to one and another, the power of contingency, the continuing deconstruction of the Italian political system, and in particular, the initiative launched by Francesco Cossiga.

Initially D'Alema was particularly harsh on this development, stating that 'the UDR is a dangerous and troubling initiative for Italian democracy' (March 1998). Nevertheless, the collapse of the *Bicamerale*, the fragility of the government (due mainly to RC's lack of consistent support), and the blandishments of the UDR (anxious to establish its political importance), quickly led D'Alema to change his attitude. As a realist, D'Alema was prepared to make use of the opportunity which the UDR offered the government. In his concluding speech to the National Festival of *L'Unità* (the party newspaper) in September, he went as far as to declare Francesco Cossiga 'a man above the fray' (*super-partes*). Thus it was that, in the face of the fall of the Prodi government, the PDS leadership, having rejected both early elections and a government of technocrats, accepted that realistically the existing *Ulivo* majority was finished, and made its bid to put D'Alema himself in the prime minister's office.

From D'Alema to Veltroni

The formation of the D'Alema government had as its immediate consequence the transfer of the leadership of the party to Walter Veltroni and the reorganisation of its internal executive bodies. Although D'Alema had at the same time assumed the far from honorific post of party President, the change seemed far-reaching. Since the time when they were in direct competition for the party secretaryship in July 1994, D'Alema and Veltroni continued to represent diverse strategic options regarding the identity and future of the party. The former, while being the real architect of the *Ulivo* electoral alliance, had emphasised the idea of the social-democratic party and *Cosa 2*. The latter had always dismissed *Cosa 2*, citing the limitations of the social-democratic tradition and was more attracted to the elusive notion of a 'world *Ulivo*' movement, the basis of which, according to an exclusively Italian reading of the event, would be laid at the much-publicised 'Third Way' seminar to be held in June in New York between Clinton, Blair and Prodi and Veltroni. In short, while D'Alema represented the claims of European socialism, Veltroni was drawn towards a more optimistic view of the *Ulivo* experience and by the idea of a broadly-based Italian 'democratic party'.

The novelty of a 'post-communist' politician at the head of the government forced the two leaders to define a new division of roles. Swapping roles between government and party did, however, allow Veltroni to put the issue of the party's future – which hitherto had been put on hold during the continuing national political emergency – at the top of his agenda. The party had suffered (and still suffers) from the imbalance between on the one hand both its role in government (which absorbs the energies of most of its key figures at all levels of government) and its general influence on political life, and yet on the other its still relatively modest level of electoral support. The difficulties it faces in this regard are also shown by the low level of participation in party life shown by its members. Commenting on the negative results of the autumn local elections, the group leader of the DS in the Chamber of Deputies, Fabio Mussi, put the problem thus, 'we are more able than we are powerful'. D'Alema himself was forced to admit that, 'the party is tired out, top heavy in its dealings with the voters. It has lost its shine and its idealistic charge. It has paid more attention to the routine of individual careers than to collective arguments.'[7]

Even though the centre-left coalition as a whole had improved on its previous performance, the autumn administrative elections were a warning for the DS. Its electoral losses were all too apparent, and it came as particularly galling that the party was defeated in the elections for the Rome provincial council, where the centre-left had previously held power and where the DS candidate for President was beaten by a candidate from *Alleanza Nazionale* and the *Polo*. Another alarm bell was the loss of membership. It was calculated that between 1992 and 1997 the party lost almost 100,000 members. Allowing for those who joined for the first time, the number of non-renewals rose to 200,000 over the same period.[8] The new secretary declared his intention to start dealing with the problem immediately, and without any further sensitivity to the party's allies in government. Although a commission to revise the party statute and its internal rules in preparation for *Cosa 2* had produced significant proposals for change, the project was set aside in favour of a revitalisation of the existing party. Veltroni's evident priority was to increase the party's share of the vote, rectify the imbalance between political centrality and organisational weakness, thwart the tendency to take shelter in government office, and generally to relaunch the party's role and presence in Italian society.[9]

The reorganisation of executive bodies within the party was intended to fulfil these objectives. For example, in order to fill the post of head of party organisation, an outsider – the Catholic Franco Passuello, the former president of ACLI – was appointed for the first time. The aim was not only to revive grass-roots participation through a special membership drive (the *Centosezioni* – or Hundred Branches) where the party secretary would make a personal appearance at certain selected local branches, but also to reach areas of society where traditionally the party had found itself excluded. However, the major sign of discontinuity between the new leadership and its predecessor was provided by the party's open and explicit support for the referendum campaign to abolish the proportional element in the voting system, a proposal to which D'Alema had responded in a noncommittal if not hostile manner.

All these initiatives served to confirm the new leadership's intention to adopt a strategy that was less constrained by the restrictions imposed on it by the centre-left alliance and – while mindful of the conflicts with the government's new alliance partner in the shape of Francesco Cossiga's UDR – to act in such a way that the need for party growth was no longer sacrificed. The possibility that this might be in conflict with the D'Alema government's desire for stability remained to be tested; certainly the possibility could not be excluded.

The Unhappy Marriage of the PRC and the Ulivo

Relations between Communist Refoundation and the broad coalition government which came to power under the premiership of Romano Prodi in April 1996 had never been harmonious. Unlike in 1994, the PRC did not formally join the *Ulivo* electoral pact as it had done with the *'Progressisti'*, but it did agree to stand-down arrangements with the *Ulivo* in constituency races where a conflict on the left would have given victory to the right. This grudging cooperation was to carry over to the parliamentary arena where the PRC's 34 deputies were crucial for the government's parliamentary majority.

From the beginning, however, both Bertinotti and his party adopted attitudes that were intended to underline the strategic and ideological differences between itself, and the *Ulivo* and PDS. Bertinotti repeatedly accused the *Ulivo* government of lacking any real drive for reform, and lamented its 'progressive reduction of politics to the confines of government'.[10] For Bertinotti, *Rifondazione*'s role was to galvanise the working class and anti-capitalist forces in civil society while using its parliamentary strength to defend the poor and the vulnerable.

The strategy for the development of this *'partito di massa'* was outlined at the party congress in July 1997 at Chianciano. It could not take the form that it had in the past since, as *Rifondazione*'s head of organisation pointed out, the historic conditions for the construction of a mass party on a Bolshevik model no longer existed.[11] Instead, the party had to search for new ways of bringing together those subjects who had a stake in opposing capitalist globalisation. However, as *Corriere della Sera* reported, the signs were not encouraging since the grass-roots organisation of the PRC appeared to be in a steep decline. By July 1998 only 73 percent of the membership had renewed its subscriptions, which even allowing for additional renewals before the year's end was not a promising statistic.[12] *L'Espresso* described *Rifondazione* as a party with a membership which, unlike the old PCI, was not mostly made up of industrial workers but instead chiefly comprised 'white-collar employees and health workers'. This Caprili denied, claiming that the PRC was increasingly recruiting students and manual workers while building its number of local associations (*circoli*) to nearly 3,000.[13] Nevertheless, it was undeniable that *Rifondazione*'s militants were predominantly well-educated radicals in secure public-sector jobs. A profile which conformed perfectly to that of far left groups in the rest of Europe, but hardly one which reflected the subaltern masses the party aspired to represent.

The PRC's aspirations to play the role of mass party made it all too aware of the need to establish a significant presence within the organised labour movement. The party had long been critical of the moderate leadership of Sergio Cofferati, the national secretary of the CGIL federation which had previously been a bastion of support for the old PCI, but which now took a more independent stance and favoured joint negotiations with the Catholic CISL federation and the moderate UIL. *Rifondazione* attacked the CGIL's involvement in national negotiations with employers dating back to the early 1990s which the party saw as offering a corporatist solution to the crisis of capitalism at the expense of workers' wages and conditions. Ciampi's proposals to establish a pact between employers and trade unions on prices and incomes in the summer of 1998 was further proof for the Communists that organized labour had lost its capacity to fight for the interests of workers whether employed or not. Hence, Bertinotti argued, the moderate leadership of Cofferati and company must be opposed while better links needed to be established with shop stewards and union activists on the ground as a key foundation for the building of a radical mass party.[14]

Before the events of October 1998 which were finally to bring down prime minister Prodi's government, the PRC had already demonstrated its willingness to show its teeth over, for example, pensions and employment rights in 1997 and over the issue of the dispatch of Italian troops as part of a UN peacekeeping force in Albania in the same year, although neither issue was sufficiently critical for Bertinotti and Cossutta to vote down the government itself. Nonetheless there was increasing resentment among the leadership and many party supporters over the government's perceived close relations with big business, and its cooperation with the parties of the centre-right over the issue of constitutional reform.

On the issue of constitutional reform itself, however, there was almost complete unanimity within the party leadership. The PRC, as Cossutta pointed out, was the only party to present a minority report to the Bicameral Commission on Constitutional Reform. The party's main objections concerned the proposal to adopt a presidential or semipresidential executive and the reform of the justice system which envisaged separate career paths for judges and prosecuting magistrates. The party also objected to what it called the 'absurd bicameralism' of the parliamentary reforms and the introduction of a system of federal government which would result in such a confused form of regionalism that conflicts were bound to emerge between different levels of government.[15] On the issue of electoral reform, the PRC was united in its opposition to the removal of the last vestiges of proportional representation in the parliamentary electoral system. A proposed referendum calling for its abolition promoted by Segni, Di Pietro and Cossiga was strongly attacked by Cossutta, who claimed it would wipe out the tradition of pluralism which, he argued, was a strength rather than a weakness for Italian democracy. His suspicion was that D'Alema's public opposition to the referendum masked his ambition to replace the existing electoral law with a double ballot system (which already existed for the election of city mayors).[16]

Although none of these issues was seen by Bertinotti or Cossutta and likely to bring down the government, the party's strategy of having one foot in and one foot outside the arena of government was to prove increasingly unsustainable as Bertinotti led the party down the path of opposition, while the government's centrist allies made overtures to Cossiga's UDR as a moderate alternative to PRC support.

'Svolta o rottura'

As early as July 1996 according to some party activists, the slogan 'svolta o rottura'[17] had been recited mantra-like at meetings of the national political committee in penance for the party's support of what was to remain a prudent, moderate and determinedly unradical coalition government.[18] By the following July, Bertinotti's position (and that of most of the party) was hardening in the direction of '*rottura*' (withdrawal).

In January the PRC launched a policy document which spelt out in some detail what it believed should be the priorities for the Prodi government in its 'second phase' after the difficulties of entry into the European Monetary System had been surmounted. *Rifondazione* saw unemployment as a major failure of the Prodi government which it believed had failed to tackle the structural and strongly regionalised problems of the Italian labour market. The party thus called for the immediate introduction of the thirty-five-hour working week, the introduction of public-works schemes aimed predominantly at the more economically deprived communities in the south, and government-financed employment schemes which would provide socially useful work (such as environmental protection, social welfare, community development programmes and so on). It also called for better services and support for the unemployed in order to help reintegrate them back into society, and for the eventual introduction of a basic right to work which would guarantee a minimum level of employment and wage for all those in a position to benefit. For Cossutta the policy document formed the basis of a negotiating strategy with the government over the pace and extent of social and economic reforms: for Bertinotti, however, demands such as the implementation of the thirty-five-hour working week and enhanced welfare protection for those on low incomes was increasingly deployed as a ransom demand for continuing PRC support for the *Ulivo* administration.

At a meeting of the national political committee in March 1998, Bertinotti explained how the balance sheet of the PRC's involvement in the government since the crisis of the previous October was 'very critical' and 'substantially negative'. Rather than embarking on a phase of reform, he claimed that the government's actions and attitudes showed 'signs of deterioration' which the party needed to reflect on with concern and attention.[19]

In concrete terms, *Rifondazione* opposed the government's policy towards the reconstitution of the state holding company, IRI, its programme of privatisation, its school reform proposals, the state railways, and the government's handling of the U.S.-Iraq crisis. In the latter case, Bertinotti criticised the government for adopting such a low profile in its dealings with other European partners and for guaranteeing the Americans use of their Italian bases for military operations against the Iraqis. Finally, Bertinotti attacked the behaviour of the centre-left towards the reform package put forward by the *Bicamerale* which, he claimed, was intended to establish a 'rightist hegemony'.

However, the problem for Bertinotti was to identify a suitable *causus belli* given that previous confrontations over, for example, a more progressive distribution of the Eurotax had been amicably settled and that war had not been declared over the content of the government's economic programme (*DPEF*) in the spring or the 'July review' (*'verifica di luglio'*) when the party's national political committee had once again passed a negative assessment of the government's performance.[20] Cossutta certainly believed that *Rifondazione*'s strength lay in its ability to press for greater concessions as part of the 'area of government' rather than as a radical voice in the wilderness. Bertinotti, however, favoured a strategy of confrontation and he knew that the disillusionment with the *Ulivo* government felt by many activists and supporters could be mobilised to his advantage.

Ironically, given his future position, Cossutta had, in the spring, argued that 'the idea that the PRC should enter the government in order to wield more influence is absurd. The conditions do not exist and it is illusory to think such a choice exists.'[21] In the same address Cossutta favoured the strategy of radicalising the centre-left government from the outside in order for it to become a genuine reforming administration. This task, he argued, was being hampered by the 'deafness' of the trade-union movement to the social and economic problems which *Rifondazione* argued the government needed urgently to tackle in order to create a fairer society.

However, as spring gave way to summer it was increasingly obvious that Prodi's government had no intention of marching to Bertinotti's tune. Over NATO enlargement the government made it clear that it would not allow *Rifondazione* to veto Italy's support for the project even if, as with the Albanian crisis, Prodi had to rely on votes from the opposition parties. Meanwhile the Foreign Minister, Lamberto Dini, was becoming increasingly vocal about his antipathy towards the communists as a governmental ally.[22] Dini was not alone in seeing the emergence of a new Catholic centre party (the UDR) by former president Cossiga as a potential moderate ally and a means of calling *Rifondazione*'s bluff should the Communists ultimately decide to bring down the government. Less directly, the DS Secretary, Massimo D'Alema, also let it be known that widening the coalition in a moderate direction could not be ruled out if *Rifondazione* refused to cooperate with the Prodi administration.

Unlike the previous October when *Rifondazione* had managed to force the government to back down on aspects of the finance bill, Bertinotti did not feel that a strike of this kind would succeed again since the government had ruled out further compromise.[23] Instead he called for the construction of new political relationships and a change in the balance of power within the government's majority. Bertinotti also rejected the participation of the PRC in a reformulated centre-left whether it went under the guise of *Cosa 2* or any other label. He argued that the party's general programme was incompatible with the creation of a bipolarised political system built around the two barely differentiated coalitions on the centre-left and the centre-right. Instead the PRC must actively become a real opposition of the left, working as a radicalising influence within civil society and among the labour and social movements as much as in parliament and in the other political institutions where *Rifondazione* had a presence.[24]

A Party at War

The clash between the pro and anti-government factions within the PRC really emerged in a dramatic and public fashion during the vote on the previous year's finance bill. Subsequently, Cossutta sought to map out a possible reform strategy which could be negotiated with the current coalition. Meanwhile Bertinotti, as a good former trade unionist, while appearing to be a 'take it or leave it' uncompromising hard-head, continued to negotiate behind the scenes over every aspect of government policy. Throughout 1998 the conflict between Bertinotti and his supporters, and those of Cossutta, had become increasingly bitter. Cossutta, who had made a much publicised visit to Russia in the summer, meeting the leader of the Russian Communist Party, was publicly accused of neo-Stalinism by activists within his own party.[25] He was also attacked for suggesting that an annex could be added to the finance bill which would introduce a progressive economic planning policy thus avoiding the need to vote down the legislation itself. This move, it was claimed, had not been approved by the national political committee and the party president was exceeding his powers in making such an approach, which would be viewed as a preliminary to eventual PRC participation in the government itself.[26] Cossutta, while insisting on the importance of party unity, also let it be known in interviews and off-the-record briefings to journalists that Bertinotti's maverick stance was damaging the interests of the party and the left in general – to the great delight of Berlusconi, Fini and Cossiga.

It would, however, be an error to see the conflict between Cossutta and Bertinotti in strictly ideological terms, since both leaders were reformists rather than revolutionaries. Bertinotti denied being a 'maximalist' – even describing his position as 'neo-Keynesian'.[27] The objective was always a vaguely defined French-style social welfare state which Bertinotti insisted would disappear for ever as a prospect unless the government was forced to sign up to *Rifondazione*'s demands immediately. As someone who saw himself as the guardian of the PCI's 'high politics' tradition, Cossutta's line could be seen as an affirmation of Enrico Berlinguer's strategy, under which socialism would be achieved in Italy at the end of a 'long march through the institutions'. Inevitably such an enterprise would involve cooperation with noncommunist elements within the government, as had been the case during the historic compromise of 1976-79 between the PCI and the DC in which Cossutta had played a prominent role. For Cossutta and his supporters, if the defence of working-class interests and the exclusion of the right from government had to be bought at the expense of ideological purity, then it was a price worth paying. Bertinotti, in contrast, believed that even the risk of early elections and the return to power of Berlusconi and Fini was justified in order to prevent the finance bill from being passed.

Among the activists of the PRC's national political committee and in many of the federations in key regions such as Emilia-Romagna, Lombardy, and Liguria, it was Bertinotti's defiant stance which won popular backing. Bertinotti was also able to win support from half the Trotskyist minority which had joined *Rifondazione* from the former Proletarian Democracy Party (*Democrazia Proletaria*).[28] At the national political committee's meeting in Rome on 4 October, the party secretary's resolution calling for the withdrawal of *Rifondazione*'s support for the government won the support of 188 out of a total of 332 (56.6 percent) delegates. While Cossutta's motion which pledged continuing constructively-critical support for the government received only 112 votes (33.7 percent) and was defeated. A crisis for both Communist Refoundation and the *Ulivo* government now looked inevitable.

On the eve of the vote of no confidence, newspapers were predicting that with Cossutta's twenty deputies, only two dissidents from Bertinotti's camp would be needed to save the government. But as the deputies lined up to vote on the morning of Friday 9 October, it was clear that none of Bertinotti's troops was having second thoughts. With the 'no' of Tiziana Valpiana who had been absent during the first roll call, Prodi realised that the game was up, and resigned in short order. Only twelve of the PRC's deputies had voted with the opposition, and Bertinotti had to sit poker-faced as the leader of PRC's deputies, Oliviero Dililberto, after an impassioned plea not to sink the government received a congratulatory handshake from Cossutta.

Bertinotti declared himself satisfied with the result of the no confidence vote, but he continued to offer the prospect of renewed

PRC cooperation if a second Prodi government came back with a new Finance Bill which met Bertinotti's demands. However, as Bertinotti knew as well as anyone, the ground had already been prepared for the installation of Massimo D'Alema as President of the Council of Ministers. Ironically, by his actions, Bertinotti had promoted a much tougher prime ministerial candidate who had made no secret of the fact that there would be no reconciliation with Bertinotti's apostates if he carried out his threat to wreck the government. With only a dozen deputies, the reduced PRC parliamentary group lacked the numbers required to form a group in their own right and were obliged to seek sanctuary among the homeless deputies of the '*gruppo misto*' (mixed group). The PRC's press office also complained of a virtual news blackout which was seen as a conspiracy to marginalise *Rifondazione,* and to deny it access to its voters and supporters.

Meanwhile, Cossutta and his followers set about the establishment of a rival party, provisionally named the *Partito dei Comunisti Italiani,* which was to have had appropriated the ancient hammer and sickle symbol of the PCI until Massimo D'Alema's office objected. Bertinotti's respone was to exclude the *Cossuttiani* from the party headquarters while battle was joined for control of the party newspaper *Liberazione* and the periodical *Rifondazione,* which in the past had been strongly identified with Cossutta. As with the schism of 1991 during the founding of the PDS, the fight for control of the patrimony and resources of the party reached right down to the smallest federation, and in the case of Cagliari actually degenerated into a physical confrontation between the rival factions.[29]

Both sides claimed victory in the 'battle of the faxes' for grass roots support, although the *Manifesto* newspaper and the radical broadcaster *Radio Popolare* found that readers and listeners were fairly evenly split over the vote. Speaking to a demonstration in Rome on 17 October, Bertinotti claimed to have reaffirmed the PRC as a revolutionary mass party and to have won the popular backing for the '*rottura*' among the party rank-and-file. Rather more bizarrely Bertinotti rounded on his critics for saying that the right would be the only beneficiaries of the collapse of the Prodi government and claimed the credit for installing D'Alema in Palazzo Chigi as Italy's first genuinely left-wing prime minister.

Far from producing a '*svolta*' (change), Bertinotti's '*rottura*' (withdrawal) had failed to halt the passage of the Finance Bill and had strengthened the position of his rival Cossutta as D'Alema's one reliable ally on the left. Romano Prodi was the most obvious casualty of the no confidence vote, although his departure from Palazzo Chigi ironically paved the way for him to succeed Jacques

Santer as President-designate of the European Commission. Having played his one and only card, Bertinotti's brief time in the spotlight came to an end as the glare of publicity turned on D'Alema and discussion moved to the 'opening to the centre' with talk of a German-style 'grand coalition'. Understandably, Cossutta was more concerned with the long-awaited opening to the left, and his spokesman, Nerio Nesi, was quick to confirm that in return for their support the Communist loyalists would expect to be offered seats on the boards of the powerful state undertakings and public authorities by the D'Alema government.[30]

Conclusion

Not surprisingly, the main losers from the political crisis of October 1998 – beyond the *Ulivo* – were *Rifondazione Comunista*, and any hope of launching a reconciliation of the two branches of the Italian left. The bitter divorce that marked the establishment of RC in 1991 repeated itself after Cossutta's resignation, with the same long legal battles, and the decline of members and voters that were the unavoidable price of the split. Although it would be easy to attribute this failure to a clash of personalities, in the final analysis the conflict inside *Rifondazione* reflected the mentality of a large part of the Italian left, which has always been more comfortable with the militant battles of opposition than with participation in government, despite its regular loud lamentation at being excluded from the real centres of power – a condition which Lenin in one of his wittier essays referred to as 'an infantile disorder'.

Reconciling and rebuilding the left will perhaps be possible only at the end of a process of self-destruction on the part of *Rifondazione*, and only if the reformist left were to succeed in expanding fully into the electoral space occupied by what is today still the extreme left. But the reformist left still looks organisationally weak, electorally stalled, and locked in by the unending political emergency of the long Italian transition and by a seemingly unstoppable process of party system fragmentation. In this perspective, it is particularly clear that the failure of the *Bicamerale* implies, for the DS and for D'Alema, the end of any immediate prospect of institutional stabilisation through which they might have played a key role in the reform and modernisation of Italian political life.

Because of the way it has happened, Prodi's replacement by D'Alema has not been and will not be painless for the *Ulivo* coalition. In the context of a still very fluid structure of the party system, and of a new coalition as heterogeneous at its predecessor, taking charge of the prime minister's office could be a serious risk for the DS. In any case, it places a heavy responsibility on the party, which has now visibly become the cornerstone of governability in Italy. The replacement of D'Alema by Veltroni as party leader may be an opportunity to relaunch the party both organisationally and politically, but it also risks provoking serious internal tensions, and further blurring the party's uncertain identity, organisation, and overall direction. As never before, therefore, the fate of the Italian left, in its various manifestations, will be strictly tied to the fate of the Italian political transition as a whole.

Notes

1. The initiative partially took its inspiration from the 1989 launch of a post-communist 'Project' by the Italian Communist Party secretary, Achille Occhetto, which came to be known (in the initial absence of any other name) as '*La Cosa*' ('The Thing'). *La Cosa (1)* eventually led to the dissolution of the PCI and to the foundation of the Democratic Party of the Left (PDS) in 1991.

2. On the events and documentation concerning the *Forum della Sinistra*, see *Un nuovo partito della Sinistra. Documenti e materiali*, edited by the *Direzione del PDS*, Rome 1997.

3. 'Parties have a function ... in the fragmented and complex world of post-industrial society; if we wish politics to have a structured relationship with society they have a utility which is a condition for building consensus around a project and not merely as a means for mediating corporatist interests.' Massimo D'Alema's concluding address to the *Stati Generali della Sinistra*, Florence, 12-14 February 1998, reported in *L'Unità*, 15 February 1998.

4. See Gianfranco Pasquino, 'La Cosa infinita', *Il Mulino* 1, 1998: 71-81 and Stefano Folli, 'Cosa Due, bella senz'anima', *Ideazione*, 2, 1998, pp.105-108. However, the negative limits of *Cosa 2* had been acknowledged by the leadership of the PDS itself.

5. *Un nuovo ciclo riformatore dell'azione di governo*, internal document of the Direzione dei DS, 7 July 1998.

6. Interview with Walter Veltroni in *Corriere della Sera*, 4 October 1998.

7. Quotation taken from Enrico Melchionda, 'Il partito routine', *Aprile*, 4 November 1998.

8. Report of the Organisational Director, Franco Passuello, to the Direction of the DS on 17 December 1998, mimeograph.

9. For an account of the ideas of the new party secretary see, 'Una sinistra aperta e moderna, intervento all'assemblea congressuale dei DS', Rome, 6 November 1998 reported in *L'Unità*, 7 November 1998. It was at this assembly that Veltroni was elected secretary.

10. Fausto Bertinotti, 'Sette temi sul partito di massa', *Rifondazione*, Anno II, No.1, January 1999.

11. Milziade Caprili, interviewed by Anubi D'Avossa Lussurgiu in *Liberazione*, 29 July 1998.

12. The newspaper reported that at the end of 1997 *Rifondazione*'s membership stood at 130,000, while in the first six months of 1998 only 81,000 members had renewed their membership. Source: *Corriere della Sera*, 8 October 1998, p. 2.

13. *Ibid.*

14. Fausto Bertinotti, 'Sintesi della relazione del segretario Bertinotti al Comitato politico nazionale 3-4 ottobre 1998', *Liberazione*, 4 October 1998. However, it was significant that during the leadership crisis, the leader of the PRC grouping within the CGIL, 'Alternativa Sindacale', Gian Paolo Patta was critical of both Bertinotti and Cossutta in allowing internal divisions to weaken the organizing capacity of the party within the trade union movement. Reported in *Corriere della Sera*, 8 October 1998, p. 2.

15. Armando Cossutta, interviewed by Andrea Fabozzi in *Liberazione*, 11 January 1998.

16. Armando Cossutta, interviewed by Piergiorgio Bergonzi in *Liberazione*, 11 March 1998.

17. The phrase is roughly and inelegantly translatable as 'either the government's policy changes, or we break away from the government'.

18. See for example, Maria Pelegatta, 'Non è l'ora X' *Liberazione*, 29 September 1998.

19. Intervention of Fausto Bertinotti during the meeting of the PRC national executive in Rome, 2/3 March 1998 reported in *Liberazione*, 20 March 1998.

20. See Armando Cossutta, 'Rifondazione Comunista: La parola al Presidente', *Liberazione*, 2 September 1998.

21. Intervention of Armando Cossutta in *ibid.*

22. Interview with Lamberto Dini, *Corriere della Sera*, 28 March 1998.

23. Fausto Bertinotti, 'Sintesi della relazione del segretario Bertinotti al Comitato politico nazionale 3-4 ottobre 1998', *Liberazione*, 4 October 1998.

24. Bertinotti's concluding speech in *ibid.*

25. See Anubi D'Avossa Lussurgiu, 'Le parole della separazione' *Liberazione*, 3 October 1998.

26. See Marco Nesci, 'Basta risse. Discutere seriamente' *Liberazione*, 3 September 1998.

27. A concept which Bertinotti had trouble defining although he claimed to be more 'neo' than Keynesian. Fausto Bertinotti, 'Sintesi della relazione del segretario Bertinotti al Comitato politico nazionale 3-4 ottobre 1998', *Liberazione*, 4 October 1998.

28. *Corriere della Sera*, 5 October 1998.

29. Reported in *Corriere della Sera*, 8 October 1998, p.2.

30. *Corriere della Sera*, 9 October 1998, p.7.

2

THE PARTIES OF THE *POLO*: UNITED TO WHAT END?

Marco Tarchi and Emanuela Poli

At the close of the budget debate in the lower house in October 1997, the chance that the Prodi government might collapse was averted. Had it collapsed, the entire political strategy of the *Ulivo* (Olive Tree) coalition would have been placed in doubt, and the possibility of early elections would have increased. Without the prospect of such a favourable turn of events, the *Polo per la Libertà* alliance settled back down to the routine of opposition. Its leaders took it for granted that the Prodi government would run the full course of its five-year mandate without further tremors, except for the possibility that an underground battle for the leadership of the coalition might break out anew between its PDS and Catholic wings. Berlusconi's view was that the discord between the governing parties and the *Rifondazione Comunista* was nothing more than an act, and that by concluding a basic agreement for the reduction of the working week to thirty-five hours, Prodi had taken out an insurance policy against possible acts of rashness on the part of Bertinotti and Cossuta. Fini spoke of a long battle which would be taken up in the 1999 European elections, and would come to a close only when the legislature came to its natural end in 2001. The *Polo* therefore had to equip itself for a long siege.

The passage of time showed these forecasts to be mistaken and costly. Abandoning its strategy of direct confrontation with its political opponents was to cost the centre-right dear on two occasions, and on two fronts, during the course of 1998. Firstly, it exposed the *Polo* to the charge that it lacked political initiative and realistic short-term objectives, and had no better tactic than simply to await the electoral day of judgement. This provoked ever more frequent and open attacks from both moderate and conservative critics, and led to the open challenge launched by Francesco Cossiga, whose aim was to curb the power of both sides of the left-right divide (starting, however, with the right), and to draw up a new broad-based alternative, built on a social-democratic left and a liberal-Catholic centre. This challenge subsequently reduced the centre-right to the role of spectator, (albeit an interested and active one), of the crisis that led to the resignation of the Prodi government. This crisis was triggered by the extreme left, brought to a conclusion by the defection from the *Ulivo* of a Deputy from the *Rinnovamento Italiano* group, and resolved by the subtle tactics of political flexibility of the Cossiga group.

The creation of the UDR was a particularly serious blow for the parties of the *Polo*. Firstly, the two Catholic members of the Alliance were decimated by defections – the CDU has been absorbed, practically speaking, by Cossiga, while the CCD lost half of its parliamentary strength. Secondly, not only did *Forza Italia* suffer an increase in the losses to which it had already been exposed, to the advantage of the Dini group inside the *Ulivo*, but the entire profile of the Alliance was upset by Cossiga's initiative. In one fell swoop, its centre of gravity shifted to the right, its claim to represent the majority of the Catholic electorate was once again challenged (notwithstanding Berlusconi's references to de Gasperi and the 'spirit of 18 April 1948' during *Forza Italia's* National Congress) and the possibility of a single, moderate opposition to the 'government of the left' was undermined. Furthermore, the UDR appeared from the outset better placed to reach an agreement with the right-wing groups in the *Ulivo* (*Rinnovamento Italiano* and the *Partito Popolare*) which the CCD and CDU had never succeeded in developing. It was even able to keep open a fragile dialogue with the *Lega Nord*, which electoral arithmetic suggested was still the only way for the opposition to defeat the centre-left in a future election. Finally, the emergence of an increasingly bitter controversy between Cossiga and the *Polo*, and the subsequent decision of the former President to support the government formed by Massimo D'Alema, removed the only hope the centre-right had of electoral expansion into the territory of the centre-left, on the back of the individual issues which divided the *Ulivo* – prominent among which were public support for Catholic schools, foreign policy and judicial reform.

The consequences of this new political context for the positions and strategies of the *Polo* may be better understood by examining separately how the two pillars of the Alliance have faced it, and have tried to find an at least provisional solution.

Alleanza Nazionale: Between Hopes and Fears

Under the timetable laid down by its leaders, 1998 should have marked a further stage on the road to ideological revisionism for *Alleanza Nazionale*. It was the year in which another *Fiuggi* (the convention which first launched AN's ideological modernisation) had been expected, enabling the party, still only recently risen from the ashes of neo-Fascism, to celebrate its full entry into the framework of Italian democracy, and to mark publicly a further clear break with its past.[1] The chances of the party regaining a significant political role seemed favourable: its participation in the work of the Bicameral Commission, which had initially been viewed with extreme distrust, gave Fini and his group the welcome chance to play a role among the signatories to the new constitutional accord, and was expected to give them public credit as the party which had always been the strongest supporter of a presidential form of government. The reasonableness displayed during the dispute between Berlusconi and the judiciary also earned them credit as mediators in the eyes of the *Ulivo*. The tensions which developed between the government and the *Rifondazione Comunista* (first on the Budget, and then on foreign policy) led them to hope that Prodi's five-year term might be cut short, and that the *Polo* might insert itself once more in the power game. There were three pillars to this pro-active strategy, which the party hoped would give it a better grip on the external factors[2] of the political environmental in which it was operating: firstly the completion of the process of domestic and international recognition; secondly, a more favourable redefinition of the balance of power within the centre-right coalition;[3] and finally, the relaunching of the party organisation. But unexpected developments upset these plans, and, with the process already under way, forced the party to make hurried modifications.

The political season opened for *Alleanza Nazionale* a few weeks earlier than expected. The outcome of the administrative elections held the previous November, which saw the party lose ground in nearly all the cities where voting took place, and which saw the *Polo* lose a large number of the seats it was contesting, strongly influenced the initial moves of the new year. This unexpected electoral debacle sparked off a fierce internal debate. Defeats in certain of the party's traditional strongholds were felt especially deeply – most notably in Rome and Naples, where, four years earlier, the MSI had laid the foundations for its relaunch. There were heated discussions about the lack of representativeness of the *Polo*'s candidates for the mayoral elections. The consequences of these recriminations were not long in coming. In December, Fini reorganised the party leadership, and named two new figures as national party co-ordinators in place of the tried and tested Maurizio Gasparri and Publio Fiori. These 'new men', Manlio Contento and Alfredo Mantovano, were given the task of reorganising the party and its strategy in the northern and southern halves of the country. There was also a growing sense of discontent about the unsatisfactory state of relationships with other parties in the *Polo* alliance. There was much criticism of the party's subordination to the strategic choices of its allies, and especially to those of *Forza Italia*.[4] Those who believed in a stance closer to the political culture of the former MSI accused the party leadership of talking to the electorate in a language it did not understand. They saw the *Polo* alliance as suffering from serious leadership failures, the solutions to which could no longer be delayed, and they denounced Berlusconi as someone the party could not trust.[5] Even those in the party most attracted to the idea of dialogue with the centrists and moderates agreed that it was now time to move 'beyond the *Polo*',[6] though the basis on which this should be done remained unclear, as did the allies the coalition might be widened and reconstructed to include. The overtures towards the *Lega Nord* proposed by Berlusconi were viewed with suspicion. Rather, there was a preference in AN for widening discussions with those representatives of Catholicism who could not find a home in the *Ulivo* and whose priority was institutional reform. These included Mario Segni and, above all, Francesco Cossiga, towards whom the centre-right electorate seemed to be particularly well-disposed,[7] and who was, according to Fini, 'working for a modern democratic alternative'.[8]

The opportunity to respond to these demands presented itself at the party's Policy Conference held between 29 February and 1 March. This event had been planned for some time, only to be postponed. It eventually took the place of the congress which, according to party rules, should have been held by the end of January. It was conceived with the principal aim of packaging the party as part of the European mainstream right, temporarily re*Le*g*a*ted to an opposition role, but ready to resume its governmental vocation. The press, which dubbed the conference 'Fiuggi 2' and focused on the delays in holding it, fed rumours that Fini intended to use the Conference to make a further and more far-reaching public departure from MSI tradition. According to some sources, a Thatcherite conversion to neo-liberal values would be announced. Others believed that Fini would complete the passage towards policy and programmatic renewal set out at the first Congress in January 1995, and at the same time would issue a public repudiation of the Italian Social Republic of 1943-45 – the last act of interwar Italian Fascism. As it turned out, the event was far less memorable, and consisted more than anything else of an astute, image-building make-over. In all probability, circumstances dictated a healthy dose of prudence on Fini's part: the militant core, already unhappy with the recent poor showing in elections, greeted with an evident sense of irritation the first signs of the feared 'abjuration' of the last adventure of Fascism, of which the post-war MSI has always considered itself a continuation. Even more significantly, Cossiga unexpectedly gave the go-ahead for the formation of the Democratic Union for the Republic (UDR), taking tens of deputies away from the *Polo* (AN itself had to pay a price, with the departure of two senators Valentino Martelli and Romano Misserville). There was, therefore, a clear double-sided risk of future defections: on one hand, by burying the historical memory of the MSI, there was the danger of encouraging the flow of party members and local party organisations to the small *Movimento Sociale–Fiamma Tricolore* led by Pino Rauti; on the other, by criticising its allies at a delicate moment, there was a danger that the party might be playing into the hands of its new centrist competitors.

The Verona conference therefore reasserted and re-launched *AN's* national ambitions at the level of mass media, but created no ideological or strategic break with its recent past. The symbol chosen for the presentation of candidates (a ladybird) did not, as had been anticipated, replace the logo of the three-coloured flame of the MSI; the role of the one thousand invited nonmembers, fancifully described as 'delegates of a civil society', was limited to that of observers; and Domenico Fisichella's draft policy conclusions for the conference proved little more than starting points for discussion on current themes – focusing primarily on general economic problems and public policy in the era of globalisation – without seriously questioning any of the traditional party beliefs.[9] The opening and closing speeches by Fini laid out the focal points of the programme through which AN sought to establish its new electoral identity,[10] but all controversial issues were left for another day. The sensitive question of the party's historical roots was finessed first with the slogan 'what is past is past, but the memories remain', and secondly in a comparison of the genocide of the Jews with the *foibe*,[11] both, in equal measure, said to be typical examples of the horrors of totalitarianism. As for the relationship with the other parties of the *Polo*, the tone was ambivalent. Berlusconi was greeted from the floor with a lengthy ovation,[12] and Fini obliged him with a powerful attack on the Milan prosecutor's office (which had been Berlusconi's judicial tormentors), but Berlusconi himself publicly dissented from Fini's view that anti-communism was now an anachronism, and to stress their differences on this question, he distributed to all those present a freshly-printed copy of his '*Libro Nero del Comunismo*'. The intersecting expressions of loyalty to the *Polo* coalition easily prevailed over fine distinctions, however, and the concern to re-establish the collaborative relationship among the allies on a new and better footing, which had seemed so urgent on the eve of the conference, was not even voiced during the speeches by members of the minority within the party.

Much emphasis was placed on the presence at the Conference of de*Leg*ations from many Italian and foreign parties – including the Gaullists from France, the Spanish *Partido Popolar*, the English Conservative Party, the German Christian Democrats, leaders of the U.S. Republican Party,[13] and members of the Israeli Likud – and of representatives of institutions such as the Presidents of the Senate, Nicola Mancino, and the Chamber, Luciano Violante.[14] The emphasis placed on the allegedly legitimising effect of the presence of these outsiders was evidence of the party's lasting fear that it is not yet 'a party like all the rest', and that notwithstanding its solid electoral performance it might once again be pushed out to the fringes by the activities of the new centrists, and relegated to a position of isolation corresponding to that of *Rifondazione Comunista*. This fear became almost a *leitmotiv* during the course of the year, intensifying in proportion to the growing UDR criticism of the lack of political initiative from the *Polo*, and prevented the party from dramatising its differences from Berlusconi even on issues where he was vulnerable.

The threat of possible exile to the political far right was brought menacingly on to the scene as early as February in fact, when Francesco Cossiga launched his new political group. It went away for a couple of months, when it seemed that the former President's project would be shipwrecked on the rocks of the personal ambitions and rivalries of his followers, but then returned more starkly than before. When Cossiga spoke of the need to build a new centre that would be 'distinct and distant' from the right, in relation to which it would limit itself to concluding electoral agreements on a case-by-case basis, *Alleanza Nazionale* grew deeply alarmed. Already anxious about the repeated rumours of the formation of a 'constituent assembly of moderates' inspired by FI, the CCD and the CDU – rumours which never seem to have had much foundation, it should be added – *Alleanza Nazionale* felt that it was being specifically singled out for attack. Its reaction was to draw its larger alliance partner into an ever tighter embrace, distracting it from the enticements of potential new allies in the centre by offering support even on issues where it had severe doubts about so doing. There were continuous instances of the leadership's excessive level of compliance, generating outbursts of open dissent inside the party.

This dissent first emerged over the fate of the Bicameral Commission, which soon exposed sharp differences of opinion between *Alleanza Nazionale* and *Forza Italia*. In less than a year, the Bicameral Commission was transformed, in the words of Fini, from a tricky and difficult 'path' to a 'motorway' towards an overdue modernisation of Italy. After 'reluctantly'[15] abandoning its calls for a Constituent Assembly – which would have permitted it to link up directly with Cossiga – AN established, through the work of the commission, a covert working relationship with the PDS, the aim of which was to acquire further legitimacy for AN in the eyes of other parties. As one of the founding members of a new constitutional agreement, the party believed it would be able to relaunch the image of pragmatism and trustworthiness which had been damaged by the party's opposition to Antonio Maccanico's attempt to form a 'government of reform' in early 1995. But its path was often hindered by the reticence, or open opposition, of *Forza Italia*. The positions of the two parties during the work of the commission diverged over federalism, presidentialism, or electoral reform, but above all over reform of the judicial system. Fini and his followers nonetheless tried hard to find solutions which would overcome the differences between the two parties, and Berlusconi's decision to abandon the work which had been done up until then in the Bicameral Commission could not but irritate AN. To the extent that the split occurred around the insoluble question of the conflict between the leader of *Forza Italia* and the judiciary, which has always been the stumbling block between the two largest parties of the centre-right coalition, the irritation was even more profound.

The problems experienced by *Alleanza Nazionale* and *Forza Italia* in their attempts to work together were not limited to this episode, however. The borders between competition and cooperation were jeopardised more than once during the year, and it was generally AN which had to adapt its positions to those of its partner. In addition to the definition of the relationship between politics and judicial power – a topic on which its spokesperson, an ex-judge Alfredo Mantovano, refused to abandon demands for a margin of autonomy, thereby provoking periodic friction – *Alleanza Nazionale* was obliged to soften its line on immigration, and on the process of Euro-

pean monetary union, and grudgingly to accept Berlusconi's periodic hints regarding the possibility of forming a 'government of
broad understanding' if the Prodi government were to fall. At times,
the dissent bubbled to the surface, and became an open struggle to
push the general policy of the *Polo* in one direction or another. This
occurred, for example, with the re-emergence of the question of
changes to the electoral system following the failure of the Bicameral
Commission. After some uncertainty, Fini espoused the cause of the
promoters of the referendum against proportional representation,
postponing decisions on new electoral rules which might strengthen
bipolarity in the party system until after the referendum itself.
Berlusconi's insistence on reviving the deal on a second-ballot system, agreed with the centre-left before the collapse of the Bicameral
Commission, did not persuade him to change his mind. AN had
fought too hard to present itself as the standard-bearer of reform to
allow the initiative to be seized by potential electoral rivals such as
Di Pietro or other exponents of the referendum movement.

The consequence of all these tensions inside the *Polo* was that the
periodic proposals to create a formal coordination mechanism for the
alliance once more fell into abeyance. The proposal was first made
after the defeat in the regional elections of 1995, and polls suggested
it was popular with voters.[16] It reappeared in its original form before
the Verona Conference – as the idea of a fully-integrated single party
for the entire *Polo* – and was greeted in different ways within
Alleanza Nazionale: the radicals of the '*movimentista*' wing condemned it as 'a depressing utopia';[17] moderates adopted it as a highly
desirable objective, at least in the medium term. Fini argued that the
issue could only be faced when bipolarity in the party system was
sufficiently far advanced that the possibility of evolution to a two-
party system could seriously be contemplated. The idea subsequently
reappeared in two more modest versions, which were limited to the
parliamentary arena, and were backed up by arguments which were
more technical than political. First, it was suggested that there should
be a common spokesman for all the party groups in the *Polo* alliance.
Later, thought was given to the idea of the constitution of joint parliamentary groups in the Senate and the Chamber of Deputies. No
agreement was reached, however. On the contrary, the range of reactions which greeted Berlusconi's suggestion of mass resignations by
centre-right members of Parliament, in protest against the appointment of Massimo D'Alema as Prime Minister, made it apparent that
the senators and deputies of the *Polo* were a very long way from
being willing to accept a single leadership.

While *Alleanza Nazionale* and *Forza Italia* were promoting the
cause of unification, however, certain factions were clearly pro-

ceeding along other paths. The main evidence of this was found in the international strategies the two parties were cultivating. When, for example, to underline its centrist connotations, *Forza Italia* succeeded in joining the Christian Democrat Group of the European Parliament (PPE), abandoning the *Union pour l'Europe*, where they sat beside representatives of the RPR, Fianna Fàil, the Portuguese CDS and certain Greek and Dutch deputies, *Alleanza Nazionale* lost no time in trying to take their place. AN had been busy establishing good contacts with the UPE since the *Fiuggi* Congress,[18] and, through an official collaborative relationship with the Gaullists, it hoped to be able to achieve further respectability, this time at the European level. To this end, Fini first arranged a meeting in Paris with the newly elected Secretary of the RPR, Philippe Séguin, stressing the common principles shared by their two movements. He then presented a request for his party to be admitted to the union, and finally, to give weight to this request, met the Irish Prime Minister, Bertie Ahern, in Dublin. During this meeting, an agreement was signed for the drafting of 'a common programme for the parties of the right in Europe', in anticipation of the imminent European Parliamentary elections. It seems clear, therefore, that in this area, AN was attempting to distinguish its image from that of its ally, and to underline its calling to occupy a political space on the right, giving weight to those differences in content over which, due to tactical concerns, it tended to draw a veil in the context of national politics.

In certain areas the existence of disagreements between AN and FI was hard to disguise. One case was clear in AN's opposition to the possibility of a second term of office for President Scalfaro, in contrast to FI's willingness to consider it. Another was the mini-crisis which arose from the defeat (aided by the deliberate absence from Parliament of many *Forza Italia* deputies) of a bill by Mirko Tremaglia on the right to vote of Italians resident abroad. Yet another was on the differing interpretations of the relationship between Italy and the United States which emerged from the parliamentary debate on the U.S. attack on Iraq. In any event, the party-system context obliged both sides to tone down the controversy and to continue to revive the message of bipolarity. This was to be seen in the parliamentary opposition to the draft budget proposed by the *Ulivo*, and again during the Prodi government crisis, when *Alleanza Nazionale* again felt threatened by Berlusconi's penchant for broad-based governments, a penchant which AN sought to tone down, and, finally, on the occasion of the organisation of the successful mass anti-government demonstration in Rome on 24 October. AN confronted the differences of opinion with the party with which it was forced to work by following two parallel strategies: publicly minimising the significance of the disagreements,[19] while working towards a strengthening of its rank- and file- structure so as to be more competitive electorally. To this end, we see the active intervention in support of the 'rebellion' of Rome's taxi drivers against the city council, the adoption of primary elections for the selection of AN candidates for the provincial elections in Rome (a system which, it has been stated explicitly, it would like to extend to the whole of the *Polo* in the future, especially in the light of the selection of the candidate for premier), and the successful efforts to back its candidate Silvano Moffa for the presidency of the province of Rome. AN is clearly aware, therefore, that as a party of the Italian right it has not yet maximised its electoral potential, and believes that it can compete with the UDR in the battle to win the support of voters who are beginning to detach themselves from *Forza Italia*. There is, however, a paradox which limits its range of activity: it must hope for an erosion of the support enjoyed by the alliance if it is to overtake it in electoral terms and thereby be able to dictate moves more decisively, but at the same time it must hope that *Forza Italia* is not excessively weakened, because a destabilisation of Berlusconi's party would favour a readjustment of the political system towards the centre, and would bring with it the risk of a reduction in its power inside the coalition. There was much here to complicate the tasks of AN's leaders as the year drew to an end. The electoral gains brought by the collapse of the 'First Republic' were no longer the main issue; a new, more extensive field of battle remained to be identified, and the fences were still to be built.

Forza Italia: Reorganisation, the Temptations of the Political Centre, and Lost Opportunities

For *Forza Italia*, 1998 was to be a year of internal reorganisation. Hitherto the party had been fairly weak at the centre and poorly established at the periphery. Its relaunch began in 1997 with the approval of proper by-laws and regulations for internal elections and for the enrolment of members.[20] This reorganisation was the wish of many inside the party, and was accelerated at the behest of its leader after the electoral defeat of April 1996. The year thus closed with the holding of the first provincial and city congresses for the election of local leaders and of delegates to the first national congress. The latter had been long delayed, and was finally scheduled for the spring of 1998. Approximately 90,000 of the 140,000 members who joined FI in 1997 voted, electing (on the basis of the votes obtained by the FI list at the most recent provincial or city elections[21]) a total of 1,704 delegates to the congress. To these should be added 1,372 delegates who attended *ex officio* (members of parliament, and the various levels of elected officials and party leaders). The two groups together elected, by direct vote, the president of the party, fifty members of the national congress and six members of the executive committee *(Comitato di Presidenza)*.[22] There was much interest in the composition of the elected component of the executive committee, which was expected to become a powerful group within the party. The remaining fifteen members of the committee would, however, still be nominated, directly or indirectly, by the president of the party (Silvio Berlusconi). Moreover, during the course of the congress Berlusconi warned delegates not to stir up controversy in the presence of journalists, and to put on a show of party unity rather than express publicly preferences for particular candidates. And in the end he opted for a balanced outcome, with no particular group emerging as dominant.[23]

There were eleven candidates for the six places. Their support tended to be mainly based in particular regions, though some of it came from past political loyalties (the former Christian Democrat group was a powerful force, for example). Those elected were: Gianni Pilo, with votes from Emilia, Campania and, in part, Lombardy (though Lombardy had four candidates in the running, and split its votes accordingly); Franco Frattini (who won fewer votes expected, possibly due to Berlusconi's efforts to secure a balanced slate); Donato Bruno (whose support from Lazio, taken from Frattini, was decisive to his election); Maria Teresa Armosino (Piedmont); Lombardy regional counsellor Maurizio Bernardo (whose votes came from Lombardy and in part, the Veneto and Friulia), and Filippo Cingolani (a businessman with support in Tuscany, the Marches and Umbria). The majority of those elected were members of Parliament, and thus were better known by the deLegates as a whole, and when added to the other members of the committee (almost all of whom were also members of Parliament), provided a continuation of the overlapping of parliamentary and party élites which has distinguished the party since its formation in 1994. It is difficult, nonetheless, to argue that during 1998 this body, which was formally summoned to meet only four times, and whose size was subsequently increased by cooption to fifty members, played any significant political role, or succeeded in achieving independence from the influence of the president, in whose hands the real powers remained.

The election of Berlusconi as president, by acclamation and under a hail of confetti, was largely a formality. So was the approval of the only political motion presented at the close of the congress, which included a commitment to strong semi-presidentialism, a separation of the career paths and regulatory bodies for judges and prosecutors, devolution, tax reduction, and opposition to the thirty-five hour week and to the *Ulivo*. The motion synthesised the conclusions of seven working parties which had met during the three days of the congress to discuss the reports presented by Professors Marzano (economy), Urbani (state institutions), Brunetta (labour policy), Mathieu (education and training), Martino (foreign affairs), Pera (justice), and Tremonti (federalism). The impression, nevertheless, is that the influence of the congress on party policy was rather limited: the working parties did not produce any new ideas, and the final reports proved very similar to the printed copies which the delegates had found in their conference folders. The debate never took up policy issues, and political events subsequent to the congress demonstrated that the decisions – or often the indecision – on public policy remained the preserve of the leader and the tight but variable group of advisers which surrounds him.

The congress also became the catalyst for criticism, not only from outside (Prodi defined it as 'the congress of nothing'[24]), but also from within. Berlusconi himself was accused of populism. *Forza Italia*'s uncertain policy platforms and uncertain political strategy, and claims of the bureaucratisation of the party also came under attack. The congress witnessed an explosion of discontent by those against turning *Forza Italia* into a mass political party with a locally rooted nationwide branch structure (as strongly proposed by the head of organisation Claudio Scajola), and who believe, like the leader of the party group in the Chamber Giorgio Pisanu, that FI needs a very small but efficient organisation which 'uses the prestige of its leader to the best effect',[25] in the conviction that 'bureaucracy suffocates *Berlusconismo*'.[26]

Most of the criticism came from members of Parliament who had already found themselves in dispute with the FI leadership in the past – for example Parenti, Matranga, Colletti, Vertone, Rebuffa, Taradash, Mezzaroma, Caligaris and Guidi – nearly all of whom were to leave the party during the course of 1998.[27] The year was, in fact, noteworthy for great tension within the parliamentary groups, between these groups and the President. Twice Berlusconi accused his own members of parliament of absenteeism, opportunism and lack of discipline[28]), and and there were tensions between MPs and Scajola's staff, though the latter retained the loyalty of regional and local party organisations. October saw the birth within FI of a lay-liberal grouping led by ex-radicals Calderisi and Taradash, and of the so-called 'professors', unhappy about 'a political policy entirely handed down from the top of the party', is focused solely on elections, and within which 'the real modernising inspiration of the *Polo* has been lost'.[29]

Dissent also emerged on the subject of Berlusconi's centrist leanings. It was more visible in the first half of the year, which was marked by problems in FI's relationship with AN and by worries about Cossiga's own centrist strategy. Berlusconi's references to FI as the heir to the Christian Democrat tradition (at a public meeting in Milan at the conclusion of the national congress, coinciding with the fiftieth anniversary of the victory of the DC over the leftist Popular Front) was unpopular with many MPs. Similar misgivings were expressed on policy towards the family, bioethics and private schools, and towards Berlusconi's periodic hints at the desirability of a return to proportional representation along German lines (PR, with extra seats to the winning coalition, and a 5 percent threshold) which in Parliament might lead to an opposition front which would include portions of the PPI, the *Lega* and the extreme left.

The minor masterpiece of Berlusconi's centrist policy came in mid-June, with the entry of *Forza Italia* representatives into the European People's Party group, to which four Italian groups (PPI, the Patto Segni, the CDU and the SVP) already belonged. With the support of José Maria Aznar and Helmut Kohl, anxious to widen the parliamentary base of the European Christian Democrats before the German elections (and with the strong opposition of the left wing of the EPP, and above all of PPI and Prodi), entry into the group allowed Berlusconi to obtain greater credit among European centrists, to end his international isolation, and to regain stature at a moment when the Italian left was accusing him of burying the Bicameral Commission. Three FI European deputies (Caligaris, Caccavale and De Luca) dissented, and refused to join.

Berlusconi's desire to widen the electoral base of *Forza Italia* at the centre also explained his intermittent attempts at dialogue with the *Lega Nord*. Bossi himself was not averse to these overtures. He had been trying to reinsert himself into the FI-AN alliance in order to destroy it, and was enticed by the positions FI assumed on federalism, subsidiarity, tax reduction, the rejection of 'Stalinism', and the general scepticism towards the reforms proposed by the Bicameral Commission.[30] The Bossi-Berlusconi front was an improvisation born out of unfolding events, especially those inside parliament. In March, for example, *Forza Italia* voted with the *Lega* in the Senate Justice Commission in favour of *Lega's* draft bill to decriminalise attacks against the unity of Italy – provoking an icy comment from Fini in the process. At the beginning of April, *Forza Italia* and the *Lega* voted together in the full Senate against the abolition of the possibility of life sentences for attacks against the unity of Italy, while AN sided with the centre-left. A few days later, the parties were again united in the Chamber on the vote to give Veneto the status of a semiautonomous region. Despite this, the restrictions which both sides placed on the agreement (Berlusconi requested the abandonment of the *Lega's* secessionist goals, while Bossi demanded the shelving of the Bicameral Commission) and Bossi's accusation that Berlusconi only wanted a deal for his own personal purposes, namely to use the *Lega* to form a political alliance against the judiciary, made it impossible to come to an electoral deal in the spring local elections. Bossi's approaches to Cossiga beginning in the summer marked the definitive end of any such plan.

The relationship between *Forza Italia* and the Cossiga's UDR was similarly complex and troubled. Notwithstanding the fact that the polls indicated that the powers of attraction exerted by the ex-President of the Republic over the *Forza Italia* electorate was limited (a Datamedia poll found only 1.2 percent of FI voters were prepared to vote for the UDR, and that fewer than 3 percent wanted Cossiga as the leader of the *Polo*[31]), Berlusconi was justifiably convinced that the same did not apply at the parliamentary level, where, in fact, Cossiga succeeded in the course of a year in taking ten deputies away from FI (Danese, Del Barone, Filograna, Meluzzi, Parenti, Rebuffa, Savelli, Scirea, Scognamiglio and Vertone). In the spring, during one of the difficult periods in the relationship with AN, Berlusconi declared himself disposed to consider Cossiga's offer of a joint list for the centrist parties in anticipation of the European elections: 'common political and organisational initiatives for the building of a moderate alliance, to be distinguished, where appropriate, from positions taken by a right wing, which though evolving, is still on occasion seduced by the appeal of a slow and inopportune process of recognition when it comes to translating its process of maturation into political action'.[32] Events following the fall of the Prodi government, and in particular the decisive support offered to Massimo D'Alema by the UDR in the confidence vote in Parliament, definitively compromised this dialogue however, and deepened the personal hostility between the two leaders with Cossiga's return to the attack on the issue of conflict of interest, seeking to widen the scope of a pending parliamentary bill on the subject which had already been approved by the Chamber, and had been blocked in the Senate since April.

Berlusconi's refusal to detach *Forza Italia* from AN and bring it to the centre, which became evident in the autumn, had the effect of bringing the *Polo* back together, and drawing it out of the half-concealed crisis of mutual trust which had characterised the first half of the year. The reconciliation was the result of reciprocal concessions: Berlusconi gave up his special relationship with Cossiga, and Fini gave up the relationship with D'Alema which had so concerned Berlusconi during the work of the Bicameral Commission. Berlusconi's attitude towards the Bicameral Commission remained variable and ambivalent, with regard both to single issues, and to the general working relationship with D'Alema, in contrast to the greater consistency and interest shown by Fini.[33] For Berlusconi '(institutional) reforms are not self-evidently required (*non ce le ha ordinate il medico)*', while for Fini 'it is the Italians who are asking for them'. In the Bicameral Commission, Berlusconi lacked the will – perhaps even more than the strength – to reach agreement with D'Alema. This applied to the priority to be given to changes in electoral law through the so-called *'casa Letta'* pact (a coalition-based second-ballot system, compensated for with a PR element, and a bonus to the largest coalition list). It also applied to the scope of the powers of the Head of State (especially those accorded in a political crisis) in the context of a semi-presidential system, and to the principles governing a (for Berlusconi indispensible) reform of the judicial system. Fini was opposed to the almost obsessive pre-eminence attributed to judicial reform, which so badly hampered *Forza Italia's* bargaining position in the Bicameral Commission, and distanced himself from the numerous attacks on 'political justice' launched by Berlusconi during the year.

From the legal point of view 1998 was, in fact, one of Berlusconi's most difficult years. Some of the initial investigations begun against him in earlier years led to criminal sentences – though they were still subject to a long appeals process. Having already been given a remitted sixteen-months sentence on charges of improper budget statements relating to the acquisition of the Medusa film production company, in mid-July, he received another two lower-court sentences within a few hours of one another: two years and nine months for bribes paid to the *Guardia di Finanza*, and two years and four months for illegal currency transfers to former prime minister Bettino Craxi. At the beginning of May, he was served with two further indictments for corruption in relation to the legal documentation connected to the purchase of Mondadori and Sme.

However, as in the past, what Berlusconi sees as judicial persecution appears to have benefited both his standing as party leader, and the popularity of the party, which a poll in mid-July put at 31.5 percent.[34] The 'true' level of support evidenced by the administrative elections in May and June had already given encouragement to the *Polo* and, above all, to FI, which showed itself capable of renewed vitality at the local level, where it had traditionally had difficulty in establishing itself. The results of the second round of voting gave fourteen provincial capitals out of the twenty-three which voted to the *Polo*, with FI the largest party in these cities, winning 153 seats against the 134 of the PDS.[35] At the administrative elections of November and December, the results were less encouraging, above all for FI, which lost ground against AN. In the second round, the *Polo* took the Province of Rome and took eleven mayoral posts from the centre-left.

It is probable that FI's problems were partly organisational (as Fini suggested), and linked to the continuing difficulty in finding good-quality candidates in the provinces, and in building local networks which could compete with the established organisations on the left. FI's problems were certainly also linked to its internal democratic deficiencies and to the poor performance of its national decision-making bodies, as evidenced by the frequent disorder on the part of the parliamentary group when faced with the political decisions imposed, often without chance of discussion, by their leader. The general crisis of policy and strategy which became evident in the course of 1998, and which affected the party from top to bottom, were more damaging than these management problems. The rudimentary policy proposals produced at the congress did little to carry forward into concrete and convincing policy proposals of long-term value the liberal values which had been propounded by Berlusconi since the party's launch in 1994. FI's plans for 1999 included many focused initiatives and demonstrations similar to its 'national campaign for jobs' and the successful demonstration against the D'Alema government organised on 24 October 1998 in Rome. There were initiatives aimed at the grass roots of the party and opportunities for lively internal debates through municipal party congresses and of 'tough and unceasing' opposition in Parliament. The doubt remained, however, that these solutions, though imaginative, were insufficient to solve the problems of a party which was culturally and structurally unprepared for a long spell in opposition. Frequently the party seemed obsessed with the next general election and the alliance strategy it should adopt. Victim of the eclectic vacillation of its leader, who was himself the victim of his own contradictions generated by conflicts of interest and judicial vulnerability, *Forza Italia* frequently failed to seize the chances it was offered to play any really incisive role in parliament.

Conclusions

The events of 1998 demonstrate that the motives behind the unity of the two largest parties of the *Polo* are, for the moment, more *neg-*

ative and defensive than *positive and proactive.* They are tied to the need of both parties to show voters that, given their agreement, any concession to the temptations of neocentrism would only translate into a damaging dispersion of energy, which would simply play into the hands of the left. During the year, not only was the foundation for better policy understanding not laid, but it became even more evident that the strategic objectives of the two main allies did not coincide. *Alleanza Nazionale* is aware that it can gain an advantage from a renewal of the dialogue with the democratic left in the area of institutional reforms, and does not intend to submit to the campaign of *Forza Italia* on the issue of anti-communism, as was clearly seen in the brief moment when the *Polo* called into doubt the right of D'Alema to become prime minister. It would have been senseless and suicidal for a party which has the imprint of nostalgia for the fascist regime in its genes to question the democratic credentials of the former communists. On the contrary, burying the legacy of the great ideological conflicts of the earlier part of the twentieth century is a necessary condition for AN to be able one day to assume full autonomy in political initiatives and cease to depend on the respectability endowed by the allies it can persuade to work with it. On the other hand, *Forza Italia* has an interest in maintaining a high level of conflictuality with the left, and especially the DS, so as to differentiate itself from its centrist competitors. Its most dangerous competitor for the immediate future, the UDR, has allowed its own image to become unbalanced, and this may affect its support among moderate voters. Unable to steer the crisis of the Prodi government towards a broad-based 'institutional' solution, the UDR was forced to align itself with the D'Alema candidacy for the office of Prime Minister.

If the general context of party life in Italy has strengthened the, albeit unenthusiastic, tendency towards cohabitation on the part of most of the parties which make up the *Polo* (the problem is more complicated for CCD, given the attraction which any kind of successful neo-Christian Democrat *rassemblement* would exert upon its leaders and its electorate), their attempts to face common difficulties collectively have worked in the opposite direction. Among these various unresolved problems, at least two appear, from a short-term perspective, to be particularly difficult: the referendum on the electoral system, and the choices to be made in the election for the President of the Republic. The messages which FI and AN have exchanged so far on these two arguments have not always been friendly, and are marked by their common desire to keep their hands free. In particular, agreement on the subject of the referendum appears improbable. From the time when Fini and the CCD threw caution to the wind and offered public support to the Segni-Di Pietro referendum proposal (thereby also forming an unwelcome *de facto* alliance with the DS) a sharp clash with *Forza Italia*, (which had itself offered support to Giuliano Urbani's proposal to form a committee to vote 'no') became inevitable. In any event, with the referendum proposal approved by the Supreme Court, if it were not possible to find a compromise solution in parliament, both parties would have to consider carefully the costs and benefits of campaigning on opposing sides in the campaign. AN might, in fact, be attracted (as has happened in the past) by a second-ballot system if it perceived that FI itself was in renewed electoral decline, as suggested by the administrative elections held in the autumn. Equally FI would have to weigh the risks of reintroducing proportional representation, since this would give potentially undesirable opportunites for political mediation in the centre of the spectrum to the UDR.

In the presence of these divergent views, and given the problems in resolving certain weighty questions which remain on the table (such as the identification of a future candidate for Prime Minister, or the position to be adopted towards the *Lega*), the prospects that the *Polo* can recover the political initiative in the short term look poor. The temptation of pitching for the populist causes has been much in evidence in efforts to politicise any form of social discontent available, from the desperation of cancer sufferers anxious to try Professor Di Bella's miracle cure, to the efforts of taxi drivers to hold the Rutelli administration in the city of Rome to ransom. There is a risk that this will become the only strategy that holds the coalition together, against centrifugal pressures driving its parties apart in parliament and elsewhere. As things stand, the idea of forming a single party of the right, which would secure the tactical and strategic co-ordination which is currently so lacking, has no appeal for the *Alleanza Nazionale*.

The centre-right's chances of returning to government, which polls suggest remain good, are therefore more tied to the misadventures of its adversaries and competitors – and the decision by Cossiga to support the D'Alema government is potentially one such – than to its own efforts. As for the future, and the path which the *Polo*'s opposition will follow in the second half of the legislature, much will depend on the results which its component parties secure in the European elections in June 1999. And for both *Forza Italia* and *Alleanza Nazionale*, what still counts much more in the short term is that each emerges with more votes than the other, than that together they are able to defeat their enemies on the left.

Translated by Simon Dix

Notes

1. On the stages in the creation of *Alleanza Nazionale*, and on related problems, see M. Tarchi, *Fuori dal 'ghetto': il caso di Alleanza Nazionale*, in M. Fedele and R. Leonardi (eds), *La politica senza i partiti*, Roma: Seam, 1996, pp. 77-93; Piero Ignazi, *Postfascisti?*, Bologna: Il Mulino, 1994; M. Tarchi, *Cinquant'anni di nostalgia. La destra italiana dopo il fascismo*, Milano: Rizzoli, 1995.

2. The analytical categories used here are those developed in A. Panebianco, *Modelli di partito*, Bologna: Il Mulino, 1982.

3. Some commentators, in using this phase, believed that in Italy they saw 'a series of circumstances capable of bestowing on ... Fini a potential destiny as leader of the conservative bloc in our country'. Thus G. Lerner, *I due punti deboli di Fini*, in *La Stampa*, 3 December 1997, p. 1.

4. The 'national-liberal' faction spoke in terms of a 'serious political and numerical defeat' (see for example the cover story ('Quattro anni fa') by A. Urso in *Charta minuta*, 2 November, 1997); *Area*, the periodical published by the so-called 'social-right' faction even evoked the image of Caporetto on its cover. On the intensification of conflicts between FI, AN, CCD, and CDU following the poor election results, cfr. P. Ignazi, *Polo, il paradosso di una crisi*, in *Il Sole 24 ore*, 3 December 1997, p. 5.

5. See M. de Angelis, *Appuntamento sul Piave*, *Area*, II, 20, December 1997, p. 1; A. Terranova, *Una sconfitta annunciata*, *Area*, II, 20, December 1997, p. 13-15; G. Alemanno, *Uscire dalla palude: tre punti per Fiuggi/2*, *Area*, II, 20, December 1997, p. 17.

6. Significantly, the second volume (November 1997) of 'Charta Minuta' is dedicated to the question '*Un*do the *Polo* o *Re*do the *Polo?*'.

7. A Luxor poll indicated that a high percentage of *Polo* voters (49percent) saw in Cossiga 'the personality, outside the centre-right, who should be used in the political relaunching of the moderates'; after Cossiga, favourable votes went to the former *Amministratore Delegato* of Fiat, Cesare Romiti (30percent), and Antonio Di Pietro (17percent). These data are reported and commented on in an article entitled 'Berlusconi, il Polo ed oltre', in *Ideazione*, V, 1, January-February 1998, pp. 32-33.

8. F. Guiglia, 'Parla Fini. Ecco il mio liberismo per la nuova destra', in *Il Borghese*, 29 October 1997.

9. Alleanza Nazionale, *Rimetti in cammino la speranza nell'Italia*, Roma: RGS, 1998.

10. On the possibility of an evolution of *Alleanza Nazionale* towards the model of the '*partito programmatico*', see. M. Tarchi, *Dal Msi ad An. Organizzazione e strategie*, Bologna: Il Mulino, 1997, pp. 408-415.

11. *Le foibe* are naturally-occurring ditches. At the end of the second world war they were used as mass graves by 'communist partisans' (Italians included) for murdered Italian nationalists who opposed the new border and the transfer of Istria and Dalmatia to the Yugoslav Republic. In Italy they have provoked a heated historical and political debate since, until few years ago, left-wing historians and politicians denied the 'existence of the foibe' (the use of the foibe as mass grave) or minimised the number of cases.

12. This event was confirmed by F. Storace, 'Il grande progetto della destra nuova', in *Area*, III, 24, April 1998, p. 9.

13. By the end of November 1997, Fini had already met the deputy leader of the Congressional Republicans, the President of the Justice Commission, Henry Hyde, who was invited to Italy by Aelle, the parliamentary research organof the

Polo directed by Adolfo Urso. See B. Jerkov, 'La benedizione di Mr. Hyde: Gianfranco, tutto ok', in *Il Messaggero*, 24 November 1997, and V. Cus., 'Le idee della destra Usa simili a quelle del Polo', in *Il Giornale*, 24 November1997.

14. The meeting between Fini and Violante on the issue of the *foibe*, organised by the University of Trieste two weeks after the Verona Conference (on March 14) was also presented by the party as a further sign of the normalisation of its relationships with the political forces of the former *arco costituzionale*.

15. The expression is reported in a document approved by the national leadership of AN in January 1997, after seven hours of debate. See G. Alemanno, 'Tra Verona e Cossiga', in *Area*, III, 23, March 1998, p. 7.

16. In December 1997, according to an Ispo-Cra Nielsen poll, 52,2 percent of the *Alleanza Nazionale* electorate (and 51,9 percent of the *Forza Italia* electorate) approved of it. See R. Mannheimer, 'L'elettore incalza: no a un Polo frammentato, meglio un partito unico', in *Corriere della Sera*, 8 December 1997, p. 7.

17. G. Alemanno, 'Cercasi premier disperatamente', in *Area*, III, 21, January 1998, p. 10.

18. For a review of the joint initiatives which have already been attempted, see M. Cellai, 'An e l'Upe: un avvenimento storico', in *Charta Minuta*, II, 9, July 1998, pp. 15-16.

19. See, in this regard, the low-profile reaction of the president of *Alleanza Nazionale* to the lack of success of the FI in the autumn administrative elections. See M. Nese, 'Fini: gli azzurri si devono organizzare', in *Corriere della Sera*, 2 December 1998, p. 10. On the prospects of electoral competition between the two parties, see M. Nese, 'Martino: attenti, per la prima volta An ci ha tolto consenso' 2 December 1998, p. 10.

20. On the organisational evolution of *Forza Italia*, see E. Poli, 'Forza Italia: i modelli organizzativi', in D. Mennitti (ed.), *Forza Italia. Radiografia di un evento*, Roma: Ideazione Editrice, 1997, pp. 79-109; C. Golia, *Dentro Forza Italia*, Venezia: Marsilio, 1997; P. McCarthy, 'Forza Italia: i vecchi problemi rimangono', in R. D'Alimonte and D. Nelken (eds.), *Politica in Italia. Edizione 1997*, Bologna: Il Mulino, 1997, pp. 65-84.

21. See *Forza Italia, Regolamento dei Congressi Provinciali e delle Grandi Città*, Roma: 1997, Article 5.

22. See *Forza Italia, Statuto*, Roma: 1997, Articles 15 and 16. See also P. Di Caro, 'Berlusconi vuole un partito vero', *Il Corriere della Sera*, 10 April 1998.

23. See M. Conti, 'E il Cavaliere ordinò: nessuno deve stravincere', in *Il Messaggero*, 7 April 1998.

24. See M. Marozzi, 'Prodi: congresso del nulla', in *La Repubblica*, 19 April 1998.

25. See P. Di Caro, 'Il leader di Forza Italia: abbiamo sette anime', in *Il Corriere della Sera*, 21 February 1998.

26. This opinion is expressed by On. Giorgio Rebuffa in an interview given to P. Di Caro, 'Rebuffa: Berlusconi è troppo buono, ma ha commesso un errore...', in *Il Corriere della Sera*, 9 April 1998.

27. On the emergence of critical voices close to the *Forza Italia*, see G. Fregonara, 'Colletti, deluso, snobba il congresso azzurro', *Il Corriere della Sera*, 15 April 1998; F. Alberti, *Forza Italia, via al congresso dei litigi*, Il Corriere della Sera, 18 April 1998; P. Di Caro, 'Matranga: Tra di noi c'è un malessere profondo', *Il Corriere della Sera*, April 18, 1998; F. Alberti, 'Taradash: un congresso? E' stato una messa', *Il Corriere della Sera*, 20 April 1998; F. Sa., 'Vertone vascia Forza Italia: al congresso solo urla e culto del capo', *Il Corriere della Sera*, 22 April 1998.

28. See P. Di Caro, 'Berlusconi duro con i suoi', in *Il Corriere della Sera*, 18 September 1998.

29. See B. Jerkov, 'Nasce la corrente dei profesori: stufi di Berlusconi', *Il Corriere della Sera*, 1 October 1998; P. Di Caro, 'Da Rebuffa a Colletti, cresce il malessere dei liberal azzurr', *Il Corriere della Sera*, 4 October 1998.

30. The polling organisation run by Gianni Pilo claims that the electorate of FI would react favourably to an agreement with the *Lega*, and that in the north 3percent of the electorate has remained without party identity since the breaking of the *Polo della Libertà*, the 1994 agreement between FI and the *Lega*. See R. Delera, 'Pilo: se ci accordiamo con il Carroccio al Nord vittoria sicura in tutti i collegi', *Il Corriere della Sera*, 5 March 1998. Renato Menneimer, on the basis of a simulation of the 1996 election results, also calculates there would be a significant increase for the *Polo* (58 seats) in the event of an agreement in the north with the *Lega*, notwithstanding some loss of votes in the south. See R. Mannheimer, 'Il Carroccio con il centrodestra sottrarrebbe 58 seggi all'Ulivo', *Il Corriere della Sera*, 9 March 1998.

31. See R. P., 'Berlusconi: Cossiga non attrae Forza Italia', *Il Corriere della Sera*, 25 January 1998.

32. See P. Di Caro, 'Berlusconi: oltre il Polo con i moderati', in *Il Corriere della Sera*, 16 March 1998.

33. The relationship between Berlusconi and D'Alema, which had begun to develop at the beginning of 1996 with the attempt to form a government 'of broad understanding', and which had started off constructively in the Bicameral Commission, deteriorated in the course of the work of the commission, to the point where there was a mutual loss of trust. Berlusconi commented on the Bicameral Commission in the following way: 'The majority in the government was against carrying out the reforms; the alternative, therefore, was to do away with the coalition and build a new one with the aim of rewriting certain political rules' D'Alema, however, 'ended up surrendering' to the more conservative positions. See the interview with Silvio Berlusconi by Domenico Mennitti, 'Ecco perchè l'Italia non è un Paese normale', *Ideazione*, 5, September-October, 1998, pp. 30-31.

34. See P. Di Caro, 'Berlusconi: pieni poteri alla commissione', *Il Corriere della Sera*, 15 July 1998.

35. See L. Fuccaro, 'Berlusconi: dobbiamo mandare a casa Prodi', *Il Corriere della Sera*, 9 June 1998. See also, in the same newspaper, the analysis by R. Mannheimer, 'Quando la Lega non da indicazioni politiche, i suoi elettori scelgono il centrodestra'.

3

REASSEMBLING THE CENTRE
AND THE ELECTORAL SPECTRUM

Renato Mannheimer and Giacomo Sani

Introduction

The characteristics of the so-called 'First Republic' – today of interest more to scholars of contemporary history than to political scientists – can be described in different ways according to the approach adopted. But its nature and dynamics are difficult to analyse without reference to the substantially 'tripolar' pattern assumed by the Italian political system in the years between 1946 and 1992. For more than four decades, the successful players in elections, coalitions, governments, policy agendas, reshuffles, and crises (and subsequent realignments) were the political groups occupying more central, or less peripheral, positions in the political spectrum. Only occasionally did the groups located further to the left or right come to the fore. For more than forty years the political stage was dominated by the centre party *par excellence* (the DC) accompanied first by the three lay parties (PSDI, PRI, PLI), and then from the early 1970s on also by the PSI (following that party's shift towards the centre).

This arrangement began to break down in the early 1980s as the DC went into electoral decline (the result of numerous factors, but mainly the erosion of voting by 'subcultural membership'), and as the PSI gained increasing political (and governmental) importance. Then, in the early 1990s, with the crisis of the First Republic and the advent of transition, there emerged a tendency towards bipolarity that was induced partly by the crisis of the parties caught up in the '*Tangentopoli*' (Bribesville) scandal and partly by the electoral reform law of 1993. When the first elections were held under the new rules (on 27 March 1994), the political centre represented by the parties that defined themselves '*al centro*' (and had been positioned as such by the electors) still stood as an independent electoral alternative. But it emerged crushed, indeed almost annihilated, when the votes were counted. Despite receiving more than 15 percent of votes, the grouping comprised of Martinazzoli's PPI, Segni's *Patto per l'Italia* and other minor parties won only four seats for single-member constituencies in the Chamber and three in the Senate. Its parliamentary representation was only ensured by the proportional quota system, which allocated it a further forty-two deputies and twenty-eight senators.

Two years later, on the occasion of the elections of 21 April 1996, the trend towards bipolarity became even more apparent. After a further split in the PPI which gave rise to the CDU, the remainder of the previous centre joined the two principal alignments of the *Polo* and the *Ulivo*. As a consequence, when voters inspected the symbols on their ballot slips identifying the candidates' party allegiances they no longer found one denoting a political group belonging explicitly to the centre – even less the Catholic centre – and standing in opposition to the other two poles. Of course, *Forza Italia*, CCD and CDU, on the one hand, and *Rinnovamento* and PPI on the other, could present themselves to voters as the true heirs of centrism, but these groups were in fact integral parts (and decidedly minor partners) of two opposing alignments on, respectively, the political centre-right and the centre-left. In short, by the spring of 1996 a freestanding centre 'pole' had disappeared from the electoral scene.

However, although evident at the electoral level (despite the awkward presence of the *Lega*), this tendency towards bipolarity had not yet taken concrete form in terms of alignments at the parliamentary level. In the course of 1998, first with the creation of the UDR and then more strikingly with the formation of the D'Alema government, neo-centrist strategies or (as their opponents called them) 'temptations' once again appeared. Although the details of the UDR's policy programme are as yet unclear, there is no doubt as to its overall goal: to dismantle (or at least to undercut) the two poles that arose in the early phase of transition, and to construct (or reconstruct) a political grouping at the centre of the political spectrum which will play a pivotal role – or which will at least condition the strategies of the left and right political groups in the country and in parliament. Its intention, that is to say, is to instigate a retreat from bipolarity and to restore a tripolar configuration to the system.

How likely is the UDR to succeed? Obviously, fulfilment or otherwise of its neo-centrist project depends on numerous factors. Although it is difficult to determine the weight of these various factors, one indispensable condition for the reconstruction of the centre is obviously endorsement by the general public, and therefore the response of the electorate when, sooner or later, it is asked to pronounce on the matter. This is the question addressed by this chapter: do the conditions exist for a central pole to re-emerge? Can the electoral space available for fulfilment of the neo-centrist project be identified, and its size estimated (or, so to speak, 'quantified')?

Does a Centre Electorate Still Exist?

That an electorate of the political centre existed throughout the First Republic was amply documented by research carried out from the 1960s onwards.

The size of the section of the electorate made up of interviewees who declared themselves as belonging to the centre varied from period to period, and also according to the survey techniques employed. Nevertheless in the course of those decades, the overall distribution was substantially uniform, with the largest proportion of interviewees locating themselves in the central segment of the political spectrum. In the light of these surveys one may say that during the First Republic the size of the centre electorate amounted to at least one-third of the electoral body and, according to the results of some surveys, it was even as high as 40 percent.

Against this background, statistics gathered in recent years have demonstrated the emergence of a number of novel features. In particular, they have highlighted a certain shrinkage in the central segment of the political spectrum with a corresponding growth of its two inner segments constituted by the centre-right and centre-left. It seems that the electoral alignments that arose prior to the elections of the transition years were reflected in (and may also have resulted from) mass opinion, and thus matched the bipolarity then emerging. In other words, the bipolar system has been readily accepted by the Italian electorate, as documented by the numerous surveys that have shown the distinct preference of Italians for a two-party system.

This therefore seems to be a pattern that has consolidated itself in public opinion. And yet, although the central segment has shrunk, it still maintains a certain quantitative weight. On the basis of the figures used for the purposes of this chapter, and relating to the autumn of 1998, the number of citizens defining themselves as belonging to the political centre can be estimated at between one fifth and one quarter of the electorate. And since there are around forty-nine million voters enrolled on the electoral register, the amount of potential votes for the centre parties can be calculated at no fewer than ten million. Even taking account of the probable amount of 'no votes' (abstentions and spoilt ballot slips, calculated on the figures for the 1996 election), this still leaves approximately 7.5 million potential votes for the central segment of the political spectrum (1996 electors: 48.8 million; 1996 valid votes in the proportional quota: 37.5 million).

This is obviously a sizable amount of electoral support, especially since it is roughly equal to the number of votes cast for the two largest political parties – the PDS (7.9 million) and *Forza Italia* (7.7 million) – at the last elections. In a completely bipolar set-up, a mass of centrist votes of such proportions could play an extremely important, indeed decisive, role in swinging the electoral outcome to either the centre-left or the centre-right. If the two largest poles were evenly matched, then even a slightly unequal distribution of the centre votes between them would decide the result of the election.

Yet this block of centrist votes could move in a third direction. It could, in fact, deliver massive support to those endeavouring to construct an alternative lying midway between the two main centre-right and centre-left alignments. Of course, the likelihood of this third alternative coming about depends not only on initiatives by the political elite but also on the nature, composition and degree of homogeneity/heterogeneity of the group of voters who consider themselves '*di centro*'. But what are the social characteristics and political attitudes of this segment of the electorate?

The Social Characteristics of the Electorate of the Political Centre

Age is the most striking of the demographic features that socially connote the portion of the electorate that describes itself as belonging to the political centre. Specifically, those who place themselves at the centre of a hypothetical political spectrum ranging from right to left tend in the main to belong to the older age classes. Whereas relatively fewer young people – roughly one fifth – declare themselves to be politically centrist, almost one third of the population aged over sixty does so. Moreover, a much larger proportion of young people compared with other age groups refuses to assign itself to a particular political position, thereby rejecting the conventional antithesis between left and right and implicitly proposing a different reading of the political spectrum. Almost 20 percent of the population aged under twenty-nine, in fact, declare that they are unable to (or does not wish to) specify their position on the left-right continuum. This percentage diminishes significantly with age, falling to just above 8 percent among the population aged over sixty. This is a further sign of the 'withdrawal' of young people from politics, as also evidenced by the relatively larger number of them who do not vote at elections. There remains the fact that those young people who do express some form or other political opinion (and therefore place themselves somewhere along the continuum) prefer to define themselves as more distinctly on the left or the right, rather than in the centre. Among the less young, by contrast, centrist positions grow progressively more frequent until they account for the largest share of the over-sixties.

There are obviously numerous reasons for this phenomenon, but it is reasonable to suppose that it is mainly due to voting tradition – and not, as some have maintained, to the difficulty encountered by those, like the elderly, with lower average levels of schooling when they are asked to locate themselves in a 'clear-cut' manner on the left-right spectrum. This is confirmed by comparative analysis of the subgroups formed by possession of educational qualifications, which reveals only minimal percentage differences (at the limits of statistical significance) among those placing themselves in the central positions on the left-right continuum.

Figure 3.1 *The percentages of persons locating themselves in the political centre by age class. Variations with respect to the sample.*

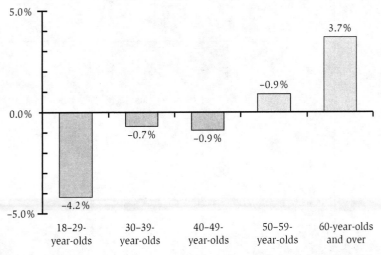

Source: SPO-CRA/AC Nielsen. Osservatorio socio-politico del 5 July 1998. (Number of cases = 3401)

Figure 3.2 *The percentages of persons locating themselves in the political centre by sex. Variations with respect to the sample.*

Source: SPO-CRA/AC Nielsen. Osservatorio socio-politico del 5 July 1998. (Number of cases = 3401)

Figure 3.3 *The percentages of persons locating themselves in the political centre by profession. Variations with respect to the sample.*

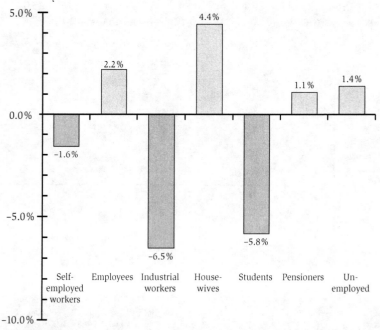

Source: SPO-CRA/AC Nielsen. Osservatorio socio-politico del 5 July 1998. (Number of cases = 3401)

Gender is another distinguishing feature of subjects who locate themselves in the political centre, of whom a much larger proportion are females. But once again it is very likely that this difference is due less to gender than to the fact that a much larger proportion of women are (to their great good fortune) elderly. The distribution of voters by occupational situation again confirms the findings set out so far. The largest concentration – relatively – of those who declare that they belong to the political centre is among housewives, while the smallest is found among students, who by their very nature (and age) tend to take up more 'radical' positions.

The Political Orientations of the Centre

We have seen that a relatively broad sector of the Italian electorate places itself in the political middle ground. But what does the way in which these voters self-locate themselves signify from the point of view of political orientation? Put differently: are the voters of the centre politically distinct from those who express other positions? And if so, how and to what extent? Providing exhaustive answers to these questions would require detailed analysis beyond the scope of this chapter. We shall accordingly only examine some aspects of the matter, providing a preliminary and provisional answer to the question of the difference between the centre voters and others.

The figures that we analysed displayed clear differences, especially as regards attitudes. A recent survey (early October 1998) has shown that 'centrist' voters are on average less involved in politics, both subjectively and objectively, than the rest of the electorate. Only 25 percent of this group declared itself 'very' or 'quite' interested in politics, as opposed to 34 percent of the overall sample. This group's lower level of political involvement was also in evidence in its more infrequent reading of newspapers. Those centre voters who reported that they read a newspaper 'every day' or 'often' amounted to 37 percent, compared with 45 percent of all interviewees. As expected, the 'gap' widened even further when they were asked, not just about newspaper readership in general, but about their reading of pages specifically devoted to political news.

Voters who placed themselves at the centre of the left-right spectrum were also more religious, being distinguished in particular by their more frequent attendance at Mass (53 percent declared that they went to church at least once a month, compared with 43 percent of all interviewees). Consistently with this finding, this group also displayed the highest levels of faith in the Catholic Church (73 percent declared that they had 'very much' and 'much' faith as opposed to 59 percent of the overall sample).

Another survey, carried out in the autumn of 1997, yielded further information on the differences between centre voters and the others. Examination of the distributions of the replies to questions concerning, for example, the death penalty for serious crimes, the presence of immigrants in the country, or the provision of incentives for private enterprise, showed that centre voters again differ, not only from those taking up politically more clear-cut positions ('left' or 'right') but also from those on the 'centre-left' or 'centre-right'.

Figure 3.4a *In favour of the death penalty for the most serious crimes. Variations with respect to sample.*

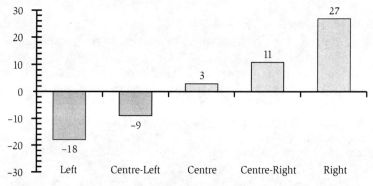

Source: G. Sani, 'Otto domande a cinque campioni: una comparazione tra indagini demoscopiche' in *POLIS* XII, 2, August 1998.

Figure 3.4b *'The presence of immigrants in the country worries me'. Variations with respect to sample.*

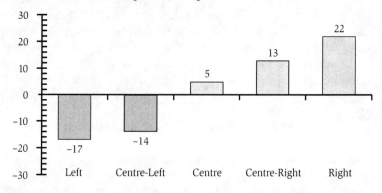

Source: G. Sani, 'Otto domande a cinque campioni: una comparazione tra indagini demoscopiche' in *POLIS* XII, 2, August 1998.

Figure 3.4c *'North, Centre, South should be more independent'. Variations with respect to sample.*

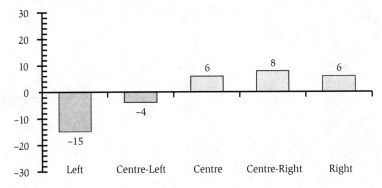

Source: G. Sani, 'Otto domande a cinque campioni: una comparazione tra indagini demoscopiche' in *POLIS* XII, 2, August 1998.

The same pattern emerges with respect to two further thematic areas covered by the survey.

In short, these results highlight that these voters occupy the political middle ground not only from a purely ideological (or 'ideal') point of view but also, and much more concretely, in terms of the specific topics on which they were asked to express their opinions. And obviously the attitudes that these centre voters expressed tend in many cases to resemble those of the electorate as a whole.

Figure 3.5a *'More opportunities for private enterprise'. Variations with respect to sample.*

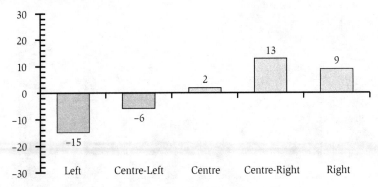

Source: G. Sani, 'Otto domande a cinque campioni: una comparazione tra indagini demoscopiche' in *POLIS* XII, 2, August 1998.

Figure 3.5b *'Greater power to the workers'. Variations with respect to sample.*

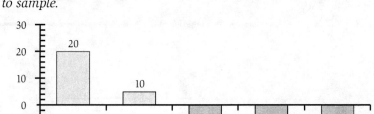

Source: G. Sani, 'Otto domande a cinque campioni: una comparazione tra indagini demoscopiche' in *POLIS* XII, 2, August 1998.

This differentiation – and median position – is naturally (and markedly) evident when attitudes relate even more explicitly to politics. This is exemplified by the interviewees' opinions of the main protagonists of Italian public life. As was to be expected, the public images of D'Alema and Berlusconi, Prodi and Fini, to mention of some of the most prominent personalities, differed sharply across the various segments of the political spectrum.

Figure 3.6 *Percentages of positive opinions concerning four leaders in the five segments of the continuum*

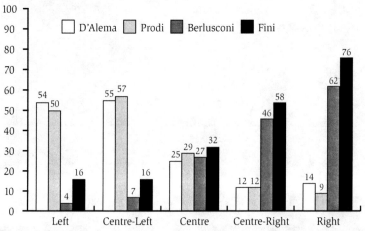

Source: SPO-CRA/AC Nielsen. Osservatorio socio-politico del 5 July 1998. (Number of cases = 3401)

More interesting, however, are the differences between centre voters and those who declared other political positions. Whilst distinctly positive or negative opinions were expressed in the other segments, those of the centrist group appeared to be more 'tepid' or less forcefully stated.

This lack of incisiveness, however, should not be taken to imply the existence of a politically (and electorally) homogenous group. Quite the reverse. From this point of view, the centre segment appears to be relatively more heterogeneous. This emerges, for example, when one examines the retrospective declarations by interviewees concerning their voting behaviour at the 1996 elections. As Figure 3.7 shows, the distribution of votes in the two outer segments for the majoritarian quota (i.e., the single-seat constituency contests) was greatly biased towards one or other of the two main competing alignments. At the centre, by contrast, voters split three ways, with some opting for the *Polo* candidates, others for those of the *Ulivo-Rifondazione* alliance, and yet others for the leaders of the *Lega*. The same pattern is revealed by the figures on voting for the party lists for the proportional quota, where a very significant phenomenon emerges: the consequence of the heterogeneity of the choices and behaviour of those declaring themselves to be 'centre voters' is that they opt for the most diverse range of parties, so that the great majority of them end up by voting for parties which do *not* belong to the political centre. In other words, centre parties receive only a very partial proportion (well below half) of the 'target' that they have set themselves.

Figure 3.7 *The 1996 first-past-the-post vote for the* Polo *and the* Ulivo *in the five segments of the continuum*

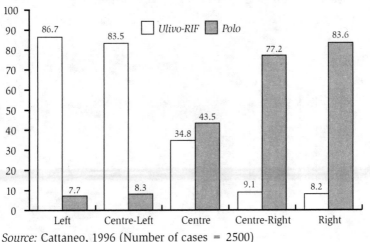

Source: Cattaneo, 1996 (Number of cases = 2500)

Table 3.1 *Voting Intentions of Voters Who Place Themselves in the Political Centre (Percentage Values)*

Forza Italia	22.2
Alleanza Nazionale	5.3
CCD	5.6
UDR (Cossiga) [a]	2.1
Lista Pannella	1.8
Democratici di Sinistra [b]	10.2
Rifondazione Comunista	0.1
Greens	3.3
Rinnovamento Italiano	2.1
PPI	6.0
Lega Nord	22.1
Movimento Sociale-Fiamma Tricolore	–
L'Italia dei Valori	3.4
Partito dei Comunisti italiani	–
Socialisti italiani (Boselli)/Laburisti (Spini)/Socialisti (Intini)	0.6
Ulivo	11.1
100 *città*	0.4
Others	3.7
Total	100.0
Base (number of cases)	278

[a] Party formed in July 1998
[b] The *Partito Democratico della Sinistra* in surveys prior to July 1998
Source: ISPO-CRA/AC Nielsen. Osservatorio socio-politico del 6 dicembre 1998. (Number of cases = 4,858.)

Figure 3.8 *Willingness to vote for the left parties*

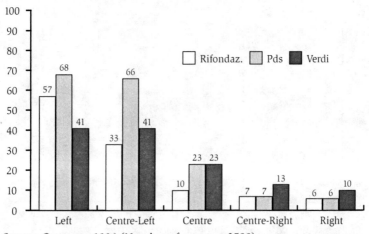

Source: Cattaneo, 1996 (Number of cases = 2500)

This characterisation of the centre as a largely heterogeneous segment of the political spectrum, or at least as much more heterogeneous than others, also concerns the so-called 'potential vote' –in other words the willingness of voters to consider other options. If voters are asked what other voting choices they would be willing to consider, besides their actual one, analysis of their replies yields a pattern very similar to that illustrated above. Inspection of Figures 3.8 and 3.9 shows that groups of voters on the left or right express very distinct preferences and exclusions. Vice versa, interviewees from the political centre are much more divided from the point of view of the centre-right and centre-left options that they would include among, or exclude from, the alternatives considered.

Figure 3.9 *Willingness to vote for the* Polo *parties.*

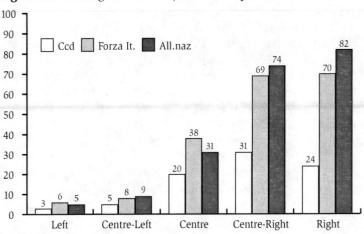

Source: Cattaneo, 1996 (Number of cases = 2500)

A Divided Pole: For Whom is There Space at the Centre?

The results of our analysis suggest that the group of centre voters differs in many respects from those located in other segments of the political spectrum. But analysis also highlights a further three points of a certain relevance to the question addressed here.

The first concerns the difference between the centre and the two segments contiguous to it. Overall, at least as regards the features considered here, it seems that centrist voters more closely resemble their 'cousins' on the centre-right than they do those on the centre-left.

The second point concerns the 'median' nature, so to speak, of centre voters. In theory, the fact that they occupy the middle ground as far as the rankings of attitudes are concerned may be

due to the prevalence of voters who express moderate positions
along the various dimensions considered. But the median nature of
the group occupying this segment may more simply be the result of
the combination in different 'doses' of entirely different positions.
This second hypothesis, which strikes us as more plausible, states
that the diversity of the centre is nothing but a reflection of the
divisions internal to it. The centre appears to be different not
because it is made up of moderates but because it is divided –
because, that is, it comprises a diversified mix of political opinions.

But if this really is the case – and this is the third point – the
problem arises of the compatibility among the centre's various
components. Put otherwise, a divided pole is, as said, a 'target'
that is very difficult to achieve, given its numerous and perhaps
incompatible fragments. How many of the PPI's potential voters
would be willing to vote for a centrist grouping which also comprised the followers of Cossiga and Mastella? And vice versa?

Only a few. Among the PPI's potential voters (i.e., those who
declare that they would consider the party as an option at the next
elections), a substantially larger proportion declare that they would
also consider the DS (20 percent of the PPI's potential electorate)
or Di Pietro's *Italia dei Valori* (28 percent) than those whose potential vote would go to the CCD (considered by 5 percent of the PPI's
potential voters) or Cossiga's UDR (less than 1 percent).

The reverse also applies, of course. The PPI is considered an
option by 2 percent of the CCD's potential electorate, which in its
turn is much more favourable towards *Forza Italia* (considered by
40 percent).

A Necessary but not Sufficient Condition

The voters of the centre exist, therefore, and they are distinct from
voters who locate themselves in other segments of the political spectrum. Hence, at the general level they constitute a substantial section
of the electorate. But the existence of a central pole at this level is
only one of the conditions for the emergence of a central pole at the
parliamentary level. It is a necessary condition but not a sufficient
one. Transformation of this potential into real support depends on
the presence or otherwise of other factors or conditions, and most
notably: the incentives and risks inherent in the electoral system; the
strategies of the parties when they formulate their programmes; and
the ability of the competing groups to communicate effectively.

These conditions are not yet in place, and centre voters prefer,
as we have seen, to vote for political forces more distinctly located
on the left or on the right.

4

A POSTMORTEM OF THE BICAMERALE

Gianfranco Pasquino

'We have other things to do; we have to govern'. With these angry, revealing and, in the light of his future unexpected nomination as Prime Minister, unwittingly prophetic words to the lower house of Parliament on 10 June 1998, the president of the Bicameral Commission on Constitutional Reform, Massimo D'Alema, acknowledged that Silvio Berlusconi, leader of the *Polo per le Libertà* (Pole for Freedom), had decided to shelve the commission, and institutional reform, for good. Thus it was that 480 hours of work conducted in 185 sessions held by the commission in full, by its committees and by the officers of the commission presidency (the president himself, his vice-presidents and rapporteurs) all eventually came to nought. There had been thirty-six plenary sessions of the commission, and twenty-two sessions of joint committees. The commission spent twenty-two sessions discussing the form of the State, eleven discussing the form of government, twenty-two discussing Parliament, regulatory agencies and Italy's participation in the EU, and twenty-two discussing the system of justice. A joint committee session was also held on the state and government, one on the state and Parliament, two on the state and the judicial system, fourteen sessions of the Office of the Presidency were held to draft the agenda and ten were devoted to hearings of expert witnesses.

Finally, a large volume of documentary evidence was produced, although calculating the exact amount appears complex and unreliable since in many sessions informal material was circulated. It appears that thirty-eight drafts were produced on the form of the state, nine on the form of government, twenty-seven on the Parliament, regulatory agencies and the EU and just two on justice.[1]

The failure of the Bicameral Commission was in no way a foregone conclusion from the outset. On the contrary, for a long time a majority of observers and analysts seemed fairly optimistic about the possibility of finally achieving some kind of reform, even if not a ground-breaking one. Thus, while reform was expected, if anything it was the coherence and incisiveness of reforms to be approved and applied that was in question. Most observers and analysts held that politicians would settle for the lowest common denominator – common just because the lowest – and consequently, the overall reform would not be clear-cut, coherent or sufficiently adequate to change the form of state, the form of government or the structure and powers of Parliament. It was not unanticipated therefore that politicians would be incapable of producing a broader reform, and worries about contents were well-grounded, but the overall failure still went well beyond expectations.

Laboriously launched in January 1997, the commission – the third of its kind[2] – completed its work at the end of June 1997 and submitted its elaborated and approved texts[3] to the Parliament. These texts were accompanied by 36,300 amendments from members of the Chamber of Deputies, of which 28,400 were presented by one individual, Mara Malavenda, formerly of *Rifondazione Comunista*, and 3,600 drafted by senators. In the twenty-six days devoted to the texts approved by the commission, the committee of nineteen, which represented the commission in the lower house of Parliament, made substantial changes only to the articles on federalism. In the meantime, no conclusive or stable agreement was reached on the other topics, in particular justice and form of government.[4] At least in appearance, the definitive break between the leader of the *Polo* and the Bicameral Commission President D'Alema, were the result of a disagreement on the powers of the President of the Republic in the constitutional framework of a so-called 'moderated' semi-presidential system. Most members of the *Ulivo* (Olive Tree Coalition) wanted these powers to be very limited or effectively non-existent, even more limited than those that the constitution currently accords to the Italian President. Nonetheless, it was and is commonly held that Berlusconi was mainly, if not exclusively, interested in obtaining a sort of judicial 'safe-conduct' from D'Alema. As President of the Bicameral Commission, D'Alema may have wanted to concede this within certain limits, but as Leader of the *Partito Democratico della Sinistra* (Democratic Left), he could not do so. This contradictory tension characterised the whole work of the Bicameral Commission, and had highly negative consequences on relations between the *Polo* (opposition) and the *Ulivo* (government).

D'Alema's concluding words – cited above – were so angry because as President of the Bicameral Commission, he saw the work to which he had devoted all his energy for almost eighteen months, disappear in one fell swoop. He had deliberately taken on this work in order to upgrade his stature from professional politician to statesman and from party leader to constitutional reformer. The words also revealed D'Alema's – subsequently resolved – dilemma. This arose from his dual role as Bicameral Commission President and PDS leader. On one hand, the President of the Bicameral Commission could not but strive to achieve the main aim of the commission, that is, to formulate efficient and clear-cut constitutional reforms. On the other, as leader of the largest party in the *Ulivo*, he had to avoid any reform that created dissent in the coalition and led to a governmental crisis.

Given the extremely heterogeneous nature of the *Ulivo*, and its lack of internal consensus in relation to constitutional reforms, especially because of the valiant conservatism of the People's Party and the Greens and outside the *Ulivo*, *Rifondazione Comunista*[5] (Refounded Communists), D'Alema's room for manoeuvre was very tightly restricted.

The message to the *Polo* ('we have other things to do') was harsh, and conveyed the message that it was wasting everyone's time in its obsession with its own problems. It also conveyed a self-assured reminder of the *Ulivo*'s new governing vocation, ('we have to govern'), in the face of an uncompromisingly obstructionist opposition. As had repeatedly appeared clear, D'Alema was not willing to sacrifice the government – a tangible and historical accomplishment for the left in Italy – on the altar of uncertain, low-profile, faulty, and widely criticised reforms. His entry into the the Premier's office at the end of October demonstrated that the reforms could, in fact, be sacrificed to save the government, especially if the beneficiary was the individual who had tried – albeit unsuccessfully – to secure them.

The Priorities of Leading Politicians

Understanding the different sets of priorities of the various leaders enables us to make sense of their behaviour, and to give an explanation for the course of the Bicameral Commission's work as well as its dismal end. In fact, the complex Bicameral Commission 'game' was characterised by an often overlapping combination of the objectives of different actors at the two available negotiating tables: the Bicameral Commission and the government. Despite various appeals to keep these two tables distinct, they inevitably intersected and often leaders would opportunistically threaten negative consequences for the government if certain constitutional reforms were not approved. Others announced that they would block possible constitutional reforms if the government did not concede something at other levels. These crossovers, vetoes and attempted exchanges would probably have been inevitable in all circumstances. If so, the responsibility lies with the president of the Bicameral Commission for having underestimated the problem of overlapping tables, and for not having sought a solution ahead of time, or a means of neutralising them.

In considering the objectives and the priorities of the various actors, it is useful, for explanatory purposes, to begin with the opposition leader Silvio Berlusconi. Undoubtedly his main objective, which he continues to pursue with tenacity in several other ways, was a constitutional reform that scaled down the power of magistrates both in concrete and symbolic terms. This reform was not really aimed at the so-called 'party' of the judges, at the head of which Berlusconi unhesitatingly puts the Milan prosecuting team and Head Prosecutor Francesco Saverio Borelli along with Palermo's High-court Public Prosecutor, Giancarlo Caselli and his collaborators. Rather, it aimed to weaken, punish and eliminate all the so-called 'red robed judges' (a group he subsequently compared with the Red Brigades, ignoring the fact that Caselli himself had presided over the first trial against the historical nucleus of that terrorist organisation). Berlusconi's goal was to send a powerful signal that their powers and political influence were being cut down. This could have opened the door to the decriminalising of some existing offences, especially the illegal financing of political parties and falsification of accounts for which Berlusconi had himself been put on trial and convicted in the first degree. It could also have opened up the possibility of a generalised amnesty for all crimes associated with the *Tangentopoli* affair.

To this end, a few weeks after the failure of the Bicameral Commission Berlusconi opened a new front by proposing the establishment of a Parliamentary Commission of Inquiry into *Tangentopoli*. His intention was not for Parliament to investigate the case in point and the systemic connections within Italian corruption, but for Parliament to evaluate and pronounce on the behaviour of the judiciary.

Even supposing, though certainly not taking for granted, as Berlusconi's supporters would, that this interpretation of his motives is a misreading of his real intentions, Berlusconi's behaviour provided regular support for such a view. In fact, in the Bicameral Commission and elsewhere, Berlusconi never pursued any issue other than that of the reform of the justice system. In the end, he justified his break with the Bicameral Commission on the grounds of the inadequate powers attributed to the directly elected President. But this argument surfaced only at the eleventh hour and appears to have been used as a pretext, understandable only in the light of Berlusconi's judicial problems as a businessman.

Nonetheless, by engendering a breakdown over the powers of the President of the Republic, Berlusconi (as a politician), was trying, albeit belatedly, to foster an element of conflict inside the *Ulivo* majority, and to achieve an important political objective, albeit one which was secondary with respect to justice. When *Rifondazione Comunista* along with the Greens and the People's Party decided that the President in a semi-presidential republic would have excessive powers – a development which had negative and destructive consequences for the Prodi government – Berlusconi could have proposed to D'Alema, as in various guises he had regularly done, that the time was ripe for the formation of a large coalition government. Moreover, D'Alema's numerous statements about the benefit of securing constitutional reforms based on a large majority that included the opposition, would certainly have justified such a willingness on Berlusconi's part.

Participating in a reform process led not by Romano Prodi (who, quite rightly, would not have joined such a project) but by a new majority that took in all men of 'goodwill', would, in some eyes, D'Alema's included, have been not only a legitimate but a highly positive outcome. It would also have been promising for the future of constitutional reform, electoral competition, the Italian political system and, even if a little more difficult to guarantee, bipolar and majoritarian democracy. Naturally, a large coalition could in due course have faced or might have had to face, a decision on the amnesty question, which required a majority of two thirds of the Parliament. In this way, Berlusconi could have attained a third useful result – that is, a return to government. This was strongly desired by many of his MPs especially after both the unhappy and foreshortened experience of government in 1994 that lasted just seven-and-a-half months, and the repeated demonstrations of the incapacity of *Forza Italia* to constitute an alternative and effective opposition to the Prodi government.

Among the numerous obstacles that Berlusconi had to overcome in pursuit of his primary, secondary, and tertiary objectives was Gianfranco Fini's own strategy, the primary and secondary objectives of which differed considerably from his own and had many similarities with those of D'Alema. The primary objective of the *Alleanza Nazionale* (National Alliance) leader was naturally to acquire full and irreversible political legitimacy for his party organisation and for himself. The *Movimento Sociale Italiano* (Italian Social Movement) did not take part in the drafting of the Constitution of the Republic in 1948, which it had always rejected, and in the resulting formal institutional marginalisation it faced, it paid dearly. The expression 'constitutional space' was used to exclude the neo-fascists. It included all parliamentary forces irrespective of whether they were in government or opposition, and therefore included the communists because they had actively participated in and contributed to the process of drafting the Republican Constitution. Consequently, Fini firmly sought not only to participate in the process of rewriting the Constitution, but to contribute to it in order to receive, in equitable exchange, legitimacy for this personal and party contribution.

Fini's second and subordinate objective had already been attained and he only had to safeguard it, but not at the expense of his main one. Historically, the MSI's main constitutional objective had been a Presidential Republic, which many of its members defined simply as the direct election of the President of the Republic, possibly along the lines of Gaullist France. The President or head of the executive, would be able to destroy the 'party regime', that is, the hated '*partitocrazia*' (literally, 'partitocracy'). Naturally, in modernising AN, Fini had already scaled down the traditional MSI critique of the party regime and had effectively redefined his Presidential Republic within the framework of democratic competition. The objective of the direct election of the President in a new Republican constitutional framework was actually attained fortuitously in an eleventh-hour incident resulting from the Northern League's sudden intervention in the affairs of the Bicameral Commission. Recklessly, and without regard to the consequences, it voted in favour of direct election. Subsequently, Fini's behaviour demonstrated that he was even willing to forego incisive presidential powers as along as the process of rewriting the Constitution was not jeopardised, and as long as the President was directly elected, which for him was symbolically decisive.

In his eagerness for constitutional legitimation, the thinking of the (ex-fascist) Fini coincided with that of the (ex-communist) D'Alema, who appreciated Fini's reconciliatory line on reform of the judicial system and who relied on Fini's moderating influence on Berlusconi. Furthermore, the AN leader did not share Berlusconi's strategic goal of a large centrist coalition any more than D'Alema did. He rightly feared the outer wings of such a coalition would be clipped off, excluding from this consociational-style government both AN and *Rifondazione Comunista*. Such a strategy was a continuation of the old Christian democratic ploy of deliberately excluding from the governmental arc the two opposed extremes at the ends of the party spectrum. In this regard, Fini's fundamental worry derived not so much from a lack of access to government posts, but from the inevitable perception that his own party and the electorate would receive that AN's demanding but necessary process of legitimation had stalled or gone into reverse. Despite everything, Fini could not under any circumstances break with Berlusconi, without whom AN would never have made the progress it had. Balancing his eagerness for constitutional legitimation against the imperative of political coalition tormented Fini during the whole period of the Bicameral Commission (and beyond). In the end however, the AN leader had no choice but to maintain his privileged relationship with FI and Berlusconi. A further factor pushing in this direction was the role of the former President of the Republic, Francesco Cossiga, who threatened to cause a rift in the AN-FI relationship by brokering a more centre-oriented Pole, which was designed to be significantly freer of right-wing influence.

In a certain sense, the most marked ideological position regarding constitutional reform came from the People's Party. With the exception of Franco Marini, the party leader, most People's Party members were heirs of the Christian Democrat left-wing and Dossetti, in whose name the 'Movement for the Defence of the Constitution' was born. They have always firmly believed that political parties and their mediating role in political life are more important than electoral and institutional mechanisms. People's Party members, though by no means alone in their beliefs, continue to be the unfailing nucleus of constitutional conservatism within the *Ulivo*. They see themselves as the guardians of basic principles of proportionalism in Italian political life, more so even than as guardians of the rules of proportional representation in electoral law. Naturally, their battle was not purely ideological or even idealistic. On the contrary, their main objective was to maintain maximum bargaining power within and outside the *Ulivo*.

Direct election of the President of the Republic would run counter to their firm opposition to the personalisation of politics, which, in rare agreement with *Rifondazione Comunista* they condemned as 'plebiscitary control'. It would also have reduced the parliamentary bargaining power of the People's Party. In addition, any electoral reform that attempted to impose a simple majoritarian counting of votes made them fearful for their future influence, given their failure to expand electorally. Thus for the People's Party, the most important objective was to build reforms that ensured its survival and that did not change the existing situation for the worse. They therefore aimed to regain and consolidate a central role in the *Ulivo* coalition, or more in general, in Italian political alliances. To this end, in a decision that has not yet been completely explained, two leading figures from the People's Party, Franco Marini and Sergio Mattarella, were given the task of preparing a draft of a new electoral law – a task that went beyond the competence of the commission and thus was open to much criticism, also because it was expected that an agreement reached outside the commission be ratified in an agenda presented in the commission itself.[6] Needless to add, the collapse of the Bicameral Commission and the subsequent re-establishment of a status quo that was quite satisfactory for them, was met with much relief by the party leaders.

As for the main protagonist, Massimo D'Alema, he would probably have been able to obtain more if he had directed the commission and his party a little better. His objectives became clear – after many fluctuations – only at the end of the above-mentioned declaration: 'first the government, then the reforms' (which, as in Aesop's Fables, must have seemed rather bitter to him). Despite this outcome, the government and especially the deputy prime minister Walter Veltroni,[7] and the entourage prime minister Romano Prodi, all, though to differing degrees, reproached D'Alema for having jeopardised the survival of the government with his reforming zeal. In fact, quite which of his many worries and ambitions was uppermost in his mind was never clear. There is no doubt that D'Alema felt strongly attracted to effective, efficient, wide-ranging constitutional reform. To have achieved this would have elevated him to the rank of a subtle and intelligent statesman who knew how to take risks to resolve the problems which lay at the heart of the Italian political system. However, D'Alema also felt the weight of the responsibility of possible destructive backlashes on the government, which would not only have affected him, but could also have brought about early elections. A repeat of the *Ulivo* victory would have been very unlikely partly because the coalition itself would be difficult to reconstruct, and partly because the *Ulivo* would certainly not have been able to formulate an electoral campaign based on a stronger impulse for reform than that of the *Polo*. Therefore, D'Alema feared the breaking-up of his vital coalition relationships with both the People's Party and *Rifondazione Comunista*, since the latter two had significantly different objectives from him in relation to the reform agenda.

D'Alema vacillated between these two legitimate and substantial concerns and was obliged to defend himself from many sections of the left, in particular from the 'La Repubblica-L'Espresso' newspaper group, which accused him of opting for disreputable under-the-counter compromises with Berlusconi. He also had to convince his own party, which was still largely proportionalist in outlook, and certainly not at all presidentialist, of the real need for constitutional reform.[8] Thus, D'Alema constantly found himself in a very difficult situation and his reform drive had one serious and reliable ally – Gianfranco Fini. However, as we have already seen, Fini's interest in his own legitimation in the eyes of the left, was subordinate to other considerations. First, his acknowledgement that it was Berlusconi who was the first not only to legitimise him, but to bring him to government. Second, the need, which should not be ignored, to remain in alliance with the leader of *Forza Italia*, who was the only person with both the power to get him back into government, or conversely to despatch him back to the isolation of the far right-wing. Hence, D'Alema had no ally to help him out of the difficulty in which he found himself, partly because of his strategy, and partly because of the circumstances, which were difficult to master, and easy to underestimate. In the end, when all was lost, D'Alema put a brave face on events, and made clear that the *Ulivo* and the PDS were more concerned with the government than reforms, and that the behaviour of the *Polo* and Berlusconi had made reversing this order of priorities impossible.

The Substance of the Reforms

It might seem that this reconstruction of the objectives of the main political leaders underestimates the substance of the reforms. In particular, it might seem that none of the protagonists approached the negotiations with any serious intention of reform or was willing to take risks to obtain any appreciable advantage for their own party, or more importantly any desirable general improvement for the political system as a whole. In fact, from the beginning most impartial observers noted not only that the trauma of a constitutional break, which would have made rewriting the constitutional map necessary, was missing, but also that a wider spirit of reform was missing too. Traumas there *were* – perhaps too many. They included the fall of the Berlin Wall to *Tangentopoli* and *Mani Pulite* (Clean Hands), the hijack of the political initiative by the Northern League, the degree of support for the electoral referendum, and Berlusconi's victory and the unworkable and short-lived government he formed.[9] What seems certain is that the spirit of reform did not linger long inside the Bicameral Commission. On the contrary, most of the commission's protagonists had very limited objectives, and hoped to draw a line under Italy's political and institutional transition.

As for the substance of the reforms, it seems very clear that, in all four areas on which the Bicameral Commission worked (the form of state, the form of government, Parliament and justice) the real contents always remained of marginal concern for the majority of commission members. The extensive and repeated redrafting of the texts of all four subject areas reveals that, within the Bicameral Commission, there was an excess of opportunism, understood as improvised adaptation to the rather rigid political opportunities of the moment. The way in which it was decided to opt for a semi-presidential system – thanks to the cynical hijacking by League Commission members who had not participated for many months in the activities of the Bicameral Commission – brought the commission to its moment of greatest rashness and revealed the opportunism present inside it. The league hoped that its explosive contribution would disrupt everything. Although things did not go as they wished, the governmental arrangements that emerged from the bicameral text can be interpreted in one of two ways: either as a very blunt semi-presidential system, that is to say a system that guarantees an explicit political role of some relevance to the directly elected President, or as a premiership equipped with a constitutional guarantee of governmental stability and strong prime-ministerial leadership, though with the risk of exposure to conflict with the directly elected President. However, this new form of government, as such desired by nobody, failed as a result to win support from anyone. Moreover, given the manner of its approval, it is not surprising that the breakdown of constitutional reform negotiations occurred over the powers of the President. But it was a self-serving break. In any case, the powers of the directly elected President were unchanged with respect to the existing Constitution. They would clearly have better been curbed by an organic and solid relationship between the premier and his parliamentary majority. (That linkage, of course, was not assured either with Mattarellum-1 or Mattarellum-2, the earlier electoral reform packages.) It is curious that Fini should have been content with the sort of partisan victory in which Berlusconi was not at all interested. But it is not surprising that in the end, Fini subordinated the substance of the reform to his participation in the revision process of the Constitution rather than the quality of the result.

Temporarily putting aside the justice problem that was driving Berlusconi and hence his party, the commission focused on his interest in at least one other theme: electoral law. The reform of electoral law, which is not a constitutional issue, was deliberately kept separate from the commission's work because of the well-grounded fear that it would be explosive. It was, of course, a very delicate argument and a very important one for all politicians. It burst on to the political scene at the beginning of June 1997, at a dinner-table discussion of reform at the house of Gianni Letta – Berlusconi's closest colleague and his undersecretary while prime minister from May to December 1994. It is claimed (and the only denial has been about the dessert over which the decision was reached) that at the end of the dinner a deal was reached in relation to the modifications to be made to the electoral law, or rather the drafting of a partially new electoral law. The commission found out about this in one of the last sessions in June 1997 when D'Alema read out the underlying principles of the reform, though the commission did not even vote on it because it was not within its terms of reference to do so.

The details of the so-called '*patto della crostata*' (literally, the deal done over dessert) remained obscure, but they evidently satisfied the smaller parties. It was clear that the deal favoured them, and that, despite the importance of ensuring coherence between the electoral system and the form of government, the deal had little to do with any such coherence. In fact, those who defended the electoral deal were not interested in the form of government voted in the commission – indeed, they were openly critical of it. Furthermore, the outcome blatantly contradicted D'Alema's (erroneous) assertion that the version of the semi-presidential system chosen by the commission would logically and functionally be complemented by a French-style two-round run-off electoral system. Since the semi-presidential system selected by the commission was not the same as that in France, the significance of this automatic connection, espoused by D'Alema, escaped many of the protagonists, though the extent to which each disagreed with him varied according to extent to which it was politically expedient to do so. Equally, D'Alema lacked the power to impose the connection. Subsequently, the extensive influence enjoyed by the smaller parties enabled them to exploit the electoral law issue. They were able to force it to the top of the political agenda, and tie it first to the fate of the Bicameral Commission, and then to a resumption of the reform process in general.

Unexpectedly, and without explanation beyond their *ex cattedra* assertions, enthusiastically shared by the small parties in the *Ulivo* and *Polo*, and never adequately contested by D'Alema, Berlusconi and Fini repeatedly insisted that without that specific electoral system – as hastily drafted at the home of Gianni Letta – the entire reform project would collapse. In fact, subsequent events demonstrated how completely and utterly misplaced this conditionality was. Berlusconi's veto eventually came just at the moment when Sergio Mattarella was completing a legislative draft to give substance to the electoral system agreed in outline at the Casa Letta meeting. Mattarella presented it as a development of the earlier (1993) system he himself had also steered through Parliament (the so-called Mattellarum) – and to which he, if rather few others, was much attached. Berlusconi chose just this moment, with the new electoral law he had so strongly advocated ready to be launched, to scupper the work of the Bicameral Commission. If this was not an outright betrayal, therefore, it was certainly more than a marginal change of position.

Before Mattarella's draft was ready – though with its essential features clear – the plan already looked like a threat to the whole idea of majority-based government built around a bipolar party system, and a strong prime-ministerial figure enjoying some degree of direct electoral support. Materalla's draft was based on an extraordinary combination of a second-ballot *premio di maggioranza* (a bonus of parliamentary seats to the largest party or coalition) grafted onto a first-past-the-post simple-plurality electoral system. From any perspective, this arrangement would have strengthened the contractual power of the smaller parties, and would do nothing to commit them to support the government throughout the life of the legislature. In sum, the system entailed a second tier of majoritarianism superimposed onto a first tier but it was constructed on a fully proportional foundation inside each coalition. It was hard to believe that, in the aftermath of elections, this would contribute towards bipolarity in the party system. The compromise agreed at the infamous meeting at Gianni Letta's home thus revealed its flaws even before it was worked through into full form in the so-called 'Mattarellum 2'. Its end result was in fact the hitherto quite unexpected one of revitalising the Referendum Movement for electoral reform which grew up at the start of the decade.

An Unexpected Consequence:
A New Electoral Referendum

Significant parts of the political, intellectual and industrial class were extremely dissatisfied with the outcome of the Bicameral Commission, and (dyed-in-the-wool apologists from La Repubblica apart), editors and senior commentators of the major Italian newspapers amplified this sense of dissatisfaction. The electoral deal was the trigger that unleashed this widespread dissatisfaction. How to respond presented this group with a tactical problem, how-

ever. An electoral verdict on the results of the Bicameral Commission would be possible only in the constitutional referendum provided for by the enabling legislation setting up the commission,
and this was not due before the spring of 1999. A referendum campaign against what would be the first generalised overhaul of the
Constitution would have meant opposing the text in its entirety,
and would pose a double risk. First, there was a possibility of
defeat if party leaders were united in its defence. Second, if the
attempt succeeded, there was a possibility of delegitimising the
entire political class, which might conceivably lead to regime collapse and to a much feared – if rather unlikely – drift towards
extremist plebiscitary and populist leadership. The widely discussed prediction that the Mattarellum 2 would simply worsen the
effects of the Mattarellum 1, and in the end would be the only part
of the Bicameral Commission's work that would have any impact,
therefore lay behind the thinking of those who opted to relaunch
the referendum movement. Their strategy had two main objectives. The first was to signal the degree of the disapproval among
informed public opinion vis-à-vis the lowest-common-denominator
compromises reached in the Bicameral Commission. The second
was to intervene in the operation of the existing electoral law in
order to block the Mattarellum 2 and to design a new electoral system that, although only a little more majoritarian in operation,
would link voter choice and government output more directly.[10]

Moreover, the variety of interests represented in the ranks of the
referendum promoters, and their effective organisational capacity,
demonstrated that it was possible to operate in a very broadly
based way, linking political initiatives emanating from civil society
to the more forward-looking elements of the political class. In fact,
the promoting Committee brought together the original leader of
the referendum Movement, Mario Segni (who had no links with
the *Ulivo*), the *Ulivo* senator and the leader of Italia dei Valori ('For
an Italy of Values') Antonio Di Pietro, the former leader of the PDS
Achille Occhetto, the former *Polo* Minister of Foreign Affairs Antonio Martino, the PDS constitutional expert and one-time Minister
of Institutional Reform Augusto Barbera, and the former president
of Confindustria and founder –promoter of the earlier referendum
movement, Luigi Abete. Other leading industrialists actively helped
the collection of signatures.

Undaunted by the danger that the parties night try to thwart the
referendum by encouraging abstentionism,[11] the promoters initiated the signature campaign on 24 April 1998 and completed it
successfully three months later with the unexpected figure of
almost 700,000 signatures. This was accompanied by Di Pietro's

collection of the necessary 50,000 signatures for a bill based on popular initiative proposing a French-style second-ballot run-off electoral system. In fact, the initiative quickly gathered more than 350,000 signatures, and – under pressure from *Ulivo* supporters in his own party – even PDS leader Massimo D'Alema was eventually forced to support it. The Bicameral was therefore dead, though not buried since its burial would have required a new constitutional law and hence the double-reading constitutional-reform procedure that would have taken up a great deal of time and exacerbated tensions inside Parliament. But the reform process was not completely undermined as a result. It still faced all the constraints of the bottom-up process of electoral initiative in Italy – limited as it is to the abrogation of existing laws or parts of laws. And the few convinced constitutional reformers who promoted it were indeed forced to act outside, and often necessarily against political parties, given that in relation to electoral laws and public financing of parties, political parties rapidly became a fragile but self-defensive 'partitocratic' front. But for all that, the movement had succeeded in keeping the reform initiative alive, indeed reviving it.

What Is Left of the Bicameral Commission?

Along with the electoral law, there were three other important institutional questions left unsolved by the death of the Bicameral Commission. These now returned to the realm of daily political life in an untidy and confrontational manner. The three issues were federalism, the judicial system and the powers of the President of the Republic. In relation to the possibilities of federalism, Franco Bassanini,[12] the Minister of the Civil Service and Regional Affairs, sought by means of institutional simplification and decentralisation, to edge the Italian political and administrative system towards something approaching the limits of federalism – until he was replaced in the change of government in October. He worked with great tenaciousness and precision, and his legacy is now a pressing need to intervene and reform the Constitution in the directions he pursued, despite the Bicameral Commission's complete failure in this direction. On the other two questions, albeit in a very polemical way, the *Polo* has taken the initiative again, forcing the *Ulivo* onto the defensive, mainly because it is mostly made up of institutional conservatives. The *Ulivo*'s defensive stance has some justification in the case of judicial reform but unjustifiable in the case of the reform of the Presidency of the Republic, and thus of the form of government.

The *Polo* first proposed a commission of inquiry into *Tangentopoli* and then through Berlusconi attacked the President of the Republic. In relation to the first point, the *Polo* attempted to sanction the behaviour of hostile judges, intimidate the investigating judges and put the request for necessary reforms of the Italian judicial system on the wrong track. Some exponents of the *Polo* have affirmed their apparently instrumental willingness to resume discussion of reform only after the establishment of the commission of inquiry into *Tangentopoli*. In the *Ulivo*, confusion immediately appeared widespread. The socialists and exponents of *Rinnovamento* some of which are former Christian democrats, as well as the People's Party, which is almost entirely made up of former Christian democrats, were willing to back the *Polo* and make a clean sweep of *Mani Pulite*, whereas the Greens and the majority of the PDS were unwilling to do so. D'Alema appeared to be tempted to renew his relationship with Berlusconi who had received his second conviction in court and awaited a third trial. The simple affirmation that history and even more so, contemporary incomplete history, is better written by historians (and even sociologists and political scientists), would be enough to defeat any kind of commission of inquiry into *Tangentopoli*, which was beaten by the lower house of Parliament in October 1998. In any case, that this kind of request has survived for so long demonstrates that the Bicameral Commission left behind many degenerative germs.

One of these is very much alive in the field of presidential powers. According to Berlusconi, President Scalfaro committed a very serious constitutional violation when in December 1994, during the crisis of his government, he denied the immediate dissolution of Parliament and an early election. Fini deplored this alleged 'democratic coup d'état'. In fact, in relation to the nature and functioning of parliamentary forms of government, this is a non-problem.[13] In non-rationalised forms of parliamentary government such as the Italian one[14], in situations of crisis and the resignation of government, the Head of State has, if not the constitutional duty, at least the opportunity of exploring whether a parliamentary majority exists to support another government. Only if this does not exist can he dissolve Parliament.

In accordance with his oft-underlined parliamentarian inclinations and his explicit declarations in this regard, when the Prodi government was defeated in Parliament on an unusual and explicit vote of confidence requested by the premier, Scalfaro followed a preordained path, which was certainly not the only possible one, but likewise was certainly constitutionally practicable. Thus, in relation to the issue at hand, a controversy like that which led to the accusations hurled at President Scalfaro would not make sense in clearly regulated situations like that of the French semi-presidential system. Under certain conditions that are not very open to partisan manipulation, which would be damaging and even counterproductive, the President can nominate and dissolve Parliament. For this reason, it appears evident that the evolution of the form of government in Italy cannot rely exclusively on the sort of contingent behavioural outcomes that were at issue in Scalfaros's case – where the right course of action derives partly from necessity and partly from utility, and constitutionally is unimpeachable.

Unfortunately the demise of the Bicameral Commission has left this problem open and has placed undefined and burdensome tasks on the shoulders of the current president of the Republic,[15] and in the very likely absence of any kind of reform on those of his successor. Thus, since all the problems seem unresolved, it is desirable useful to conclude with a brief examination of the prospects for the future, and the possibility of and conditions for a resumption of reform.

Beyond the Bicameral Commission

The paths of constitutional reform continue to be those that predated the formation of the Bicameral Commission, that is, Article 138 and the Constituent Assembly. Article 138 regulates a procedure that can be used to reform single articles of the Constitution. Since it requires cohesive majorities that are currently absent from the Italian Parliament, it stands in contrast to the Bicameral Commission, which enjoyed the power to submit an entire project first to the Parliament and then to the electorate, to be accepted or rejected *en bloc*. However, although Italian constitutional debate seems divided on its interpretation of almost everything, some authoritative experts believe that Article 138 of the Constitution is the only path to a reform that really corresponds to the spirit of the Italian Constitution. For those who believe that a small number of incisive modifications are all that is necessary significantly to improve the Constitution (for example, the direct election of the President of the Republic, strengthening the form of government, and the reversal of the powers and functions entrusted to the state and Regions generating real federalism), it is necessary and possible to act through Article 138.

That said however, the current parliamentary power relations between government and opposition, taken together with the priorities of the centre-left coalition aiming above all to survive as a coalition government until 2001 (priorities which were reinforced by the entry of Cossiga's Democratic Union for the Republic, but which are also 'dependent' on the UDR's political-constitutional objectives, as well as the time-frame of politics that foresee the election of the next President of the Republic in the spring of 1999), do not suggest that significant reforms will be made through the long, difficult and very juridically protected procedure of Article 138. What remains then is the election of a Constituent Assembly.

From a constitutional point of view, there are a number of Italian jurists that hold that the election of a Constituent Assembly would be the same as a break, a profound and decisive breach with the Republican Constitution and a delegitimation of the Constitution in force which might not be followed by a form of relegitimation.

From a political point of view, it is easy to identify two rather significant obstacles to the formation of a Constituent Assembly. The first is made up of the need for a prior agreement among the protagonists of reform on three aspects, that is, the role, powers and tasks of the Constituent Assembly. It is unlikely that such a procedural and substantial agreement, which was brusquely dropped in June 1998, would suddenly and miraculously arise in a few months. The second obstacle arises from the need (which may not be absolute) to use a proportional electoral system to chose the members of the Assembly, which would lead to the fragmentation of the Assembly, thus making high-profile agreements on the writing of the modern Constitution (a majority and bipolar system, as many politicians claim to want) even more unlikely. As an afterthought, it can be noted that while the prestige of the would-be protagonists of constitutional reform, in particular that of D'Alema and Fini, was damaged by their proven incapacity to achieve reform, the entire political class would face its own redundancy, since the Assembly would have to have a mandate of one year or even more, and then the possibility of failure of the Constituent Assembly. In the absence of leaders of great quality and personal charisma, the Italian political class fears not only the failure of the Constituent Assembly, but it also obsessively fears the popularity of the only person who seems capable of sweeping away and substituting the entire political class: that is, Senator Antonio Di Pietro.

In the light of the above considerations, it is foreseeable that the death of the Bicameral Commission will not in the short-term be followed by a revival of the reform initiative in Parliament either with Article 138 or a law enabling the election of a Constituent Assembly. Halted by their contradictions, conservatism, and shortsighted calculation of their profit-benefit, in 1998 and at the beginning of 1999, political leaders and parliamentarians sought hard to find ways of avoiding the electoral referendum. Moreover they endeavoured to tame the momentum of change represented above all by Antonio Di Pietro. Unfortunately, there are few cases in which a single individual has been able to end a political-institutional transition and at the same time consolidate a democratic regime. Thus the task of the ambitious new Minister of Institutional Reforms, Giuliano Amato – whose declarations, interviews and silences during the period before the electoral referendum was given the go-ahead – were not always 'reform-oriented' – seemed very difficult. The Italian political system, in conclusion, seems condemned to navigate the transition without any institutional guidance other than that of the efficient, but limited, electoral referendum instrument. Although better than other instruments, the abrogative referendum is still insufficient to make Italy a European democracy. It will, however, serve to keep alive the need for overall constitutional reform.

Translated by Claire Marie O'Neill

Notes

1. This last data is in stark contrast with journalistic accounts that consider even the smallest new drafts, and after due consideration, the insignificant variations introduced by the rapporteur, the Green former exponent of the extra-parliamentary group Lotta Continua (Continuous Struggle), Marco Boato, who in this way boasted about his unremitting but inconclusive activity, and consequently his count unjustifiably reached the ninth draft.

2. The two previous commissions were presided over by Liberal Party MP Aldo Bozzi from November 1983 to January 1985 (see my analysis 'The Debate on Institutional Reform', in R. Leonardi and e R. Nannetti (eds.) *Italian Politics*, London; Pinter, 1986, vol. 1, pp. 117-133) and by Ciriaco De Mita MP, before and after De Mita resigned because he received a judicial notice, and by Deputy Nilde Iotti (September 1992-January 1994). Insofar as both commissions and especially the first produced useful material and formulated intelligent proposals, the first one lacked any kind of parliamentary support and the second lacked even the time to reach the reform phase since Parliament was dissolved early. First useful analyses of D'Alema's Commission have been done by S. Vassallo, 'La terza Bicamerale', in L. Bardi e M. Rhodes (eds), *Politica in Italia. Edizione 98*, Bologna: Il Mulino, 1998, pp. 130-155 and by M. Gilbert, 'Transforming Italy's Institutions: The Bicameral Committee on Constitutional Reform', in *Modern Italy*, 3, no. 1 (Fall 1998) 49-66. See also my 'Reforming the Italian Constitution', *Journal of Modern Italian Studies*, 3 (March 1998): 42-54.

3. The controversial text on justice which passed through numerous, useless and often impromptu modifications, was never formally approved in its entirety by the commission.

4. The other two themes were federalism, which was radically overhauled by the work of the lower house of Parliament (see the criticisms of S. Vassallo, 'Il fed-

eralismo sedicente', in *Il Mulino*, July/August 1997: 694-707), and the Parliament, an obviously delicate theme for all parliamentarians, which was held over, tied as it was to federalism, the form of government and the electoral law. For this last one, infra.

5. Perfectly aware of this divarication and perhaps also of the higher degree of attractiveness of the *Polo*'s often simplifying constitutional proposals, the PDS's number two in command and candidate for vice-premiership, Walter Veltroni launched an appeal to exclude opposing programmes on constitutional reform from the 1996 electoral campaign, which was unfortunately answered. However, the *Ulivo*'s programme, which was also underwritten by the Popular and Green Parties, contained both a French two-round run-off electoral law and the designation of the head of the executive through a possible direct election.

6. My analysis of the text of the law, which was in the end drawn up by Deputy Sergio Mattarella is in 'Quel che rimane dell'ordine del giorno elettorale', in the acts of the Conference of Studies in Memory of Silvano Tosi, *La riforma costituzionale*, Milano: Giuffré (forthcoming).

7. The least veiled reproach, which was explosive and on the margins of subversion, was made by the vice-premier Walter Veltroni to D'Alema, who a few days after the Bicameral Commission's approval of the semi-presidential system, proposed the annulment of that vote. Veltroni's list of priorities as author of the *Ulivo* and vice-premier has always been clear: government, *Ulivo* and lastly, reforms. Since a large part and even the majority of the *Ulivo* was against a semi-presidential system (and perhaps if they understood what it was, in favour of a strong premiership) and both *Rifondazione Comunista* and the People's Party were decisively against the direct election of the President of the Republic, Veltroni aimed in particular to avoid any kind of backlash against the government. Massimo D'Alema's comment on this annulment proposal can be found in his book *La Grande Occasione. L'Italia verso le riforme*, Milano: Mondadori, 1997, 130 : 'To consider standing up suddenly and saying: "Excuse us, it was a mistake, a mere accident, let's begin all over again" was an unsustainable position which would not only have annihilated the Bicameral Commission, but would have inflicted a severe blow to the reformist credibility of the centre-left'. D'Alema's and Veltroni's very different list of priorities are evident in this passage. It is useful and fair to underline here that, since Veltroni substituted D'Alema as leader of the PDS on 5 November 1998, he has been very coherent in defending the electoral referendum and supporting real constitutional reforms.

8. D'Alema wrote the book cited in the previous note also in order to clarify his strategy, the pretexts and indispensable nature of an incisive constitutional reform, and to convince at least the upper echelons of the party and less hostile journalists. On D'Alema's more general political thought, see M. Gilbert's excellent review-article, 'In Search of Normality: the Political Strategy of Massimo D'Alema', *Journal of Modern Italian Studies*, 3, no. 3 (Fall 1998): 307-317.

9. A convincing interpretation in this sense can be found in M. Gilbert, *The Italian Revolution. The End of Politics Italian Style?*, Boulder, Colo.: Westview Press, 1995.

10. This is not the place to go into the details of a theme that merits specific and thorough analysis, which is aimed for in the next volume of *Italian Politics*.

11. The invitation to mass abstentionism was discovered as an efficient but certainly not a far-sighted strategy for parties during the last referendum, which is sharply analysed by M. Donovan, 'I referendum del 1997: il troppo stroppia?', in L. Bardi e M. Rhodes (eds), *Politica in Italia. Edizione 98*, Bologna: Il

Mulino, 1998, pp. 197-218. Leaving aside evaluations of its democratic nature, that strategy did not turn out to be at all far-sighted since it indicated to the institutional opposition the weapon to be used in the obligatory confirmative referendum against any kind of constitutionally unwelcome text.

12. On this point see the chapter by M. Gilbert, 'The Bassanini Laws: A Half-Way House in Local Government Reform', in this volume, pp. 115-27.

13. I dealt comparatively with this argument in my *Mandato popolare e governo*, Bologna: Il Mulino, 1995.

14. In rationalised parliamentary systems, in fact, the procedure is very different. For example, in Switzerland a government with a motion of no confidence has a week to decide whether or not the Parliament will be dissolved; in Spain, the King has the duty to countersign the President of the Government's request to dissolve the Parliament. I am grateful to Stefano Ceccanti for useful information in this regard.

15. David Hine and Emanuela Poli, 'La presidenza Scalfaro nel 1996: il difficile ritorno alla normalità', in *Politica in Italia. Edizione 97*, Bologna: Il Mulino, 1997, pp. 221 could also be right. However, the Scalfaro Presidency certainly had to go through abnormal time-frames, which it did quite ably, and demonstrated how flexible and well-equipped the Italian Constitution is in relation to presidential powers, but also how inadequate it is to enable the completion of the transition towards a majority system outlet.

5

FROM THE PRODI GOVERNMENT TO THE D'ALEMA GOVERNMENT: CONTINUITY OR DISCONTINUITY?

Sergio Fabbrini

From Prodi to D'Alema

Romano Prodi was appointed President of the Council of Ministers on 16 May 1996, and obtained a vote of confidence in the Senate on 24 May, and in the Chamber on 31 May of that year. He survived in office at the head of a centreleft (*centrosinistra*) government until 9 October 1998, when by a majority of 313-312 in the Chamber, a request for a vote of confidence put down by the government was rejected. Immediately after the vote, Prodi tendered his resignation to the President of the Republic, who accepted it unreservedly. For the first time in the history of the republic, a President of the Council and his government resigned after losing a formal vote of confidence in Parliament. The Prodi government had technically been in office for 861 days (or 886 days, including the so-called 'ordinary administration' which began with the confidence votes in the Senate and ended with the no confidence vote and the swearing-in of the new D'Alema government on 21 October 1998). It was the second most long-lasting government of republican Italy, behind that of Bettino Craxi, which survived for 1,093 days (4 August 1983 to 1 August 1986).

The D'Alema government was formally installed on 21 October. Massimo D'Alema, secretary of the *Democratici di Sinistra*, established the feasibility of a centre-left Parliamentary majority in inter-party consultations held on 17 and 18 October. The new D'Alema government won a vote of confidence on 23 October in the Chamber (333 votes for, 281 against, and 3 abstentions) and on 27 October in the Senate (188 for, 116 against, and 1 abstention). Addressing both houses prior to the confidence votes, the newly appointed Prime Minister announced that 'the government (intends) to adopt the 1999 Budget Law presented by Prodi in its entirety, as well as the range of measures connected to it', and that 'the government intends to encourage Parliament to undertake discussions aimed at a common search for a shared basis on which to build a new electoral law'.[1] He was also at pains to stress the explicitly political nature of the new government and its determination to remain in office until the end of the legislature in 2001.

The Prodi Government

The Prodi government was formed in the aftermath of the Parliamentary elections of 21 April 1996.[2] It comprised the various parties (PDS-DS, PPI, PD, RD and Verdi) that had put together a coalition to fight the elections (the so-called *Ulivo* or Olive Tree alliance). It relied on the Parliamentary support of the Communist Refoundation Party (PRC) for its majority in the Chamber though not in the Senate. Although too broad to be a solid or cohesive majority, it was not a post-electoral alliance of convenience. Compared with the post-electoral majority that had generated the Berlusconi government in 1994 (a majority built on two distinct electoral coalitions: FI and AN in the south, and FI and LN in the north), the alliance between the *Ulivo* and PRC was more homogeneous. Firstly it hinged on the left-right axis (unlike the one between FI, AN and the LN), and secondly it was the result of pre-electoral *desistenze* (candidate-withdrawals) by the *Ulivo* parties and the PRC in the great majority of single-member constituencies. In short, while Berlusconi's was a *post-electoral* majority, Prodi's – although it could not be called an *electoral* majority because it sprang from an agreement reached after the elections – could at any rate be called *semi-electoral* in that it was implicitly presented to the electors by means of the 'withdrawals game' of individual candidacies in single-member constituencies, in order to aggregate the votes of the centre-left area.

In any event, both as a result of this implicit agreement, and also because the PRC decided not to join the government but simply to form part of its majority, the Prodi government enjoyed substantial policy cohesion. And although, like the Berlusconi government,

Prodi's was also a *coalition*, the former operated according to a logic very different from that of the latter. This difference relates to the *processes* by which the two governments were formed: quasi-electoral in the former case, post-electoral in the latter – a difference that has largely escaped the attention of academic observers, who tend to place both coalitions in the same category.[3] *Empirically*, in fact, distinct analytical definitions are required for the two types of coalition. We might define a government like Prodi's, which results from electoral competition between two distinct coalitions, as a *coalitional government*, and one like Berlusconi's, created after elections, as a government of *coalitioned parties*. In so doing, we would distinguish between *coalitional government*, where the emphasis is on the government, and a *coalition's government,* where the emphasis is less on the government created by the coalition, and more on the coalition itself. This dovetails with the distinction made implicitly above between the 'centreleft' as a political area, and the 'centre-left' as a group of parties. In this sense, Prodi's was a government of the *centrosinistra* (not *centro-sinistra*) because it was based on a policy accord (among the *Ulivo* parties) reached before the elections and not after them.

In addition to its electoral 'mandate', a second and even more effective pressure for cohesion was the *European* constraint. This enabled the Prodi government to preserve its character as a 'coalitional' government (as opposed to a coalition's government). The need to 'join the single currency' (as the Italian expression puts it) – that is, the need to bring the deficit ratio into line with the parameters set by the Maastricht Treaty of 10-11 December 1991 – enabled the Prodi government successfully to press for a high degree of policy-making autonomy from the parties in the *Ulivo* alliance, in order to bring Italy into line with the Maastricht conditions. It thus came to acquire the form of a largely *party-independent* government (both in public policies and political appointments) not unlike the 'technocrat' governments of the period 1992-96. The difference, however, was that whereas the latter preserved their independence with the help of the prestige and protection of the President of the Republic, the former did so by relying on the twofold disciplinary pressures of an electoral majority and EU-imposed constraints.

The Prodi government was thus a government under *narrow and cohesive leadership* and this involved a break with the long tradition of Italian coalition governments connoted by *multiple and inchoate leadership.*[4] This was so, in the sense that the role played by the President of the Council of Ministers was truly that of *first (minister) among unequals.* Some ministers (notably those of the Treasury, Finance and Public Administration) and some undersecretaries (in particular those in the Prime Minister's office) were of course less unequal than others,[5] and this also flowed from the main elements of the policy programme that the government pursued. Once the decision had been taken to enter EMU as a first-wave member at almost any price (Spain having declined to support an Italian request for postponement of the date of monetary union itself), the government was bound to place economic and financial policies at the top of its agenda, and this gave major prominence to the ministers engaged in balancing the state budget, on both the accounting and administrative sides. Moreover, this factor strengthened the government's claim on Parliament for greater discretionary legislative powers (through *decreti delegati:* the power, granted by Parliament, to issue decrees having legislative force) and it increased Parliament's willingness to grant them. No fewer than seventy such authorisations were granted by Parliament to the government in just two years of the thirteenth legislature (April 1996-March 1998), compared with fifty-eight during the twelth legislature (1994-96), fifteen during the eleventh (1992-94), twenty-six during the tenth (1987-92), and fourteen during the ninth (1983-87).

Placing these facts in comparative perspective, we might note that international comparative literature tends to make use of four criteria for analysing cabinets in Parliamentary democracies. These are: *centrality of the executive, collegiality of its decision-making process, collective nature of its responsibility, type of relationship with the coalition parties.*[6] In this framework, the Prodi government can be said to have consolidated the *centrality* acquired by the executive in the previous technocrat governments. During the Prodi government, the executive figured as the central institution of the political system, thereby marginalising on the one hand Parliament and on the other the party groups in the Parliamentary majority, and their national secretaries. The Prodi government was also a *collegial* government – albeit *with a premier* (i.e., a relatively strong prime minister) – in that it was able to profit from close solidarity among the members (ministers and undersecretaries) of the executive, who regarded themselves as belonging to a single team (and as such had won the elections). In its turn, this collegiality helped strengthen the executive's independence from the parties. The less the members of an executive perceive themselves as representatives of parties, the more they will tend to emphasise what unites them as a governmental team, rather than what divides them. The opposite happens in post-electoral coalition governments, where each individual minister (party representative) seeks to protect his or her policy area against encroachment by outsiders, therefore assigning to the party leader – who is not normally part of the government – the role of mediator of the policy conflicts that inevitably arise.[7] At the same time, coalitional government has impeded tendencies towards strong personal leadership of the government, and has emphasised the continued relevance of collective principles. Finally, the independence from the parties pursued by the Prodi government obviously created competition (if not conflict) between the former and the latter – competition matched by the cooperation inside the executive itself.

Government and parties

The relationship between the government and the parties has come to function as a veritable litmus test of Italian transition. In similar fashion to the 'third-wave' transitions to democracy, in Italy this relationship has acquired a strongly conflictual character. Resolving this conflict is of crucial importance to the shape of the country's future *material Constitution*. And without such resolution it is unlikely that any revision of its *formal Constitution* will be forthcoming. In short, the Italian transition will not be completed until the conflict between parties and government over which predominates in decision making has been resolved. This conflict naturally pits political leaders with an interest in channelling power towards parties against those with an interest in transferring it to the government. The transition phase such as that through which Italy is currently passing can in this regard be seen as akin, analytically, to a *state of nature*. During it, there is arguably an (institutionally) zero-sum relationship between parties and government, whereby 'strong parties and strong executives are alternative means of providing structure to a policy-making process that, in a "state of nature", would be prone to such instability that rank-and-file politicians could not accomplish anything'.[8] The conflict, therefore, has to do with the allocation of the resources required to mobilise support: are these to remain in the hands of the parties, or will the government be able to acquire them independently of the parties, through the direct personal legitimation of the chief executive?

In cases where transition to democracy has been led by political leaders who enjoy little personal political prestige, these leaders have sought to promote the collective reputations of their parties in order to advance their own careers, engineering the approval of a formal *Parliamentary* constitution which assigns scant decision-making autonomy to the executive. There may be a popularly elected president but s/he has no direct legislative powers in such a system. By contrast, where a political transition to democracy has enhanced the personal reputations of the more influential political leaders, the latter have sought to introduce *presidential* or *semi-presidential* constitutions which assert – through the direct election of the President of the Republic – the government's decision-making autonomy from the parties and their Parliamentary group leaders. The constitutional solution adopted, therefore, springs largely from the preferences of those who have guided the transition, and not from any form of historical determinism.

In the case of Italian transition, too, the preferences of political actors play a crucial role. The relationship established between the government *qua* institution and the political parties will determine the country's future constitution. If the government is to depend on the parties, then it is obvious that the latter will in any event keep its Parliamentary character. If, instead, the government is to be independent of the parties, then it is clear that the constitution will need to be semipresidential, or at any rate to be based on an 'elective premiership'. In the latter case, the parties will not disappear, but will be substantially transformed, becoming electoral agencies of the candidate for president or prime minister, rather than organisations for the 'continuing mobilisation' of electoral support.[9] Italian events during the 1990s point to the (perhaps over-hasty) conclusion that the country's constitutional evolution is moving in the latter direction: not least because the government's decision-making autonomy from the parties indubitably strengthened during the six years between the Amato and Prodi governments (1992-98). And yet this strengthening, *precisely because it is not constitutionally protected*, has proved anything but irreversible.

Contrary to a widely-held opinion (especially outside Italy), the Clean Hands investigations did not lead to the 'demise of the parties' but rather to their redefinition. The delegitimation of the traditional parties of republican Italy and the judicial decapitation of their national leaderships gave rise to both a complex restructuring of the party system and to the emergence of a political class which, though still built on parties, had been peripheral, or at any rate of second-tier status, in the previous power set-up. Since the new-old parties were involved in this complex operation of restructuring their capacity for *representation*, they were forced for the time being to relax their (traditional) grip on *decision making*, allowing executive matters to be dealt with by the technocrats (albeit under the tutelage of the President of the Republic). But, it is important to note, this only applies for the time being.

Although the parties accepted the technocrat governments as a stop-gap measure while they redefined their relationships, they nevertheless activated (or allowed) a decision-making practice which – precisely because of the success of those governments – highlighted an alternative to the party-based decision-making system that had operated from 1953 to 1992. The Prodi government came in the wake of these developments. It naturally assumed the form of a political government, but (certainly) not that of a *party government*, although it could not have been a *leader government.*[10] Of course, Prodi insisted on his *personal* electoral legitimation, but his claim inevitably turned out to be rash: he was nominated by the *Ulivo* alliance as its candidate and not chosen by the electors as their prime minister. And this proved to be his Achilles' heel.

Thus, during the 886 days of the Prodi government, two different and competing strategies towards the definition of the institutional framework of government were in evidence, and finally came into direct conflict. On the one hand, there was the *government* strategy which sought to assert the executive's decision-making independence from the parties. This followed the model that had arisen in the major cities after the electoral reform of 1993 – though with the difference that, in the latter, this independence was protected by the direct election of the mayor, whereas the Prodi government could only count on the same source of legitimacy as the parties. On the other hand, the *party* strategy sought to assert the decision-making primacy of the coalition party leaders (or their national secretaries), since these were the concrete, rather than symbolic, recipients of the electorate's support for the government. The model in this latter case, therefore, was that of the bipolar Parliamentary democracies, where party leaders are still mainly responsible for the formation and management of governments because they have preserved their monopoly over the selection of members of Parliament.

As one might have expected (and as I had predicted elsewhere[11]), once Italy's European emergency had subsided, the second strategy forcefully asserted itself. For if the leaders of the main parties in the *Ulivo* alliance were rational actors, what interest could they have had in accepting the decision-making authority of a prime minister in direct competition with them, being himself a leader without a party?[12] Accepting his authority would have meant endorsing a *de facto* reform of the government system in the direction of *personal-electoral* prime ministerial or presidential power: a reform which, as it became institutionalised, would have pushed them to the margins of the decision-making process for a long time thereafter. Consequently, in June and July 1998, the parties made their first serious attempts to reduce the executive's autonomy and to increase their influence within it. The justification was provided by a foreign policy issue (the enlargement of NATO to include Hungary, the Czech Republic and Poland), foreign policy being an area in which the Parliamentary majority's cohesion was most vulnerable.

On 23 June, during discussions in Parliament on Italy's NATO-enlargement bill, the PRC announced that it would not vote in favour of it, and the Prodi government was forced to ask for the session to be suspended. When the debate resumed, Prodi was obliged to acknowledge that the PRC's refusal to support the bill was 'a wound in the programmatic solidarity of the majority'. The bill was eventually approved thanks to the votes cast by a new Parliamentary group (the UDR) led by the former President of the Republic, Francesco Cossiga, which included renegade deputies from the centre-right *Polo*. The group abstained (the PRC and LN voted against the bill) and the bill passed with 310 votes in favour, 169 abstentions and 79 votes against. The formation of a Parliamentary majority different from the one that had been elected in 1996 therefore provided the leaders of the (most influential) *Ulivo* parties with an incentive to put the government's decision-making autonomy to the test. Thus, under pressure from the President of the Republic and from the leaders of PDS-DS and PPI, the Prodi government was forced to verify its 'fiduciary relationship' with its own Parliamentary majority; an operation which concluded with a formal vote of confidence (on 21 July in the Senate: 176 votes in favour, 119 against, and 1 abstention; on 22 July in the Chamber: 324 votes in favour, 269 against).

However, beyond the outcome of the confidence vote, which was a foregone conclusion, the aim of the *Ulivo* party leaders was to assert what might, somewhat misleadingly, be called a point of principle: namely that the basis of the government's legitimacy is Parliament, even more than it is the electorate itself. Thereafter, the party leaders consistently sought to confirm this point of principle. The principle in question was of course anything but an abstract or neutral one. Asserting the principle of the *Parliamentary legitimation* of the government, in fact, amounted to a self-interested assertion of the decision-making primacy of the parties *over* the government. If the government could only operate because it was supported by the parties, then it had inevitably to operate by catering (in policies and appointments) to their interests (electoral and organisational). In short, in the crisis of the summer of 1998, a successful attempt was made to shift the government's legitimation *from the voters back to Parliament*.

The weaknesses of the *Ulivisti*

This shift of legitimation proved impossible to resist, not only because of the determination shown by the *Ulivo* party leaders but also (especially) because of the lack of determination shown by

Prodi. Indeed, after May 1998, he undertook no further significant political initiatives. And yet it was in his rational interest to contest the idea of the *Ulivo* as an 'electoral cartel of coalitioned parties' and to assert the conception of it by the *Ulivisti* as an 'electoral-programmatic party'. Only in this way, as leader of the government, could he have ensured that his decision-making independence would continue. Thus when the showdown came with their competitors, the *Ulivisti* and their leader proved unexpectedly ill-prepared on the political level, and politically far too timid.

Their immediate weakness lay in their belief that good management by the government was enough to convert the *Ulivo* into a 'party above the parties' (or at any rate into the prime minister's party). By concentrating on the goal of joining the single European currency, the *Ulivisti* and their government leader ended up by forgetting important aspects of the way politics is conducted in Italy. Consequently, as the putative leader of the coalition, Prodi did little to transform himself into its effective leader. Eight hundred and eighty-six days were not enough to define the political identity of the *Ulivo*, with respect either to the internal party system or (and perhaps especially) to the external, European, one. Of course, ambiguity may be a useful resource in ordinary political conditions, but it is not so in extraordinary conditions like those Italy has faced in the 1990s. And in any case, ambiguity is of no help to a regime-builder, however much it might help a regime-manager. By accepting that the dominant interpretation of the *Ulivo* was that of its competitors, the *Ulivisti* and their government leader ended up by conceding the political initiative to the latter.

Only the assertion of a (supra-)party-electoral *Ulivo* with a shared set of policies, unequivocally part of the European left, could have counteracted the efforts of the *Ulivo* parties, by upsetting the delicate balance between leaders and followers inside each component party. However, to have been credible, this assertion would have required the government to press for reforms to both *complete* the majoritarian electoral system and *introduce* the direct election of the head of the government, thereby subsuming the ideological and organisational identities of those parties under the wider *Ulivo* project.

Instead, however, the *Ulivisti* and their government leader chose to remain silent on institutional matters. And this was their strategic weakness. Probably convinced that new rules inevitably arise from practice and behaviour, they found themselves trapped in an institutional immobility, not lacking, according to some, a *conservative* justification, which played into the hands of their opponents. Since the basic institutional framework of Parliamentary democracy remained unchanged, it was the party leaders who, necessarily, controlled the resources of decision-making legitimacy. From this perspective, the Prodi government's decision not to involve itself in the longstanding debate on institutional reform, which had begun with the creation of the Bicameral Committee, and the government's professed agnosticism concerning the solutions under discussion, were extremely misconceived. For if there was any actor that had a rational interest in a reform which envisaged the strengthening (by majoritarian means) of the executive, it was the Prodi government; and if there was any actor who had a rational interest in a reform that would enhance the prime minister's powers (through his/her direct election) it was Prodi himself. Without the protection of new institutional rules, how could the government and its leader hope to conserve decision-making primacy over the Parliamentary majority and the leaders of the parties that composed it? This is not to say that determined institutional pressure would necessarily have enabled the Prodi government to come out on top, but such pressure, had it been brought to bear, would have greatly complicated matters for the proponents of a conservative, party-directed, restoration.

In short, the government's strategy was defeated by the political (and even more so cultural) weakness of the *Ulivisti*, rather than by the strategy of the leaders of the coalition parties. After all, in a parliamentary democracy there is little likelihood that the parties will grant autonomy to the government *unless they are forced to do so*. The Prodi government – because it was a government born of an inter-party accord, and because it was a government made up of party men and women – was unable to transform an opportunity (provided by specific contingent factors) into a necessity (imposed by specific institutional pressures). It believed that the winds of the electorate and of Europe would definitively bend the reed of the institutions towards the primacy of the electorate. But winds, of course, do not blow forever. And the reed of the government, in the absence of reformist pressure, sprang back towards Parliamentary government, and consequently in favour of the parties. After more than six years, the latter regained control as soon as the opportunity first presented itself – thereby fulfilling the principle that their leaders had long (and legitimately) asserted: namely that, in parliamentary democracies, governments rest mainly on indirect legitimation by the representatives and not on direct legitimation by the represented.

The D'Alema government

The opportunity arose for the *Ulivo* party leaders when the PRC refused to vote in favour of the 1999 Budget Law. The 'governmental' malaise of the PRC had been evident for some time. Already in October 1997 its secretary, Fausto Bertinotti, had declared his intention not to support the budget law 'that should take us into Europe', although he was forced to change his mind by the hostile reaction of numerous members of his own party. Nevertheless, in the summer-autumn of 1998, it was clear that the PRC's malaise could no longer be held at bay. On 31 August, Bertinotti stated the 'irrevocable conditions' of his party's support for the Prodi government's budget law. Although this non-negotiable position was not shared by all the PRC's leaders – as PRC chairman, Armando Cossutta, explained in an article published by *Liberazione* on 1 September – the stability of the Parliamentary majority grew increasingly shaky.

Following a meeting of the majority held on 16 September, the PRC secretary declared that he 'had not seen any significant change in the government's economic policy'. Indeed, on 21 September, at a meeting of the PRC executive committee, he tabled a motion withdrawing support for the government which was passed by thirty of the forty-six present – a majority which was reflected in the PRC's Political Committee, on 4 October when 188 members out of 332 voted in favour of Bertinotti's stance. The day after, therefore, Cossutta was obliged to resign his post as chairman of the PRC, an act that was the prelude to the inevitable split in the party that followed, not least because a majority across the PRC's two Parliamentary groups was unwilling to precipitate a government crisis. Nevertheless, this was not enough to avert it, and on 7 October discussion began in the Chamber on a motion of confidence in the Prodi government. The discussion concluded two days later on 9 October with the voting down of the government: 313 votes against, 312 in favour.

During the Parliamentary debate – but already while the crisis was in fermentation in previous months – the positions of the *Ulivo* party leaders (in particular Massimo D'Alema and Franco Marini) and that of prime minister Prodi grew increasingly distant. Whereas the former expressed themselves distinctly in favour of extending the Parliamentary majority to include the UDR group headed by former President Cossiga – a group consisting of deputies who had been the *Ulivo*'s adversaries in the elections of 21 April 1996 – Prodi roundly rejected the proposal, declaring it to be a grave distortion of the outcome of the elections. For Prodi, if any extension was to be envisaged, it should be an addition to the previous majority, not a substitute for parts of it. This diverse conception of how the majority should be extended highlighted the contrast between those (the party leaders) whose interest lay in defining the government majority as a *Parliamentary majority* and those (the leader of the government) whose interest instead lay in its definition as an *electoral majority*.

In reality, with the onset of the crisis brought about by the PRC secretary, the *Ulivo* party leaders had the numbers to resolve the crisis while Prodi had the symbols. And when push came to shove the former counted more than the latter. Thus, although the no-confidence motion had been carried with the slimmest of margins, the *Ulivo* party leaders were able to implement the principle that they had constantly sought to assert: namely that the legitimacy of Parliamentary governments resides in Parliament (a Parliament of the parties) and not in the electorate. This, and none other, was the significance of their announcement in the aftermath of the no-confidence vote that 'the *Ulivo* no longer exists'. The conditions were now in place, moreover, for a 'Parliamentarist' interpretation of the crisis: the 'white semester' – the final six-month period of a presidential term, in which the President may not nominate a new government – was about to begin. Constitutionally it was impossible to dissolve Parliament. European monetary union was also imminent, and hence approval of the budget law was a matter of paramount urgency. Of course, holding new elections was not the only option available, since a technocrat government, or an institutional government or a very broadly based government were also possibilities.

And yet the party system at the end of the 1990s is not the same as it was at the beginning of the decade. Today it is much more solid, at least on the centre-left side, than the system which made the 'technocrat' governments of the period 1992-96 necessary. Owing to the *representative* legitimacy furnished by the new electoral system, the parties are now able to reclaim the control over decision-making power they forfeited in 1992. Thus, after the failure of the President of the Republic's attempt to re-appoint Prodi, on 13 October, D'Alema assumed office three days later. Incidentally, one is struck that Prodi accepted the invitation to try to form a new government, for it was evident that a condition of his doing so would have been his acknowledgement of the 'end of the electoral majority of 21 April 1996'; an acknowledgement which, if forthcoming, would have delivered him 'bound hand and foot' as a political hostage to the leaders of the parties and groups in the new majority. In any event, once invited to form a government by the President of the Republic, D'Alema took only four days to do so (plus a further three to obtain the confidence of the Chamber, and a further six to gain that of the Senate).

Whilst in its formation the new D'Alema government was *post-electoral* – the outcome of agreement among distinct Parliamentary parties – as regards its composition it bears all the hallmarks of a government of *coalitioned parties*. It is, therefore, a *coalition government* rather than a *coalitional one* like Prodi's. Due to the fallout from the crisis of the Prodi government, amongst other things, D'Alema's government comprises a larger number of parties than its predecessor: whereas the former consisted of five parties (DS, PD, PPI, RI, *Verdi*), the latter consists of seven (the previous five plus UDR and the newly formed *Partito dei Comunisti Italiani*, which has arisen from the split in the PRC). The larger number of parties in D'Alema's government, combined with its character as a coalition, may also explain its larger size compared with its predecessor. The number of ministries has grown by almost 20 percent, and that of undersecretaries by just over 10 percent (see Table 5.1). By contrast there are fewer undersecretaries in the Prime Minister's Office (reduced from five to four), although the number of them with Parliamentary appointments has increased (from one to three).

As regards the distribution of undersecretaryships, there is no significant difference between the two governments, although one discerns greater emphasis by the D'Alema government on foreign policy and defence. In the latter ministry, indeed, the number of undersecretaries has been doubled from two to four. It is worth pointing out, finally, that there is a certain discontinuity in the *personal* make-up of ministerial appointments. Only 36 percent of the ministers in the previous government figure in its successor, although one notes much less discontinuity in the undersecretary appointments (almost 50 percent of whom have been reconfirmed) (see Table 5.1).

Of course, any assessment of the operational characteristics of the D'Alema government only three months after it took office would be pointless. What is evident, however, is the apparent *logic of its functioning*. Thus far, the prime minister has been unable to install the decision-making model of 'restricted and associated cabinet direction': indeed from the outset he has repeatedly had to urge his cabinet members to show greater caution in their public pronouncements, especially regarding policies which do not specifically concern them – a case in point being the views expressed by the Minister of Justice on foreign policy – views entirely at odds with those of the Foreign Minister. In the end, the ministers in a coalition government are party representatives more than they are the heads of a particular department of the national executive. And the prime minister, bereft as he is of electoral legitimation, is unable to claim any decision-making primacy in their regard. Should he do so, he would radically upset the balances on which the coalition rests. For this reason, D'Alema will find it difficult to impose himself as a *first among unequals* in his cabinet, lest he

Table 5.1 *Number of Ministers and Undersecretaries in the Prodi and D'Alema Governments*

| | Prodi Government | | D'Alema Government | |
	Ministers	Under-secretaries	Ministers	Under-secretaries
DS	9	17	5	17
PD	3	4	2	3
PPI	1	3	1	3
RI	3	3	2	5
Mixed		4		2
Greens	1	1	1	1
UDR			3	8
Communists			1	
Non-parliamentarians*	4	18	10	17
total	21	50	25	56

Ministers in both governments holding the *same* departments: seven
Ministers in both governments with *different* departments: two
Non-Parliamentary ministers confirmed in the same department:two
Undersecretaries in both governments with the *same* functions: twenty-six
Undersecretaries in both governments with *different* functions: three
Non-Parliamentary undersecretaries confirmed in the same department: seven
Non-Parliamentary undersecretaries assigned to different departments: three
*Note that these figures refer to 'non-Parliamentarians', but they cannot be considered 'technicians' in the sense of experts without identifiable party allegiance.

Abbreviations:
DS: *Democratici di Sinistra*
RI: *Rinnovamento Italiano*
PD: *Popolari Democratici – Ulivo* (Chamber)
PPI: *Partito Popolare* (Senate)

upset the stability of the inter-party accord, and he will probably have to settle for the role of *first among equals*.

The behaviour to date of D'Alema's government has highlighted the major changes that have come about in the relationship between the executive and the political system. Firstly, the inter-party accord on which it is based has made it less central, both with respect to Parliament (as exemplified by the difficult negotiations over the distribution of the chairmanships of the Parliamentary committees) and of course with respect to the parties of which it is made up. This is exemplified by the importance attributed to the talks between the prime minister and the chairman of the UDR – which has no government appointments – in order to resolve conflicts internal to the latter. Secondly, the government's peculiar inter-party basis has reduced collegiality among ministers, many of whom regard themselves as political rivals rather than as allies. Thirdly, the electorally ambiguous nature of the cabinet has inevitably reduced the executive's level of collective responsibility, amongst other things because several of its members openly acknowledge that they will (in the future) pursue different policy strategies. Finally, this factor has made the government's internal workings much less cooperative, but (compared with the previous government) it has also, as a consequence, made the relations between the members of the government and its supporting parties less competitive.

This does not mean that the institutionalisation of the executive in progress since the period of so-called 'transition' will peter out. Quite the reverse: not only because once in train this process benefits from an 'organisational inertia' which proves difficult to overcome, but also because there is an incentive towards greater organisational rationalisation of the executive (not to be confused with decision-making autonomy) from supranational systemic pressure (one thinks, for example, of the increasing need in Europe for coordination among national governments).

Continuity or discontinuity?

In his inaugural address to the Chamber of Deputies on 22 October 1998, D'Alema expressed himself as follows:[13] 'Mr President, honourable colleagues (...) the new majority combines diverse aspirations and cultures which legitimately envisage different outcomes for our bipolarity. On the one hand, there are those who maintain that an encounter between the reformist left and the centre is now the medium-to-long-term political perspective (....) On the other, there are those who are convinced that the centre-left coalition comprises both components of a future bipolarity. Frankly, I cannot say which of the two views will prevail in the end'.

D'Alema was right: it is indeed difficult to establish what the future evolution of the Italian political system will be. However, it is equally true that it was the second scenario that prevailed in the *Parliamentary* solution of the crisis: the scenario, that is, of a *declared* intent to redesign Italian bipolarity but which may instead bring it to a halt – if it is true, as Prodi has claimed,[14] that 'the government was brought down by an anti-*Ulivo* bias (which) appeals to the unity of Catholics, calls for the reconstitution of *Democrazia Cristiana*, and seeks to a form a centre alliance which shifts first to the right and then to the left as circumstances suit'. From this point of view, the D'Alema government displays a *policy continuity* with its predecessor but, simultaneously, a significant *political disconti-nuity* with it. The D'Alema government, that is to say, was born with an ambitious project to restructure, both organisationally and ideologically, the central area of the Italian party system, not only to counter the left's preponderance in the government but also to propose this new centre as the renewed 'representative point of ref-erence' for the section of the electorate which, since 1994, has supported the Berlusconian leadership of the *Polo della Libertà*. This project, judging from the declarations of those who promote it, is based on two assumptions: first that the electorate in question can be dismantled (and part of it transferred to the centre), and second that a much smaller electorate can then be reassembled on the right. The party system would thus be structured around *three poles*, although only two of them (the left and the centre) would be competitive (or, perhaps, seen as legitimate to govern). And they would *govern together*, because neither of them (the centre and the left) would ever *under the present electoral system* receive sufficient votes and seats in Parliament to be able to govern on its own.

Of course, the definitive restructuring of the party system around its traditional *party families* of centre, right and left would enable the latter to put the finishing touches to its newly acquired social-demo-cratic identity (which would no longer be threatened with cultural contamination by those reformist, *but not socialist*, traditions that bred the *Ulivo*). Moreover, this restructuring seemingly enjoys con-siderable support both inside and outside the country. It does so in Europe because the Italian parties would thus be 'normalised', with the most influential of them being incorporated into the main party coalitions of the European Parliament (the DS into the European Socialist Party; the Catholic centre parties into the European People's Party, to which – note – the *Forza Italia* MEPs already belong, albeit 'on a personal basis'; and *Alleanza Nazionale* into the Gaullist group).[15] And it enjoys consensus in Italy because influential social interest groups (primarily the Catholic hierarchies) would thus finally be able to establish a direct link of representation with those parties (the centre ones, especially) destined, over the medium period, to play a pivotal role in the government: the link, that is, abruptly severed by the changes that have taken place since the early 1990s. One should not underestimate the weight of this exter-nal and internal support, not least because it would otherwise be dif-ficult to explain the silent support in the press that has accompanied the changes wrought by the government majority. On the other hand, it would be also a mistake to overestimate it, because even in a Parliamentary democracy the last word still lies with the electorate.

To conclude, one finds it difficult to decide whether the political discontinuity represented by the D'Alema government will interrupt the bipolarisation of Italian politics set in train by the elections of 1994. Although there are substantial pressures to halt this process, there are others that could just as easily reactivate it, perhaps in unexpected ways. These latter pressures have internal and external origins: internally in a bipolar split within the electorate that is difficult to eliminate, especially now that the electoral referendum is forthcoming; externally in the bipolar dynamic which continues to determine political relationships in the leading European countries (notwithstanding the multiparty structure of the European Parliament[16]), and which gives those countries a decision-making capacity that inevitably impinges on the workings of Italy's system of government.[17] These twofold pressures converge on a single issue: what matters for the efficiency of a political system is bipolarity *per se*, not its specific party form. After all, European political unification can only spring from recognition of the distinctiveness of national histories; it cannot spring from their simple synthesis into a putative pan-European model.

Translated by Adrian Belton

Notes

1. Massimo D'Alema, *Discorso di insediamento*, Roma: Chamber of Deputies, 22 October 1998, quotations (respectively) on p. 5 and p. 14 of the transcript.
2. I have discussed the characteristics of the Prodi government in S. Fabbrini, 'Due anni di governo Prodi. Un primo bilancio istituzionale', *Il Mulino*, XLVII, no. 4, 1998: 657-72.
3. For a useful discussion of the characteristics of coalition governments see M. Laver and K. Shepsle, 'Coalitions and Cabinet Government', *American Political Science Review*, 84, no. 3, 1990: 873-90. See also the book edited by the same authors, *Cabinet Ministers and Parliamentary Government*, Cambridge: Cambridge University Press, 1994.
4. See S. Merlini, 'Il governo costituzionale', in R. Romanelli (ed.), *Storia dello stato italiano. Dall'Unità ad oggi*, Rome: Donzelli, 1997: 3-72.
5. I have used here the well-known typology proposed by G. Sartori, *Ingegneria costituzionale comparata. Strutture, incentivi ed esiti*, It. transl., Bologna: Il Mulino, 1997, p.116.
6. See L. De Winter, 'The Links between Cabinet and Parties and Cabinet Decision-Making', in J. Blondel and F. Muller-Rommel (eds.), *Governing Together. The Extent and Limits of Joint Decision-Making in Western European Cabinets*, New York: St. Martin's Press, 1993: 153-76.
7. As for example in Holland (on which see R.B. Andeweg, 'The Dutch Prime Minister: Not Just Chairman, Not Yet Chief?', *West European Politics* 14, no. 2, 1991: 116-32) or Belgium (see L. De Winter, 'Party Encroachment on the Executive and Legislative Branch in the Belgian Polity', *Res Publica*, XXXVIII, no.2, 1996: 325-52).

8. For detailed comparative analysis see M. Shugart, 'The Inverse Relationship Between Party Strength and Executive Strength: A Theory of Politicians' Constitutional Choice', *British Journal of Political Science*, 28, no.1, 1998: 1-29, quote p.1, emphasis in original.

9. As is well known, the activity of *permanent or continuing mobilisation* is pursued by mass parties, which have been organisationally structured precisely for that purpose. For a recent comparative analysis of the organisational characteristics of parties see R.S. Katz and P. Mair (eds), *How Parties Organise. Change and Adaptation in Party Organisations in Western Democracies*, London: Sage, 1994.

10. I have discussed the distinction between 'party government' and 'leader government' at length in S. Fabbrini, *Il Prìncipe democratico. La leadership nelle democrazie contemporanee*, Roma-Bari: Laterza, 1999.

11. Almost a year beforehand, I might add, given that my article, S. Fabbrini, *Due anni di governo Prodi*, op. cit., was the text of a paper presented at the Conference «Lavori in corso. Il sistema politico italiano dopo il terremoto dei primi anni novanta: politics, policy e polity nella transizione italiana», organised by the Centro Studi sul Cambiamento Politico (CIRCAP), University of Siena, Certosa di Pontignano, on 19-21 February 1998.

12. As Prodi himself acknowledged when reflecting on the crisis of his government: 'The facts are clear for those who want to see them. The *Ulivo* government was a success, it gradually opened channels of communication with society. At a certain point, rejection set in among the parties' *Corriere della Sera*, Sunday 17 January 1999, p. 9. For extensive and documented discussion of the relationships between Parliamentary cabinets and their supporting parties see J. Blondel and M. Cotta (eds), *Party and Government. An Inquiry into the Relationship between Governments and Supporting Parties in Liberal Democracies*, New York: St. Martin's Press, 1996.

13. M. D'Alema, *Discorso di insediamento*, op.cit., p.13.

14. R. Prodi, 'Perchè ci hanno fermato', *Appunti di cultura e di politica*, no. 7, November-December 1998: 1-2: an assessment which, on reading the little that has been written on the formation of the D'Alema government, is not widely shared, with the (Bolognese) exception of G. Pasquino, 'Bipolarismo addio?', *La Rivista dei Libri*, VIII, no. 12 (December) 1998: 10-11 and the editor of the journal *Il Mulino*, 'Ai lettori', *Il Mulino* XLVII, no. 5, 1998: 791-94.

15. In fact, on the few occasions when there has been a programmatic split able to override divisions (much more frequent) along national or regional lines (north vs. south) the European Parliament has also functioned according to a centre-left vs. centre-right axis (as opposed to socialists' vs. People's party lines). Strasburg has 626 seats distributed as follows (in the legislature that expires in 1999 – the centre-left: European Socialist Party, 214; European Party of Liberals, Democrats and Reformers, 42; Green Group, 27; European Unitary Left, Nordic Green Left and Communists, 34. On the centre-right: European Popular Party, 202; Union for Europe (Gaullist), 35; European Radical Alliance (with autonomists), 20; Independents for the Europe of Nations (anti-Europe right), 15. Then the Mixed Group with 37 seats.

16. This did not prevent France when it was governed by the Gaullists from coordinating with the other parties (and governments) of the centre-right, although it did not have a People's party.

17. As well argued by V. Della Salla, 'Losing the Centre?: Italy in the Shadow of the Euro', Ottawa: Carleton University, 1998, mimeo, and M. Cotta, 'Le élite politiche nazionali di fronte all'integrazione', *Il Mulino* XVVII, no. 3, 1998: 445-56.

6

The Bassanini Laws: A Half-Way House in Local Government Reform

Mark Gilbert[1]

The period March 1997 to March 1998 constitutes the busiest and most innovative period in Italian local government since the establishment of the regions in the early 1970s. Beginning with the Legge 59/97, published in the *Gazzetta Ufficiale* on 17 March 1997, through to legislative decree 112/98 issued on 31 March 1998, and published on 21 April 1998, a series of legislative acts named after the Minister for Local Government, Franco Bassanini (DS-Ulivo) has outlined a new shape to sub-national tiers of administration in Italy. It should be said, however, that this overhaul of local government has not provided anything remotely akin to federalism. Italy's regions are preoccupied by the fact that although their administrative remit has been significantly widened, their resources and economic independence have not yet been extended correspondingly and their ability to direct policy, as opposed to merely executing it, has not been systematically increased.

The collapse of the Bicameral committee on constitutional reform (Bicamerale) in the spring of 1998, moreover, has ensured that the greater institutional importance being accorded to all levels of local government by the Bassanini process will not be written into the Constitution in the foreseeable future. Not that the regions, in particular, were especially satisfied by the draft document produced by the Bicamerale on 4 November 1997. In their view, the Bicamerale should have been bold enough to follow the

German model and give both substantive powers of autonomy to the regions and territorial representation in the national parliament. Unsurprisingly, the political parties represented in the committee backed away from such a genuinely radical step.

All in all, in institutional terms the reforms to local government initiated between March 1997 and March 1998 should be characterised as a mutation in a slowly evolving process of decentralisation rather than a leap into the federalist dark. As any biologist knows, however, in times of rapid environmental transformation only those organisms able to adapt rapidly to changing circumstances manage to survive. And in this regard, the Bassanini laws, despite some well-publicised innovations which should help to cut red tape for business and citizens, emerge as a timid set of reforms. It is becoming increasingly apparent that the Italian state's bureaucracy is a major competitive disadvantage for Italian producers of goods and services. In a Europe with a single currency, tough rules on state aid to private enterprise, and a common legal framework, a bloated and inert public sector will prove a dead weight for the economy. The Bassanini laws, which initially hinted that superfluous layers of bureaucratic flab would be slimmed down, but which eventually promised to engage in political liposuction and transfer fat from one part of the body politic to another, simply do not go far enough in reducing the costs of Italian government.

The Laws of March and May 1997

The March 1997 law delegated to the government the power to 'confer functions and tasks to the regions and other local institutions with the goal of reforming and simplifying public administration'. To this end, a number of laws and decrees have been issued with the purpose of implementing the principles laid down in the initial law. In May 1997, the second Bassanini Law (127/97), dealing with 'Urgent measures for the slimming down of administrative activities and procedures of decision and control' was passed by parliament; in June 1997, decree 143/97 conferred some of the administrative responsibility for fishing and agriculture to the regional governments; on 28 August 1997, an important decree established a new 'Permanent' or 'United' conference of representatives from the central government, the regions, the provinces and other levels of local government for the discussion of all matters of mutual concern; in November and December 1997, decrees 422/97 and 469/97 conferred administrative authority over some aspects of transport and labour market issues to the regions. In the meantime, of course, the Bicamerale had presented its final draft document, containing a wealth of changes to the constitutional status of local government, to parliament for debate and amendment. In 1998, the conference of regional presidents and the National Association of Italian Municipalities (ANCI) presented a joint document containing a series of well-reasoned amendments to the Bicamerale's draft document. In March 1998, the major decree 'implementing' the transfer of functions and administrative tasks to the sub-national tiers of government was introduced. Within six months of this decree, the regions were supposed to put forward a coherent plan to absorb their new responsibilities.

The 59/97 law begins with the general statement that in keeping with the principle of subsidiarity underpinning the law, all functions and administrative tasks relative to taking care of 'local interests' and 'promoting the development of the respective communities' as well as 'all functions and tasks currently carried out at local level by any organ or administration of the state' would be transferred to the regions and other local bodies. There was a list of exceptions, however, and this list is a familiar one to students of the Bicamerale's subsequent negotiations in 1997. The central state reserved its absolute control over a number of key functions, notably foreign affairs and trade, defence questions, immigration, elections, public order, administration of justice, scientific research and the universities. The power to plan and lay down general policy was also reserved for the state in a wealth of areas, specifically motorways, infrastructure networks, the environment and so on. The gist of Bassanini's intentions with the 59/97 law was to abandon any lingering state control over legislation in the policy areas reserved for the regions by Article 117 of the Constitution and to use to the fullest the power conferred upon the central government by Article 118 of the Constitution to delegate administrative powers to the regions in other policy areas such as education.

The regions themselves, however, in keeping with their constitutional role as an allocator of services, rather than a direct provider, were given the task, in Article 4 of the 59/97 law, of transferring the actual administration down to the provinces and other layers of local government. The law, in short, was operating primarily according to the principle of subsidiarity and was insistent that services should be provided so far as possible by the layer of government (or even by families and volunteer organisations) closest to the 'people concerned'. The same article, however, also insisted upon the importance of nine other criteria for the assignation of administrative responsibilities. There is no space here to describe these criteria one by one, but the most important of them stressed that the regions should assign administrative authority according to the principle of 'efficiency and economic savings' by suppressing agencies or offices which became superfluous once lower levels of local government had been entrusted with any given administrative function. To reinforce the message, the law also underlined that any particular function should be the responsibility of 'a single agency'. Duplication of functions by two or even three levels of administration should be a thing of the past.

The logic of Law 59/97 should by now be clear. The state would devolve significant administrative and policy-making powers to the regions, who would, in turn, devolve the new powers down the line to the provinces, the municipalities and even semi-public voluntary associations. At no point in the chain of of administration should there be two layers of government doing the same thing. Such a process of subsidiarity, of course, had immense implications in terms of jobs and resources. While the law stopped short of saying that this process of bureaucratic rationalisation would lead to job losses, its language appeared to imply at the very least that the process of decentralising central government functions would not lead to an overall increase in the number of civil servants employed by the public administration. Article 7 expressly stated that within three years there would be a 'congruous' transfer of resources, both human and financial, from the state to local government and that at the same time there would be a 'parallel suppression or redimensioning' of 'peripheral' state agencies. Article 3 was even stronger in its language: it stated that 'central structures' would be 'suppressed, transformed or incorporated' and that 'state personnel' would be 'transferred' without 'extra cost' for public finances. Article 13 promised that the central government would identify offices of general, central or peripheral managerial level that could be eliminated, while Article 14 was bluntest of all. It committed the central state to 'pursue the objective of a broad reduction in administrative costs', called for the 'liquidation of useless agencies' and, in general, beat the drum for a more rational use of the state's assets and personnel.

The longest single article in the 59/97 law was Article 21, which dealt with reform in the schools. According to the law, schools were to be given far greater autonomy over the curriculum, methods of teaching, course organisation, out-of-hours programmes of adult education and teacher training. The underlying spirit of Article 21 was a compelling one. It is clear that the law's drafters understand the schools to be under-utilised community resources that are tied up in bureaucratic procedures and lacking in clear leadership. In this last regard, Article 21 called for head teachers to be 'entrusted with' the managerial autonomy that would enable them to 'coordinate and valorize' their human resources and be given direct responsibility over the budget. The schools, in short, were to be given their freedom in everything except one fundamental point: the power to hire and, what is obviously more difficult, to fire teachers. This point was simply not mentioned by Article 21, although the logic of the principles of autonomy and scholastic flexibility suffusing this part of the law surely demanded it.

The 59/97 law was followed swiftly by the second 'Bassanini law', number 127/97, which, as the law's preamble stated, was concerned with 'urgent measures for the simplification of administrative practices and procedures of decision-making and control'. This is the aspect of the Bassanini process which has won most public and press approval and which will in the short-term be the most visible feature of the reforms to public administration in Italy. Even a short glance through this hugely complex and lengthy piece of legislation reveals a vivid picture of the bureaucratic miseries that Italians have been accustomed to suffer at the counters of the various branches of the public administration. The law's vigorous slashing of the exasperating red tape surrounding the request for even the most basic documents such as the certificate of 'civil status', or the rules governing participation in public examinations, should prove to be a boon for every citizen.

In pursuit of further administrative efficiencies, Article 6 of the law authoriss both the mayors of all towns of over 15,000 inhabitants and provincial presidents to employ a 'director-general' (who was immediately baptised a 'city manager' by the press) with the specific task of obtaining 'outstanding levels of efficacy and efficiency'. The city manager, in theory, would act as chief executive officer of the municipality, implementing the mayor's directives and acting as a constant monitor of the municipality's services, whose managers would have to report directly to him. In order to ensure that this important new post is not dominated by 'insiders' and cronies of the mayor, the law insists that all city managers should be appointed on contracts not exceeding the length of the mandate of the mayor or provincial president who appoint them and that they should not previously have worked for the municipal or provincial workforce.

The 'Bassanini II', however, did not just limit itself to making local government more user-friendly. Article 16, which was a lengthy law with 140 clauses dealing with dozens of minor procedural and organisational changes to both the institutions and the legal status of various national professional associations, contained what amounted to a fundamental reform act for the universities. Over 30 clauses, many of which, admittedly, were directed towards the establishment of a new university at Bolzano and mitigating the effect of this decision on Trento, dealt explicitly with the universities and their reform. Clause 95 conferred a substantial degree of didactic autonomy to Italy's universities by permitting universities, within general guidelines laid down by the Ministry of Education, to 'discipline' their own degree courses free of ministerial interference. Italian universities will therefore be free to launch new courses and alter old ones without needing to persuade bureaucrats in Rome of the new courses' value. Clause 102, in fact, called the universities 'autonomous university institutions', a jargon phrase which for once sounds softly to the ear. Universities in the Val D'Aosta, Trentino-Alto Adige and Friuli will be permitted to reach independent accords with universities in Germany, France and Slovenia for the establishment of joint degrees with independent schemes of financing; even more strikingly, a deliberate policy of opening up Italian universities to distinguished foreign scholars is to be followed. The universities will also be given a direct role in the formulation of the general guidelines for university policy through the National Council of the Universities (CUN), a body containing representatives of the academic community, students and administrative staff. This form of organisation – a central ministry providing general guidelines to autonomously managed institutions after taking advice from the representatives of the institutions themselves – can in many ways be regarded as a model for the structure of the centre-periphery relationship. Where local government was concerned, however, this model was not always achieved.

The Enactment of the Bassanini Laws

Despite its length and formidable intricacy, the 127/97 law was much more concrete than the 59/97 law. It concerns precise changes to day-to-day procedures and its success or failure will be determined by the will of local politicians and ordinary citizens to compel the bureaucracy to make the new rules everyday practice. Inevitably, the implementation of the new guidelines will initially be patchy as a combination of bureaucratic inertia and perplexity over the exact meaning of key phrases in the law's amendments to previous local government legislation may cause confusion at the point of service.[2] Nevertheless, with time, political will and consumer vigilance, the law should eventually become fully operational.

The 59/97, by contrast, in so far as it was more a declaration of principle, has spawned a huge legislative effort by the government to turn principle into clear directives via the emanation of several major pieces of decree legislation. The first of these, legislative decree 143/97, was published in the *Gazzetta Ufficiale* on 5 June 1997. Decree 143/97 abolished the Ministry of Agricultural, Alimentary and Forestry Resources and replaced it with a 'new' Ministry for Agricultural Policy. The new ministry was given authority over general policy questions for agriculture, responsibility for representing Italy at Brussels, and tutelage over a substantial range of different policy areas ranging from product quality, import and export of agricultural products, national irrigation networks, bovine sperm banks and the right to declare a state of 'exceptionally adverse weather conditions', but hard decisions over the transfer of other functions were postponed until the end of 1997 and have not been satisfactorily resolved since. Further highly technical decrees on public transport (number 422/97), labour market responsibilities (number 469/97) and carbon fuel distribution (number 32/98) added to local government responsibilities as the year wore on. The second of these was especially interesting. In a nutshell, this decree entirely handed responsibility for professional training, the management of job centres, the flexibility of the labour market and other employment-related activities to the regions and laid down guidelines for new structures in this area of obvious and growing importance.

The crucial legislative effort to put flesh on the bones of the 59/97 law, however, was legislative decree 112/98, published on the *Gazzetta Ufficiale* on 21 April 1998. This huge piece of legislation (there are 164 articles, some of which themselves are as long as many ordinary laws) made recommendations for the division of responsibilities between centre and periphery under five main headings, each of which was subdivided into a dozen or more separate policy areas. The five headings were 'General Arrangements' (which included, importantly, indications for the distribution of resources); 'Economic Development and Productive Activities' (which dealt with, among other things, energy policy, trade fairs, mines and tourism); 'Territory, Environment and Infrastructure' (which discussed town planning, parks, waste disposal, transport and the roads among other important topics); 'Services to the Person and the Community' (which referred to social services, the schools, professional training and even sport). The fifth heading, and by far the shortest, dealt with the policing of urban areas.

Inevitably, a decree of this complexity had been the subject of an intense bargaining process. According to a leading regional official who sat at the negotiating table, the drafting of the 112/98 decree was characterised by regional eagerness and the dragging of central government feet.[3] According to the 59/97 law, all plans to consolidate its general principles should have been finished by the end of 1997. The need to coordinate the process with the work of the Bicamerale, however, permitted a three-month extension. Even so, the regions and the central government did not begin working together until January 1998. The regions, in conjunction with ANCI (the national association of municipal authorities), UPI (the parallel organisation for the provinces) and UNCEM (the national union of mountain municipalities and communities) made a joint presentation of over 300 amendments to the government's initial proposals. Some 170 of these were eventually incorporated into the final legislation.[4]

It is obviously impossible in a short article like this one to discuss the 112/98 decree in all its complexity.[5] It is possible, however, to highlight certain significant novelties and to underline some of the principal weaknesses of the decree.

Under the heading 'Economic Development and Productive Activities', for instance, a number of useful initiatives were launched. Perhaps the most important is that as a result of Articles 18 and 19, the central state will to all intents and purposes confer the administration and distribution of all public financial aid to small businesses and the interpretation and execution of European law in this field to the regions. The regions will decide (within the confines of general guidelines from the central state and the limits of European law) which businesses merit assistance in the purchase of machinery, in opening export markets and in commercialising products, and, for the most part, funds destined by the state for these purposes will be released by regional laws. Article 21, also dealing with industry, and particularly with small businesses, made a bonfire of the annual licences required by the state and the requirement to obtain state approval before investing in certain kinds of equipment or plant was abolished. In an interesting and widely discussed development, municipalities were bidden by Article 23 to establish 'one-stop shops' through which would-be investors will be able to complete the full gamut of bureaucratic procedures for the institution of a new business, including planning permission, at a single session. In the industrial sector, a lot will depend upon how the central state interprets its role as the setter of general guidelines for the concession of public aid and whether it will try to micro-manage policy by allowing the regions little room for manoeuvre. But at least in principle it does seem as if the regions and other layers of local government have won the opportunity to direct policy in an area that is of great political sensitivity.

Policy on the question of road transportation, by contrast, was dealt with much more timidly and illustrates a pervading problem in the decree as a whole: the unwillingness of the central government to transform its tough talk on the 'suppression' or 'liquidation' of state agencies into concrete action. As Roberto Bin has pointed out, decree 112/98 contains 'scant indication of structures to be dismantled or transferred'.[6] As he suggests, Article 9 of the decree talks merely of the 'reorganisation' of the state's peripheral functions and of their 'eventual' suppression or 'incorporation' into regional administrations. Article 7, meanwhile, goes out of its way to guarantee worried state employees that 'all transferred personnel are guaranteed the maintenance of the income levels they have already attained' – few savings will thus be found there, though the 59/97 law's insistence that the process of simplifying the state's bureaucracy should provide a reduction in the cost of government was clear. In the case of policy towards the road network (Articles 98 and 99), for instance, the decree shrank from limiting the state's role to financing, planning and managing the motorways (which are, in any event, scheduled for privatisation, though the decree gives no indication of how this will affect the legislation) and other national routes, and instead opted to preserve the National Roads Authority (ANAS) and hence its control over maintenance and construction. The regions were given extended powers to build and (via the provinces) maintain local roads, but were urged to reach temporary local accords with ANAS for the fulfilment of these tasks. Instead of there being, in short, a single agency in the regional governments in charge of public tenders for major works of construction and repair projects on all roads, including motorways, and satellite agencies in the provincial governments concerned primarily with carrying out road repairs, the state will continue to dabble in the business of building roads. And an entirely otiose (and notoriously corrupt) bureaucracy will remain intact for the forseeable future.

Something similar occurred with the schools. Although the state has formalised the transfer of many functions to regional level and the schools have been given an unquestioned degree of autonomy, the state retains (Article 137) its competence over the distribution of both human and financial resources. In other words, teachers will continue to be appointed through the shambolic and often murky system of infrequent public examinations while schools will continue to have no say in the employment of their staff, but will have to wait for the local *provveditorato* (state education offices) to send them new teachers at its own speed and with no possibility of ascertaining their quality. The spirit of the rhetoric of the 59/97 law surely implied that such autonomy in the selection of schoolteachers should be granted. If a school is unable to choose its teachers without having to wait upon a national bureaucracy its autonomy is circumscribed excessively. It would surely not have been impossible to establish regional offices of didactic standards, charged with organising the certification of all would-be teachers, and whose standards would be, on the model of university degrees within the European Union, recognised as valid throughout the entire national territory. Each region could publish a regular newsletter, or maintain a constantly up-dated webpage, listing available job opportunities and qualified teachers from all over Italy would be entitled to apply directly to the schools, which would make the final decision over the appointment. Instead of liberalising the appointment of teachers in this (or some other) way, the state has preferred to keep the tangled network of *provveditorati* alive – and Italian schools will remain under an inefficient central direction that has little or nothing to do with modern principles of deregulation and flexibility. Nevertheless, an important degree of decentralisation will be accorded by the attribution to the regions of the administrative task of providing professional training and the integration of education with work.

Implementing the 112/98 decree is likely to prove a huge task. Article 3 allowed the regions only six months to provide a detailed plan, articulated in regional laws, of how they would allocate the hundreds of new responsibilities within their territory. Early signs in this regard are quite good. Emilia-Romagna, for instance, by the summer of 1998 had already compiled a draft regional law, containing 233 articles, that outlined clearly which tier of local government would perform which function and which also abrogated some 117 regional statutes and numerous lesser regulations. Other regions, including Venetia, Lombardy and Tuscany, had also taken rapid steps towards implementing the 112/98 decree.[7] Some regions have lagged behind, however, and these risk having the necessary legal framework imposed upon them by the central government, which is explicitly empowered to arrogate this responsibility to itself by the 59/97 law in cases where the regional assemblies have failed to fulfil their statutory duty. In a sense, however, it is possible to make excuses for even the slowest of the regions since the central state has signally failed to specify, even in general terms, by how much local government's share of tax revenues will be increased, and therefore it is far from clear which responsibilities can be assumed and which cannot.

In this regard, the failure of the Bicamerale in the Spring of 1998 has thrown a shadow over the process of implementing the 112/98 decree. Article 62 of the draft law drawn up by the Bicamerale would possibly have provided two sources for substantial financial autonomy for the regions. Firstly, it guaranteed that tiers of subnational government would get one half of the money raised in taxation once monies for servicing the public debt, coping with natural disasters, financing defence, and providing for a solidarity fund to assist the poorer regions had been subtracted. Joined to their existing tax-raising powers these allocations would have ensured that the increased responsibilities transferred to local government could be immediately financed. Secondly, Article 62 promised to transfer all necessary state property for the fulfilment of local government's new administrative responsibilities to the regions and provinces. In the absence of this provision, local government's power to overcome bureaucratic opposition to regionalisation has been sensibly reduced. More generally, the regions, after scrambling to draft plans for the reorganisation of the responsibilities given to them by decree 112/98, will find themselves in the uncomfortable position of knowing that the extent to which they can implement their plans is at the discretion of the ministers holding the purse strings. The speed and thoroughness with which decentralisation is carried out will depend upon the amount of new money released by Rome.

The United Conference

The question of finance only underscores the crucial importance for the future of Italian local government of the most significant institutional innovation launched by the Bassanini process: the so-called 'United Conference' of representatives from local government. The need for this body was signalled in Article 9 of the 59/97 law, which delegated the government to issue a decree that 'defined and widened' the powers belonging to two already existing coordinating bodies, the 'Permanent Conference for Relations between the State, the Regions and the Autonomous Provinces of Trento and Bolzano' and the 'State-City and Local Autonomy Conference'. By decree 281/97, published in the *Gazzetta Ufficiale* on 30 August 1997, this obligation was fulfilled. Article 8 of the decree specified the composition of the new body, which is chaired by the prime minister or by either the minister of the interior or the minister for regional affairs. The ministers for the treasury, the budget, finance, public works and health may also participate. The regions are represented by their presidents; the provinces by the president of UPI and six other provincial presidents indicated by the same body; the cities by the president of ANCI and fourteen fellow mayors. This mini-legislature – the expression is chosen deliberately – was given the task in decree 281/97 of finding the common ground in any policy matter concerning local government; with expressing an opinion on the annual budget and legislation connected to it; with making a judgment on the government's long-term economic strategy; with acting as the forum for decision-making on the enactment of the two Bassanini laws. In addition, the 'Permanent Conference for Relations between the State, the Regions and the Autonomous Provinces of Trento and Bolzano' has acquired an important role in the making of European policy. Article 4 of decree 281/97 indicates that this body will meet twice a year to ensure that the foreign ministry is aware of the regional viewpoint on forthcoming European legislation, to express an opinion on the annual transformation into Italian law of Community directives, to designate representatives of the regions at Brussels, and to give the state advice on drafting legislation to harmonise Italian law with Community norms. The 'Permanent Conference' will also be in charge of ensuring that Italy finally spends the funds paid out to it by the EU for economic modernisation and social development.

As yet the United Conference is not endowed with its own secretariat (Article 10 of decree 281/97 did not provide for a permanent bureaucracy but insisted that the two subordinate conferences should provide the logistical support), but its eventual transformation into a fully fledged institution is surely only a question of time. The unified conference was the seat of the decisive meetings which hastened the passage of decree 112/98 and, in fact, a close reading of the decree reveals that the United Conference will have a tremendously significant role to play in the development of Italian local government. The eighth paragraph of Article 7 in decree 112/98 confers upon it the positive role of 'promoting agreements' between the government and the layers of local administration, while paragraphs 10 and 11 of the same article give it the task of pressing the government if the central administration proves tardy or evasive in transferring human and financial resources from the centre to the periphery. In effect, the United Conference is to be the watchdog that ensures that both the spirit and the letter of the 59/97 law is fulfilled.

The Bicamerale

A body as politically significant as the United Conference, whose powers and functions give the periphery an influential voice in central policy-making, constitutes a qualititive shift in the structure of the Italian state. This was recognised during the deliberations of the Bicamerale in 1997. The text presented to parliament on November 4, 1997, reserved Article 76 of the revised Constitution for a description of the United Conference's activities and role. The subsequent failure of the Bicamerale's proposals in the Spring of 1998 has of course rendered void this innovation along with the other changes introduced by the committee and will certainly complicate the transition of functions from the centre to the periphery.

The Bicamerale ground to a halt, moreover, right at the moment that a compromise, regarded as reasonable by the regions and by the lower tiers of administration, had been reached to reorganize the state on more overtly federal lines than conceded by the draft bill submitted to parliament by the committee on constitutional reform. This compromise emerged in the course of the parliamentary debate on the bill following representations from the Conference of Regional Presidents and ANCI, which put forward a joint list of amendments to the Chamber of Deputies.

The Bicamerale's final draft attempted in Article 58 to give a definite list of the functions that would henceforth be the prerogative of the central state and stated specifically that the regions would legislate in all other areas. Both the regions and ANCI found that the description of the state's powers in Article 58 was 'too extensive and, above all, too elastic' since it included 20 specific areas of policy and also attributed to the state the power permanently to impose general guidelines in a raft of further areas including education, the universities, work-place regulations and the environment.[8] The implication of this sweeping retention of powers was that the decentralisation process begun by the 59/97 law would end with the 112/98 decree rather than be the harbinger of a controlled further extension of responsibilities to the regions. For the regions in particular, this was not good enough. They believed strongly that the Bassanini laws should be only a starter before the main course of outright federalism and suspected that unless a federalist orientation was written into the Constitution then the gains of the Bassanini laws might be nibbled away over time by a state bureaucracy reluctant to surrender its powers.

Article 60 of the draft law (supplanting the much more centralist Article 123 of the existing Constitution) did permit the regions to define their own form of government, electoral law, principles of taxation and legislative procedures without reference to the final opinion of the central government. Following the model of the recent reforms to provincial and municipal administrations, the regions and ANCI also proposed that article 60 should contain a constitutional requirement for the direct election of regional presidents, a provision which was regarded as likely to increase the stability and authority of the regional governments. They further asked for the creation of 'Regional Councils of the Autonomies', local 'senates' composed of mayors, provincial presidents and regional councillors that would involve the main authorities *within* each region in the process of guiding and managing the extended powers being conferred upon all levels of local government. In another step that was clearly inspired by the German model, it was further proposed that certain big cities (Rome, Bari, Bologna, Florence, Genoa, Naples, Turin and Venice), already designated as metropolitan areas by the 1990 local government reforms, should become mini-regions, like Hamburg, Bremen and Berlin, able to determine their own statute and to substitute municipal government for the wasteful layer of provincial government.

Further amendments proposed by the regions and ANCI, in fact, would have deconstitutionalised the provincial level of government. Article 114 of the 1948 Constitution states that the Italian Republic is divided into 'regions, provinces and municipalities'. In the amendments suggested by ANCI and the regions, the provinces would simply have become 'intercommunal associative forms': mere extensions of the municipalities controlled by the local mayors. The chief source of bureaucratic overlap at present clearly is at provincial level, with this older tier of local government retaining responsibilities and decision-making powers that have become anachronistic. The regions' desire to downgrade the provincial authorities, however, was fraught with political consequences and unsurprisingly was not given a proper hearing. Bowing to political realities, ANCI and the regions have since taken the opposite route and are distributing significant responsibilities to the provinces as part of the process set in motion by the 112/98 decree. Nevertheless, as in the cases of ANAS and the *provveditorati*, the political cost of root-and-branch reform to ingrained bureaucracies can be seen to have prevailed over the eminently rational reform initially proposed.

The regions and the municipal authorities were also anxious to write the prospect of a further expansion of regional authority into the Constitution. Article 57 of the draft produced by the Bicamerale stated that 'particular forms and conditions of autonomy' *might* be extended to regions other than those already possessing a special statute (Trentino-Alto Adige, Val D'Aosta, Friuli-Venezia-Giulia, Sicily and Sardinia). The regions' proposed amendment pinned down this ambiguity and insisted that regions currently subject to 'ordinary' status would have the right to ask parliament to grant them powers over policy areas reserved for the state in Article 58: in effect, to ask for 'special' status. In the case of Venetia, where frustration with the inadequacies of central government is by now almost at boiling point, this question became a political issue within a few weeks of the regions' submitting their amendment. The pressure coming from the north east led to the powers-that-be in the Bicamerale to make further changes to the articles dealing with the 'Form of the State' and to secure parliamentary approval for an amendment to article 57 which would have allowed 'ordinary' regions to be granted special status upon a majority vote by both chambers of parliament and subsequent approval in a regional referendum.

Moreover, after much hesitation, the leading lights in the presidency of the Bicamerale had also seemingly come to the conclusion that it was necessary to transform the Senate into a chamber that represented regional interests, rather than go along with the frankly unconvincing reform (the establishment of special sessions of the Senate, attended by representatives from the regions in addition to ordinary senators) proposed by the Bicamerale in November of the previous year. This softening towards one of the most longstanding demands put forward by local government was regarded as being a major shift towards federalism.

Federalism or Decentralisation?

There is a sense in which the current debate over the organisation of the functions of the state reproposes an antique debate that is nearly as old as Italy itself. After the Risorgimento, the politicians of the so-called 'historic right' had to deal with the problem of governing a country that was deeply divided geographically, economically, linguistically and socially. At the risk of over-simplifying, they were faced with a choice between three main options: tight centralisation, administrative decentralisation or outright federalism. The first of these methods, which was the one chosen, is associated, historically, with the names of Urbano Rattazzi and Bettino Ricasoli. The second option was that preferred by Marco Minghetti, the third by radicals such as Carlo Cattaneo. The Bassanini laws essentially constitute a large step in Republican Italy's overdue transition from a centralised to a Minghettian state. As even a brief study of Minghetti's minor classic of institutional analysis, *I partiti politici e la loro ingerenze nella pubblica amministrazione* (1883), illustrates, for Minghetti, decentralisation of government was the most practical method of ensuring that the delicate relationship between an invasive, growing, state and the rights of the citizen was not unbalanced. He envisaged, therefore, that peripheral offices of the central state in any given territory should be managed locally, with all decisions on hiring clerks and deciding procedures being carried out by the chief local officials without reference to Rome. Provincial budgeting could be decided by a simple block grant, which the local officials then assigned according to their own, local, priorities. Regions could be established with authority over prisons, hospitals, public roads, lakes and rivers, agriculture, regulation of industry and commerce, forests, hunting, education, libraries and so on. In part, these tasks could also be filled by what Minghetti called 'moral agencies' such as the universities, religious bodies and commercial associations. His main point was that the central government should naturally handle matters of national concern such as defence, foreign policy, the legal system and general economic policy, but otherwise its principal task should be that of directing resources to the periphery either through grants or increasing local taxation rights. In Minghetti's view – which is likely to be widely shared in regional administrations over the next two years – there could be no local autonomy in the absence of clear, untrammelled sources of funding.[9]

This portrayal of Minghetti's ideas should not be regarded as being of merely historical curiosity. It depicts a quintessentially *liberal* approach to the empowering of local government. For Minghetti, the state should be decentralised because it makes the state less remote, more responsive to people's needs and, implemented properly, it allows for much greater efficiency in terms of public spending. Much of the work done by the Bassanini laws will indeed bring the state closer to its citizens and make the state work harder for its citizens' good. The laws will also free many institutions that had previously been held back by suffocating central controls to flourish and compete more effectively: the universities are the most glaring example in this regard. This is no small achievement and one that more than justifies the praise that has been directed Bassanini's way.

At the same time, far more could have been done to cut costs. A lingering fear of letting local affairs slip completely from central government control has led to too many policy areas being reserved for the competence of the state. The state will continue to set the norms in most fields while the regions scurry to apply them with whatever funds the state chooses to dole out. The experience of the USA in the 1980s, when Congress regularly established new programmes but failed to vote the funds to pay for them and burdened the states with the costs of these so-called 'unfunded mandates', seems a possible outcome of the Bassanini process. A system of mandatory block grants calculated on a pro capita basis, would have been a far more effective tool for keeping down public spending. It would, of course, make job losses certain in Rome. The same fear of job losses and social protest has also led to a number of 'useless agencies' being retained, has prevented a clear analysis of the institutional function of the provinces, and has ensured that no systematic attempt to overhaul the bureaucracy in Rome has been undertaken. How many central planners and writers of general guidelines need there be? As things stand, the right of central government officials to a four-hour day remains as intact as ever.

The Bassanini laws, in short, are a halfway house. It seems unlikely, however, that the process of building this house can be stopped abruptly now. As the amendments suggested by the regions to the Bicamerale illustrate, the Bassanini laws have not slaked the thirst of the Italian periphery for more devolution and for a more overtly 'liberal' approach to decentralisation. In a world in which dysfunctional public institutions can be a major competitive disadvantage for manufacturing industry, pressure for further local control, especially in Venetia and Lombardy, is unlikely to abate. The significance of the Bassanini laws, in other words, cannot be understood in isolation. They are a broadside in the wider battle of turning Italy into a more deregulated country. But that battle will be finally decided not in the regional, provincial and municipal assemblies, but in Rome. If the Bassanini laws are to become any more than a promising beginning, Italy's current crop of political leaders will have to make a decisive commitment to greater liberalisation of the state.

Notes

1. The author would like to thank Salvatore Vassallo for the timely and generous way in which he provided both documentary materials and advice. The main texts referred to in this article, the laws and decrees themselves, can all be downloaded from the webpage of the Italian parliament or studied in the *Gazzetta Ufficiale*. This article has deliberately tried to avoid overloading itself with footnotes by clearly referring the reader to the relevant articles of the original laws.

2. The 127/97 law, as Fabio Rugge immediately pointed out in an article in the 4/97 edition of *Il Mulino*, is essentially a continuation of the earlier 1990 restructuring of provincial and municipal administration.

3. Elena Saccenti, Sul processo di elaborazione del decreto, *Le istituzioni del federalismo*, XIX, July/August, 663-69.

4. Ibid. p. 669

5. Readers wishing to study the decree fully should read either (or both) the edition of *Le istituzioni del federalismo* cited above or the recent book edited by Giandomenico Falcon, *Lo stato autonomista*, Bologna: Il Mulino, 1998. Both volumes provide an article-by-article commentary on the decree and feature useful prefatory essays.

6. Roberto Bin, comment on the General Arrangements of the 112/98 decree in *Le istituzioni del federalismo*, op. cit. p. 495.

7. See Guerino D'Ignazio, 'L'attuazione legislativa da parte delle regioni del decreto legislativo 112/98: Struttura delle leggi e delegificazioni', forthcoming in *Le istituzioni del federalismo*.

8. *Emendamenti alla proposta della Commissione per le riforme costituzionali*, documented presented by ANCI and the Conference of Regional presidents, 20 January 1998.

9. Marco Minghetti, *I partiti politici e la loro ingerenza nell'amministrazione pubblica*, Milan: M&B Publishing, 1995, 143-53.

7

CHANGES TO THE ITALIAN BUDGETARY REGIME: THE REFORMS OF LAW NO. 94/1997

David Felsen

Introduction

A new budgetary regime governed budget preparation and management for the 1998 budget year. Law no. 94/1997 and its associated legislative decrees carried out important changes to the structure of the annual budget and the management of the budget within the public administration. The legislation also altered the structure of the ministries involved with budget management. The Ministry of the Budget and Economic Programming was incorporated into the structure of the Treasury Ministry. Law no. 94/1997 remains the most significant reform of the budgetary regime for a decade. Moreover the current legislation differs substantially from previous laws in its objectives. Whereas previous legislation aimed at increasing the efficiency and effectiveness of the budget approval process in parliament, the current legislation increases the efficiency and transparency of budget preparation and management (pre- and post-parliamentary) phases.

The implementation of law no. 94/1997 follows a period of impressive fiscal consolidation in Italy which began in the early 1990s. Confronting a debt to GDP ratio of greater than 100 percent in 1991, the country faced strong pressure from the European Union and international economic institutions to remedy its public finances. These pressures intensified in 1992 following the signing of the Maastricht Treaty on European Union. Currency turmoil in September 1992 and the lira's subsequent exit from the exchange rate mechanism forced the Italian government to implement immediate and extensive budget measures as part of a July 1992 mini-budget and the 1993 budget package. The weakened state of Italy's political parties, resulting from the discrediting of the political class by judicial investigations into corruption and the poor showing by traditional parties at the April 1992 election, facilitated the government's implementation of far-reaching budget provisions.

The reversal in public finance trends in 1992-93 began a process of fiscal consolidation which was continued by successive Italian governments during the 1993-1998 period. Italy recorded consistent primary budget surpluses, while the ratios of deficit and debt to GDP declined. Temporary one-off budget measures were accompanied by key structural reforms – most notably the two reforms to the pension system in 1992 and 1995. Following several years of deficit reduction, Italy satisfied most of the TEU convergence criteria[1] and in 1998 was invited to participate in the single currency along with ten other EU member states.

The ability of successive Italian governments to meet budget policy objectives aimed at fiscal restraint point to a strengthening of the executive's control over policy-making. The image of *penta-partito* coalitions succumbing to parliamentary resistance over budget policies during the 1980s has given way to an image of a strong executive that has the capacity to implement budget measures which conform to initial government targets and objectives. The current reforms implemented by law no. 94/1997 further consolidate the executive's control over budget management and increases centralised control over expenditure decisions. While the reforms also increase the transparency of the budget structure and the autonomy of spending ministries in the management of budget resources, they leave overall expenditure control within the hands of the Treasury Ministry.

Context of the Current Budget Reforms

Budgeting and public accounting practices of the Italian state were codified by the De Stefani legislation of 1923 and 1924. These norms underpinned budgeting and public finance management for over half a century.[2] Under the De Stefani laws the *Ragioneria generale dello Stato* (General Accounts Office or RGS) was given direct responsibility within the Treasury for budget preparation and management as well as for the verification of expenditure commitments. The RGS retains this central role in the budgetary process to this day.

The Republic's Constitution does not alter the norms governing budget preparation and management within the executive. Article 81 of the Constitution stipulates that the government must present an annual budget and its final budget accounts for parliamentary approval. It also stipulates that no new or higher expenditure may be introduced during the budget approval phase in parliament, but rather must be introduced with separate expenditure laws. Moreover, expenditure laws must indicate the financial means to cover the expenditure.

Article 81's restriction on the introduction of new expenditure into the annual budget effectively prevented the budget from becoming anything more than a formal authorisation law that recorded expenditure decisions already taken and inserted into individual expenditure laws. Parliament simply gave its approval to a formal document that it could not modify. Since the budget could not be used as an instrument of policy, the budget approval process in parliament remained a 'pointless ritual'.[3]

The late 1970s saw the introduction of a budget approval process more responsive to policy needs. The international economic crisis of that decade necessitated the implementation of legislative measures designed to increase domestic budget policy coordination between decision-makers in the executive and legislature with the aim of containing public expenditure and government deficits. The economic slowdown of this period, sparked by exchange rate instability stemming from the collapse of the Bretton Woods system and exacerbated by the oil price rise of 1973-74, manifested itself in terms of a decline in international trade and investment, financial and monetary instability and persistent inflation.[4]

Policy-makers of industrialised countries responded by implementing measures to control public expenditure. In the world's largest industrialised economy, the American Congress responded to the crisis by implementing the 1974 Budget and Impoundment Act with a view to altering expenditure practices. Two new budget committees were instituted and charged with approving binding budget resolutions that would shape the overall parameters of the annual budget. The new budget resolutions included figures for total spending, revenue, deficit and debt, as well as functional subtotals.[5]

In Italy, the inflationary effects of the global economic crisis were compounded by a strong rise in public expenditure which resulted from domestic policy choices made in the late 1960s and early 1970s. During this period there was a sharp increase in social spending due to the gradual extension of welfare coverage to private sector workers, the increase in budget transfers to welfare and local authorities, and the signing of new indexed wage agreements with trade unions – agreements that were more generous in Italy than elsewhere in the industrialised world.[6] As a consequence, while the country attempted to pursue more restrictive macro-economic policies geared towards stabilising the domestic economy during this period of international crisis, it was confronted by rising obligatory expenditure on social protection which served to increase overall deficit and debt levels during the 1970s and 1980s.

In the late 1970s Italy introduced legislative measures aimed at increasing budget policy coordination and containing public expenditure and deficit levels. Law no. 468/1978 reformed the system of budgeting and public accounting, introducing innovations to permit better short- and medium-term budget planning.[7] The legislation instituted the finance law as an instrument to reflect the annual financial and budget choices of government and parliament. The finance law was to be presented each year by government to parliament alongside the budget law. Unlike the formal budget authorisation law, the finance law could contain new substantive expenditure (and revenue) measures. These measures could be amended by parliament and in turn modify the budget authorisation law. Thus the introduction of the finance law created a more important role for parliament in the budget approval process and a mechanism for government and parliament to participate in the formulation of annual budget policy.

Law no. 468/1978 also introduced a three-year budget to enhance medium-term budget planning. The document was to provide policy-makers with a longer term perspective of budget trends based on existing legislation. However the new three-year budget had a limited impact on medium-term budget planning not least of all because the document was not binding on policy-makers. Its contents and objectives received considerably less attention from policy-makers than the annual financial law.

First presented as part of the 1979 budget package, the finance law quickly became the source of intense political conflict in the council of ministers and in parliament. Parliamentary groups exercised their new capacity to modify budget provisions through the finance law by inserting vast amounts of micro-amendments in order to satisfy a plethora of interests. The finance law had become a sort of 'omnibus' law that proved ineffective in controlling spending, deficit and debt totals.

During the 1980s the government was often forced to authorise provisional budgets as a result of parliament's failing to approve the budget and finance laws by the 31 December deadline. The government saw its policy objectives repeatedly diluted as it was forced to make concessions or face delays in the budget approval process in parliament. Since the finance law was generally approved in a form much different from how it was presented by the government, policies aimed at public expenditure containment met with failure. The 1980s witnessed a rise in deficit and debt totals due to the growth in social spending and high real interest rates. Budget outturns saw deficit/GDP ratios of around 10 percent or higher throughout most of the 1980s.[8]

The 1980s also witnessed changes to parliamentary procedures and legislation geared towards increasing discipline in the parliamentary approval process. In 1983 the 'budget session' was introduced into the parliamentary rules of the Chamber of Deputies.[9] These new rules introduced a strict timetable for the discussion and approval of the budget and finance laws in the permanent commissions, budget commissions and assemblies. The budget session was to last from 1 October until 31 December during which parliamentary activity was to focus on the annual budget package.[10] In the late 1980s further modifications were carried out to parliamentary procedures. A more rigorous timetable for the presentation of budget and financial documents was introduced as were stricter limits on the introduction of amendments to the budget package.[11]

In addition to changes in parliamentary procedures, further legislative changes to the budgeting regime were carried out in 1988. Law no. 362/1988 introduced measures to correct the flaws of the budgetary regime created by law no. 468/1978.[12] The key objective of the legislation was to return to the finance law its original function as an instrument primarily designed to set public finance targets and limits. Substantive budget measures were removed from the annual finance law so that the document would only indicate public finance objectives and targets that set overall limits to budget choices. The substantive budget measures were inserted into *leggi collegati* or 'accompanying provisions' to the budget package. The provisions were to be presented with the finance and budget laws. The removal of substantive budget measures from the finance law was intended to reduce the political conflict surrounding this document, thereby improving the efficiency of the budget approval process in parliament.

Law no. 362 also implemented the Economic and Financial Planning Document (DPEF) to improve medium-term planning effectiveness. The DPEF would be presented by the Treasury Minister to parliament each spring and would set three-year public finance objectives and limits. The document was to be examined in budget commissions and in the assemblies in a 'mini-budget session'. Moreover, Parliament would be obliged to approve a binding resolution on the DPEF. The budget package presented in autumn-would be bound to the objectives and targets stipulated in the previous spring's DPEF for both short- and medium-term expenditure decisions.

These innovations to Italy's budgetary regime that were designed to contain public finances in the short and medium terms were employed in the preparation and presentation of the 1989 budget. However it was plain to observers that these legislative and procedural reforms would not be sufficient to bring about an improvement in public finances and a reversal in deficit and debt levels in relation to GDP.[13] Following the initial year of operation of law no. 362 the public sector deficit fell to 9.9 percent of GDP, but rose to over 10 percent of GDP in 1990 and 1991. Improvement to Italy's public finance position could not result merely from changes to the budgetary regime.

Public Finances in the 1990s

During the early 1990s budget reform remained high on the political agenda and numerous proposals were presented aimed at rationalising the budgetary process by simplifying budget management procedures and increasing the transparency of budget classification.[14] While additional fundamental changes to the budgetary regime were not implemented during this period, a reversal in public expenditure trends did indeed come about as a result of external pressures and domestic political developments.[15]

Italy's public finances worsened considerably at the end of 1991. Its debt/GDP ratio stood at over 100 percent while its budget out-turn overshot estimates by L20,000 billion.[16] Italy's signing of the Maastricht Treaty in February 1992 increased the financial market and EU scrutiny of its public finance position.[17] The EU and other international institutions such as the OECD issued warnings to Italy to remedy its public finance situation. Scepticism over Italy's commitment to fiscal restraint was compounded by growing uncertainty over the Maastricht project in general following the Danish rejection of the treaty in a referendum and the potential French rejection of the treaty in a September referendum. These factors contributed to continued Lira instability, forcing the Bank of Italy to hike up interest rates. The instability eventually culminated in the Lira's devaluation and exit from the exchange rate mechanism in September 1992.

Accompanying these strong external pressures was growing turmoil on the domestic political front. The judicial investigations into political corruption which began in February 1992 led to the resignation of many politicians and the discrediting and weakening of the old political party system. Furthermore, the April 1992 vote saw a decline in electoral support for traditional parties and the concurrent rise in support for anti-system political parties such as the separatist Northern League.[18] As a result, the Amato government which was formed in June 1992 found itself in a position of far greater autonomy vis-à-vis political parties than its predecessors as regards budget policy choices.

Amid financial crisis and confronting a divided and discredited Parliament, the Amato government successfully implemented by decree a July mini-budget to curb public finance trends for 1992.[19] The Amato government forced through the package employing repeated warnings to politicians and the Italian public of the dire consequences of failing to solve Italy's crisis in public finances. Following the September exit of the lira from the ERM and in an attempt to regain the confidence of financial markets and the EU, the Amato government pushed the 1993 budget package through Parliament, employing threats and warnings in order to ensure that the far-reaching measures were passed.

The budget package for 1993 consisted of provisions to cut expenditure and increase revenue over current public finance trends by a combined total of L93,000bn ($51bn). The government implemented the legislation by employing a series of decree laws and by obtaining delegated authority from parliament to issue legislative decrees. The package consisted of one-off measures and structural reforms, most notably the first significant reform of the pension system. The mini-budget of July 1992 reduced the overall borrowing requirement for 1992 to below 10 percent and resulted in a primary budget surplus of 1.9 percent. This was followed by a primary budget surplus for 1993 of 2.6 percent.[20]

Fiscal restraint was continued under successive governments during the 1993-98 period. The 'technical' government led by former Bank of Italy governor Carlo Azeglio Ciampi, relying on the support of the Left in Parliament, exploited the external pressures on Italy to force through tough fiscal measures in the 1994 budget aimed at reducing the deficit. Subsequently, the short-lived Berlusconi government elected in March 1994 was also able to obtain parliamentary support for the 1995 budget in spite of the inherent weaknesses in the coalition and Berlusconi's personal legal troubles. The 1995 budget outturn resulted in a primary budget balance of 4.4 percent and a reduction of the deficit to 7.0 percent of GDP.[21]

The mandate of the 'technical' government led by Lamberto Dini was to make further progress in deficit reduction in order to meet the convergence criteria as well as to carry out a second structural reform of the pension system. In the summer of 1995, the Dini government successfully negotiated changes to the pension system with trade unions, resulting in a more rapid harmonisation of the pension system across worker categories and the gradual elimination of seniority pensions.[22] The pension reform was inserted into the 1996 budget package which obtained rapid parliamentary approval with the support of the Left. The 1996 budget outturn saw a primary surplus of 4.0 percent and while the deficit fell to 6.7 percent of GDP.[23]

The process of fiscal consolidation was continued by the government of Romano Prodi, whose centre-left *Ulivo* coalition came to power after the April 1996 election with the support of the PDS and centrist parties, and with the outside support of the refounded communists (RC). The government aimed to bring the deficit/GDP ratio down to the 3 percent level required by the convergence criteria with its 1997 budget package measures. The L78,500 billion ($47.5 billion) budget package received the coalition's support and the external support of the RC in Parliament, passing rapidly through the two assemblies. However additional corrective measures during the 1997 budget exercise were necessary to ensure that the government met its target objectives. The budget outturn saw a primary surplus of 6.7 percent of GDP in 1997 and a deficit/GDP ratio of 3 percent. Debt levels also continued to decline, falling from a peak of 124.9 percent of GDP in 1995 to 123.8 percent in 1996 to 122.6 percent in 1997.[24]

The 1998 budget package was approved amidst intense political conflict. The differences in budget priorities between *Ulivo* and RC came to the surface as RC demanded economic policies geared towards employment creation and the implementation of a thirty-five-hour week, while *Ulivo* impressed upon Parliament the need to continue prioritising fiscal consolidation in order to ensure Italy's participation in the single currency. Following Bertinotti's decision to oppose the 1998 budget package, the RC was criticised not only by the government and the PDS, but also by the Italian public and trade unions for attempting to sabotage Italy's efforts at fiscal consolidation. The RC had underestimated the significance of the European constraint and the importance that participation in the single currency held for Italian policy-makers, interest groups and the electorate at large. In the end, *Ulivo* obtained parliamentary support for the 1998 budget package by the end of December. The 1998 budget is expected to bring the deficit down to 2.7 percent of GDP.[25]

The consistent deficit-reducing policies pursued by successive Italian governments during the 1990s resulted in consistent primary surpluses and the gradual reduction of borrowing to below 3 percent of GDP. In addition, it set into motion the gradual reduction of debt/GDP ratios in 1996 and 1997. Italy also satisfied Maastricht criteria for inflation, interest rates and exchange rate stability, and demonstrated that its debt/GDP ratio was declining at a sufficient rate.[26] In May 1998, the country was selected to participate in the single currency set to come into existence in January 1999.

The process of fiscal consolidation witnessed in recent years was carried out by successive governments who were able to exercise greater control over budget policy and the management of public finances. The emergence of stronger executive policy coordination and more favourable budget outcomes came in the wake of strong external pressures which forced Italy to implement deficit-cutting measures, and was facilitated by the existence of a weakened and divided parliament that acquiesced to measures aimed at fiscal restraint. Following the initial 1992-93 period of financial crisis and domestic instability, a series of strong political and 'technical' executives emerged to continue the process of fiscal consolidation under EU scrutiny, utilising the convergence criteria as public finance targets.

The current measures implemented with law no. 94/1997 aim to reinforce and complement the process of fiscal consolidation through the modification and strengthening of the administrative structures within the executive that manage public finances. Law no. 94/1997 increases efficiency, transparency and administrative autonomy in budget management and strengthens centralised control within the ministries involved in public expenditure coordination.

The Current Reforms

Italy's public finance efforts throughout the 1990s have permitted the country to participate in the single currency. In addition, these efforts have also set into motion a process of strengthening the institutions responsible for budget management. Previous reforms focused on improving the effectiveness of the budget approval phase in parliament. However law no. 94/1997 increases the efficiency and transparency in budget management and simplifies the budget classification structure in order to link the new budget structure more closely to the administrative centres that manage budget resources and to the centres responsible for budget accounting. In this way, public policy objectives of government may better correspond to the activities of the public administration and to the evaluation of budget accounts. The current reforms also rationalise the ministerial structures responsible for public finance management by incorporating the offices of the Ministry for the Budget and Economic Programming into the Treasury Ministry.

Law no. 94/1997 is preceded by other recent reforms to the public administration that served to increase transparency and efficiency of services. Law no. 241/1990 adopted a uniform system of administrative procedures to simplify bureaucracy in order to increase the efficiency and transparency of the administration and its links to citizens. Law no. 142/1990 simplified procedures at the local level and created new institutional arrangements between the central state and communes and provinces. Legislative decree no. 29/1993 introduced a series of reforms to the state administration, including the privatisation of public employment, in order to increase the efficiency and bring the Italian administration in line with other European systems. The reform of public finance management within local authorities was carried out with legislative decree no. 77/1995.[27]

The most recent reforms, law no. 59/1997 (the Bassanini reforms) and law no. 127/1997, introduced some of the most important innovations, the former legislation presenting to parliament a request for delegated authority to issue legislative decrees to carry out extensive modifications of the public administration (see the contribution by Mark Gilbert in this volume).

Building upon previous reforms to the public administration, law no. 94/1997 introduces greater transparency and efficiency in budget management. The legislation presented by the Prodi government in 1997 included a request for 'delegated authority'. This legislative instrument sanctioned by Articles 76 and 77 of the Constitution allows government to ask parliament to authorise the issue of further 'legislative decrees' without further parliamentary approval in order to implement large-scale reform measures rapidly and efficiently. In its request for delegated authority, the government is required to indicate the objectives of the reform measures, the extent of the measures and the time required to exercise the delegated authority.[28]

Two key legislative decrees were issued based upon the delegated authority that the Prodi government was granted by Parliament. Legislative decree no. 279/1997 outlined the reform for the budget classification structure and budget management. Legislative decree no. 430/1997, as well as the implementing presidential decrees (DPRs) no. 38/1998 and no. 154/1998, outlined the structure of the new Ministry of the Treasury, Budget and Economic Programming.

Legislative decree no. 279/1997 was implemented prior to the approval of the 1998 budget.[29] The decree aims to increase the transparency of the budget structure by reducing the number of budget classification units that require parliamentary approval and by increasing the relevance of the budget structure to government policy implementation. The new units subject to parliamentary approval are aggregated in such a way that they correspond to administrative centres of budget resource management.

Budget classification of expenditure changes from the previous four-tiered system to a three-tiered one which corresponds to centres of budget management within the public administration. The old budget classification system comprised: *titles*, which divided expenditure by current spending, capital investments and loan repayments; *rubrics*, which divided expenditure according to the administrative apparatus charged with managing the resources; *categories*, which divided expenditure according to its economic nature; and *chapters*, the basic units of expenditure, divided according to individual expenditure items. Under the old budget classification system, parliament was charged with approving the 5,000 chapters of expenditure. As a consequence, it proved difficult for policy-makers to view how the individual budget chapters subject to parliamentary approval related to overall policy objectives and spending choices.

The key innovation of the budget classification reform is that parliament now approves more aggregate units of expenditure. The 1998 budget is divided into three classifications. The 'functions-objective' classification is the most aggregate level of expenditure and indicates the total public resources committed to particular sectors of public administration intervention. The 'basic forecasting units' are the principal units for public accounting and budgeting and are subject to parliamentary approval. These units correspond to administrative centres responsible for the management of budget resources within the public administration. Finally, chapters remain the most basic units of classification. However, chapters no longer constitute the units subject to parliamentary approval. The current legislation also authorises the reorganisation of chapter classifications. For the 1998 budget, legislative decree no. 279/1997 has implemented approximately 800 'sub-forecasting units' to serve as the units subject to parliamentary approval – a lower level of aggregation than envisaged by law no. 94, though still a marked improvement over the previous system in terms of the transparency of the budget structure and efficiency of budget approval.

Legislative decree no. 279/1997 also changes the procedures of budget management. It increases the autonomy of spending ministries and their flexibility in budget management and control. The new administrative centres responsible for budget resource management are each headed by a director-general who is responsible for managing the budget resources which correspond to the budget's basic forecasting units. The director-general is responsible for managing all human and financial resources and has the power to limit spending of other directors within individual administrative centres. Administrative centres within spending ministries have the autonomy to reallocate budget resources between chapters within the same basic forecasting unit. The director-general that manages the administrative centre has the authority to issue a request to reallocate resources between chapters. The request must be communicated to the relevant spending minister who issues a decree and communicates the reallocation of budget resources to the Treasury and to the relevant parliamentary commissions. However, if the expenditure is reallocated between ministries, it must still be approved by the 'budget adjustment law' presented each June to parliament.[30] Thus while the spending ministries have gained greater autonomy in management and reallocation of budget resources, their independence is offset by Treasury control over the verification of financial transactions.

Legislative decree no. 279 also changes final budget accounting. The final budget accounts are also structured according to the new three-tiered classification system. The new accounting system is based on analysis which links budget resources committed to administrative centres to the results obtained in the final budget accounts. The new accounting system is better able to evaluate the efficiency and effectiveness of the management of budget resources within the public administration by monitoring costs, yields and results of administrative activity.

In sum, legislative decree no. 279/1997 permits policy-makers a better understanding of how chapters of budget expenditure translate into public policy. It increases the transparency of the link between the budget classification structure and the management of budget resources, and more effectively bridges the budget approval and budget management phases. The implementation of these measures is overseen by a bicameral commission, instituted in accordance with Article 9 of law no. 94/1997, while the new procedures are to be incorporated into a single text of procedures and legislation that discipline budgeting and public accounting. Finally, legislative decree no. 279 replaces budget planning based on incrementalism by a system of programme-based budgeting which evaluates costs and analyses resource efficiency of the public administration and its capacity for carrying out programme objectives. This legislation marks a departure away from incrementalist budget calculations in favour of non-incrementalist programme-based calculations of budget expenditure.

Legislative decree no. 430 and its implementing presidential decrees of 1998 (DPR no. 38/1998 and no. 154/1998) contain measures to incorporate the functions and offices of the budget ministry into a restructured Ministry of the Treasury, Budget and Economic Programming.[31] The Budget Ministry, whose chief role had been to promote economic development through public investment projects is incorporated into the Treasury structure. The role of the Inter-ministerial Committee for Economic Programming (CIPE) has been reduced as have the number and sizes of other inter-ministerial committees.

The new Treasury Ministry comprises four departments: department of the treasury; department of the RGS; department of development and cohesion policies; department of general administration, personnel and services. This first department comprises six directorates and is the former directorate of the treasury within the old Treasury Ministry. It is responsible for economic and financial policies including public debt issue and external economic relations. These offices played a central role in negotiating the Maastricht treaty in 1991 and the importance of these offices has increased in recent years as a result of growing European economic and financial coordination. The second department incorporates the formerly autonomous RGS into a full department. The RGS is divided into nine inspectorates and plays a pivotal role in budgeting and public finance management. The third department incorporates the offices and functions of the former Budget Ministry. The department is divided into central services that are functional equivalents to directorates. These central services are responsible for territorial development, EU structural funds policies, and the CIPE secretariat. The department manages state interventions and local development programmes, as well as the relationship between the state and regions. The fourth department is responsible for personnel, coordination of general affairs, provincial and local offices of the ministry, and information technology systems.

In addition to these four departments, the legislation establishes new technical-scientific committees. The old technical-scientific councils have been replaced by three new bodies: the technical-scientific council of experts which falls under the jurisdiction of the department of the treasury within the Ministry; the technical commission for public expenditure which is directly responsible to the minister; and the national centre for public accounts which is responsible to the department of the RGS.

Other nondepartmental organs in the new ministry include the *cabina di regia nazionale* which is directly responsible to the minister for coordinating the use of community structural funds in conjunction with the departments for development and cohesion policies and the RGS; the *nucleo tecnico di valutazione* which evaluates public investments and is responsible to the department for development and cohesion policies, and supports the activities of CIPE; and the General Budget Office which is responsible to the department of the RGS and evaluates expenditure commitments.

The restructuring of the Treasury Ministry and its incorporation of the offices of the Budget Ministry into its structure rationalises and increases the efficiency of that part of the executive most closely involved with public expenditure control. It fully institutionalises the RGS – the key actor involved in public expenditure control within the Treasury – by making this formerly autonomous agency into a full department. It further centralises control over public expenditure in the hands of the executive. It thus counterbalances the increased autonomy of spending ministries in resource management with more centralised 'guardian' control over total expenditure. This reform serves to improve executive control over public finances and further institutionalises executive budget coordination at the level of the public administration.

Conclusions

The increased administrative transparency and efficiency introduced by law no. 94 not only follows but is also a product of the process of fiscal consolidation that began in 1992. It is the first significant legislative innovation to change budgeting and public finance management in Italy since 1988 and differs from the previous reform of 1988 in its objectives. While the earlier legislation aimed to increase the efficiency of the budget approval phase in parliament, the latter changes the budget structure and budget management procedures in the public administration. In addition, it rationalises the Treasury Ministry, the key guardian in public finance management, by incorporating the Budget Ministry's offices into its structure.

While changes in the 1980s to legislation and parliamentary procedures governing the budgetary process were necessary for the observed budget discipline recorded in later years, these changes were not in themselves sufficient to reverse public finance trends of the 1980s and early 1990s. Increasing external pressures and domestic political factors were also important in bringing about a reversal in public finance trends. Growing pressures to improve public finances came from the European Union, following the signing of the Maastricht Treaty in February 1992, and from financial markets who signalled their disquiet over Italy's public finances by increasing their speculative pressure against the lira and forced its eventual exit from the exchange rate mechanism in September 1992. The strong external pressures on Italy to correct public finances limited the policy choices of the Amato government in 1992-93.

The Amato government's capacity to implement strict deficit-cutting measures was facilitated by the weakened state of the traditional political parties following the initiation of judicial investigations into political corruption and the electoral losses of the major political parties in the April 1992 poll. The government was able to instrumentalise the warnings of the EU, as well as financial market instability, to impose far-reaching measures on a weakened and divided parliament. The Amato government's mini-budget and 1993 budget package resulted in primary budget surpluses for 1992 and 1993, beginning a process of fiscal consolidation which was carried on by successive Italian governments during the 1993-98 period.

With the Maastricht convergence criteria serving as public finance targets, and persistent EU scrutiny, successive governments were able to pursue budget policies which further reduced public expenditure and deficit levels. Throughout the post-1992 period government budget policy objectives met with greater success and crucial structural reforms were carried out. Governments of the 1992-98 period demonstrated more cohesive budget policy coordination than previous Italian governments in the 1980s.

It is significant that the recent reforms come during a period of stronger executive policy coordination and that they are part of the process of ongoing fiscal consolidation. While the Italian experience has demonstrated that changes to the rules governing the budgetary regime alone are not sufficient to bring about fiscal consolidation, it may be true that these reforms, which come after a period of successful fiscal restraint that entailed strong centralised executive control, will help consolidate and strengthen that control. Law no. 94/1997 further increases the executive's control over public expenditure by improving efficiency, transparency and control in budget management. This reform is an important step in consolidating public finance gains of recent years, for while it increases the autonomy of the spending ministries, it strengthens the guardians of the budgetary process.

Notes

1. Italy has satisfied the Maastricht convergence criteria for inflation, interest rates, exchange rate stability and public sector deficits. While its debt/GDP ratio remains well above the 60 percent threshold, Italy has sufficiently demonstrated that debt levels are on the decline.
2. The De Stefani laws comprised R.D. no. 2440/1923 and R.D. no. 827/1924. see G. Vegas, 'Procedure di formazione del bilancio e della legge finanziaria: gov-

erno e Parlamento,' in D. Da Empoli, P. De Ioanna and G. Vegas, eds, *Il bilancio dello stato: La finanza pubblica tra governo e parlamento*, Milan: Il Sole-24 Ore, 1988, p.108; P. De Ioanna and G. Fotia, *Il bilancio dello stato: norme, istituzioni, prassi*, Rome: NIS, 1996, p. 25; P. Furlong, *Modern Italy: Representation and Reform*, London: Routledge, 1994, p. 205.

3. S. Cassese, 'Special Problems of Budgetary Decision-Making in Italy,' in D. Coombes, ed., *The Power of the Purse: The Role of European Parliaments in Budgetary Decisions*, London: Allen and Unwin, 1976, p. 254.

4. See A. Graziani, *Lo sviluppo dell'economia italiana*, Bologna: Mulino, 1992, pp. 102-112.

5. See Lance T. LeLoup, 'From Microbudgeting to Macrobudgeting: Evolution in Theory and Practice,' in I. Rubin, ed., *New Directions in Budget Theory*, Albany: SUNY, 1988, p. 25.

6. See G. Morcaldo, *La finanza pubblica in Italia*, Bologna: Mulino, 1993, pp. 65-73; see also M. Salvati, 'Muddling Through: Economics and Politics in Italy, 1969-1979,' in P. Lange and S. Tarrow, eds, *Italy in Transition: Conflict and Consensus*, London: Frank Cass, 1980, pp. 33-35; see also P. Lange, 'The End of an Era: The Wage Indexation Referendum of 1985,' in R. Leonardi and P. Nanetti, eds, *Italian Politics: A Review* 1, London: Pinter, 1986, p. 30.

7. For a discussion of law no. 468/1978 see R. D'Alimonte, 'Il processo di bilancio in Italia,' in G. Freddi, ed., *Scienza dell'amministrazione e politiche pubbliche*, Rome: NIS, 1989; see also Vegas 1988; see also R. Perez, 'Finanza, bilancio e contabilita pubblica,' in S. Cassese and C. Franchini, eds, *L'amministrazione pubblica italiana: un profilo*, Bologna: Mulino, 1994; see also V. Della Sala, 'The Italian Budgetary Process: Political and Institutional Constraints,' *West European Politics* 11, 3, (1988): pp. 110-125.

8. For a discussion of budgeting and budget policy in the 1980s, see L. Verzichelli, 'Le politiche di bilancio: Il debito pubblico da risorsa a vincolo' in M. Cotta and P. Isernia, eds. *Il gigante dai piedi di argilla: Le ragioni della crisi della prima repubblica. Partiti e politiche dagli anni '80 a mani pulite.* Bologna: Mulino, 1996.

9. The budget session was not incorporated into the Senate procedures until 1985. However, the timetable was employed on an experimental basis from 1983 onwards. For more details on the budget session procedures, see G. Fazio, *Il bilancio dello stato: La funzione e la gestione del bilancio nel sistema giuridico ed economico*, 4th edn, Milan: A. Giuffre, 1992, pp. 85-86; see also D'Alimonte 1989, p.184; see also Vegas 1988, p. 206.

10. Exceptions are made for international treaties which may be examined at this time.

11. See M. Meschino, 'Il Parlamento di spesa', *Quaderni costituzionali* 11, 2 (August 1991): pp. 373-74; see De Ioanna and Fotia 1996, pp.67-69; see also Perez 1994, pp.63-64.

12. For a discussion of law no. 362/1988 see P. De Ioanna, 'Dalla legge no. 468 del 1978 alla legge no. 362 del 1988: Note sul primo decennio di applicazione della "legge finanziaria"' *Quaderni costituzionali* 9, 2 (August 1989): pp. 205-27; see D'Alimonte 1989, pp. 178-80; see also F. Cavazzuti, 'Public Finance and Public Administration: Characteristics and Limitations of the New Finance Bill', in R. Catanzaro and R. Nanetti, eds, *Italian Politics: A Review*, London: Pinter, 1990.

13. Cavazzuti argued in 1990 that the changes in parliamentary procedures and legislation introduced in the late 1980s were not in themselves able to stabilise or reduce deficit and public debt in relation to GDP, and that further provisions would be needed in future; see Cavazzuti 1990, p. 22.

14. See G. Della Cananea, *Indirizzo e controllo della finanza pubblica*, Bologna: Mulino, 1996, p. 176 fn 7.

15. S. Vassallo, *La politica del bilancio: Le condizioni e gli effetti istituzionali della convergenza*. Paper presented at workshop: *Il cambiamento delle politiche e della politica nell'Italia degli anni Novanta*. Forlì, 17-18 December 1998. Forthcoming in G. Di Palma, S. Fabbrini and G. Freddi, eds., *La transizione. Politica e politiche pubbliche in Italia negli anni novanta*; see D. Felsen, 'Case Study of an Annual Budget Cycle: The Amato Government'. Contribution to ESRC Project on Core Executive Coordination. Directors: V. Wright and J. Hayward. Italy Director: D. Hine. Oxford, 1998.

16. See Bank of Italy, *Economic Bulletin* no. 18, February 1992.

17. The TEU convergence criteria for borrowing and debt in relation to GDP received the greatest scrutiny. The TEU stipulated a deficit/GDP ratio of 3 percent and a debt/GDP ratio of 60 percent. For a discussion of the Treaty on European Union, see N. Nugent, *The Government and Politics of the European Union*, 3rd edn, London: MacMillan, 1994, pp. 59-64.

18. The political changes of the early 1990s are discussed in James L. Newell and Martin Bull, *Party Organisations and Alliances in Italy in the 1990s: A Revolution of Sorts*, in M. Rhodes and M. Bull, eds, *Crisis and Transition in Italian Politics*, London: Frank Cass, 1997; see also G. Pasquino and P. McCarthy, eds, *The End of Post-War Politics in Italy: The Landmark 1992 Elections*, Boulder, Colo.: Westview Press, 1993.

19. See G. Amato, 'Un governo nella transizione. La mia esperienza di presidente del consiglio', *Quaderni costituzionali* 14, 3, December 1994.

20. Ministry of the Treasury, *Documento di programmazione Economica e Finanziaria*, 1996-98.

21. See Ministry of the Treasury, *Convergence Plan* (1997).

22. See O. Castellino, 'Pension Reform: Perhaps Not the Last Round,' *Italian Politics: A Review* 11 (1996).

23. Ministry of the Treasury, *Convergence Plan* (1997).

24. Ministero del tesoro, *Documento di programmazione Economica e Finanziario*, 1999-2001.

25. Ibid.

26. Ibid.

27. See Comitato Euro, Ministero del Tesoro, *Piano per l'Adozione dell'euro nelle Amministrazioni Pubbliche* (1997).

28. This was the legislative instrument used by the Amato government to implement parts of its 1993 budget package. see F. Sorrentino, 'Le fonti del diritto', in G. Amato and A. Barbera, eds, *Manuale di diritto pubblico*, Bologna: Mulino, 1994, pp. 143-46.

29. Legislative decree no. 279/1997 is based on article 5 of law no. 94/1997 which authorises government to issue a decree within 120 days of entry into force of law no. 94/1997 to identify new budget accounting units and new budget management procedures. see Camera dei deputati – Servizio studi, *Riforma del bilancio dello Stato. Il decreto legislativo no. 279/1997: Schede di lettura sul testo definitivo (XIII legislatura*, November 1997), pp. 3-7.

30. The *bilancio di assestamento* modifies the budget during the annual budget exercise. It is presented each June to parliament.

31. Article 7 of law no. 94/1997 authorised government to issue legislative decree no. 430/1997 within six months. See Camera dei deputati – Servizio studi, *Individuazione degli uffici di livello dirigenziale del Ministero del Tesoro, del bilancio e della programmazione economica: Schema di regolamento (XIII legislatura*, February 1998), pp.4-15.

8

Drafting the 1998
Legislation on Immigration:
A Test of Government Cohesion

David Hine

Introduction

Italy has had three major framework laws on immigration since the issue became a significant one at the start of the 1980s. The first was law no.943, 1986. The second was the so-called 'Martelli law' (law no.39, 1990). Thereafter, despite widespread agreement that the law remained seriously inadequate to cope with the fast-changing reality of Italy's exposure to new and much more intense flows of immigration, it proved impossible for eight years to secure agreement on further reform. Policy proceeded through fitful (and often unconverted) decree law, and short-term emergency provisions.

Immigration was therefore a dual challenge for the centre-left majority elected in 1996. It was firstly a test of its ability to combine a policy of social concern for the plight of desperate and vulnerable immigrants, with a policy of firm resistance to clandestine immigration to which Italy was increasingly exposed from the various sources in south-east Europe, the southern Mediterranean, and beyond. But it was also a test of executive cohesion. Immigration is a classic multidimensional, multidepartmental, and multi-institutional problem. It includes various types of problem, covers the remit of several departments of government, and is a policy area in which parliament has traditionally sought to intervene frequently and assertively in relation to the executive.

Key Policy Issues in the Immigration Sector

The background to immigration policy since Italy became a country of net inward migration in the early 1970s is well documented.[1] The problem is by European standards a recent one. Inflows exceeded outflows for the first time only in 1973. The change was partly the result of the change in the European labour market that generated a long-term rise in structural unemployment, and spelled the end of easy access for non-EC immigrants to France, Germany, and northern Europe in general. The tightening of Europe's immigration controls made Italy both a back-door route to the northern labour market, and an alternative to it for extra-EC flows of labour towards the continent as a whole.[2] Henceforth Italy became more attractive as an immigration target than in the past. These developments took place in parallel with the development of EC – enshrined in the Schengen Agreement – to remove physical borders between member states. Although not all states were required and/or permitted to participate in the arrangements from the outset, the strong Italian desire to become part of the Schengen area – finally achieved in 1998 – required the Italian authorities to begin to apply the same policies on visas, work-permits, asylum, family reunification, and external border policing as other EC states, and to cooperate closely with them.

The result of the delayed emergence of immigration meant that the changes of overall policy, legislation, structures, and social values made necessary by such developments had to be achieved more rapidly than in most other EC member states. This, and a delay in public recognition of the existence of the issue as a social problem, provoked potentially serious social tensions from the mid-1980s onwards, in a society where racial harmony had hitherto been the norm. Political instability in the former Yugoslavia, Africa, and the Middle East added to the problem in the 1990s, with periodic emergency flows of displaced persons which became very difficult to stop with the legislation and policing methods then in place.[3]

But Italy was not suddenly being swamped by immigrants it did not want. On the contrary, it is widely recognised that the Italian economy has over the last two decades had a significant need for immigrant labour. However, the nature of the need, and in particular the uncomfortable paradox that for many Italian businesses the immigrants they need are the clandestine ones, posed difficult dilemmas for the authorities. Italy in fact became an attractive location for illegal immigration not only because of its Mediterranean location, the short distance to Africa and south-east Europe, and the country's inevitably porous borders, but also because of its substantial black economy, and the growth of significant discontinuities in its labour market structure. Reconciling these conflicting tensions was thus extremely difficult. It was easy to say, as the left and the trade unions did, that the best way to combat exploitatively low wages and the black economy was to forge an alliance with illegal immigrants to bring them out of the shadows, and champion their rights to participate in the regulated labour market, and to enjoy access to social-service provision equal to that of Italian and EC workers. It was much less easy to achieve this when employers persisted in hiring on black-market terms, and threatened their clandestine migrant workers with the sack if they cooperated with the authorities.

Moreover the left itself, while against black-market labour, was nervous about the application of tough and automatic measures of arrest, detention, and forced repatriation of clandestine immigrant workers. In the 1990s, several powerful pressure groups have emerged to speak for the interests of all categories of immigrants, whether economic migrants, political refugees, or asylum-seekers, and their demands and outlooks have, by and large, been shared by trade unions and by the parties of both the left and the Catholic centre. The left's position on immigration reflected the strong commitment (at least at the ideological level) to broadly based social solidarity, as opposed to immediate job-protection, that has always characterised the union movement. The strong ideological charge which has made the unions relatively solidaristic in outlook across sectors, across income differentials, and across the divide between workers on the one hand and the unemployed and pensioners on the other, has also influenced their attitude towards immigrants, and has prevented a purely defensive response based on the maxim of 'Italian jobs for Italian workers'. The strength of the charitable sector, and the forum which it, and Italian unions, have in the CNEL, have also worked in this direction.

Policy thinking has therefore been influenced by strongly humanitarian impulses, and a relatively open approach, at least as far as entry policy, visas, and asylum have been concerned. Until the 1998 legislation, Italy had not even allowed the practice of administrative detention pending deportation hearings, except very exceptionally in the face of dramatic emergency influxes and serious manifestations of public disquiet. Yet, as almost all observers note, the humanitarian concerns have generally not been followed up with adequate measures to guarantee proper social support and social integration of immigrants, and even more seriously, a large black market in immigrant labour has continued to operate alongside the regulated market.

Policy Style in the Immigration Sector

A Multiplicity of Government Agencies

Immigration policy poses serious problems of interdepartmental coordination in the Italian context. Notwithstanding the important role played by the Ministry of the Interior, there is no dominant departmental actor in this sector. There are several reasons for this. In Italy as elsewhere, 'immigration' is a bundle of very diverse individual policies rather than a single policy. The Ministry of the Interior has responsibility for two main aspects of that bundle: physical control of admissions at the border, and internal policing of illegal residents and of social frictions. However, other no less fundamental policies are beyond its remit. These include: firstly, estimates of the labour-market needs to be filled by migrant labour, and management of the flow of such workers into jobs, which are both within the natural remit of the Ministry of Labour; secondly, relations between Italy and other countries, both within and beyond the European Union, that are affected by immigration, which are the preserve of the Ministry of Foreign Affairs; and thirdly the generation and coordination of policies to ensure the welfare and social integration of immigrants, which – since its establishment in 1990 – is primarily handled by the Department for Social Solidarity[4] inside the Presidency of the Council of Ministers.

Beyond this, there are several other aspects to immigration policy, albeit of a less central nature. For example, while the Minister of the Interior has responsibility for physical control of entry and expulsion, the civil rights' aspects of these issues are the natural preserve of the Ministry of Justice and the legal system generally. Similarly, the Minister for Social Solidarity plans and coordinates the social welfare and social integration of immigrants, but aspects of these policies are delivered by the ministries of Health and of Education, or they are delivered by sub-national tiers of government, especially the regions and the municipalities, (and in this area, returning to the national tier, the Minister for the Public Service and Regional Affairs has a role in the coordinating process). There is also a financial dimension to immigration policy, as to most other policy areas, and thus a role for the Ministry of the Treasury. Finally, there is temporary involvement of other ministries in particular circumstances. For example, efforts to police borders at times involve the navy and hence the Ministry of Defence, as well as the Ministry of the Interior.

The potential for departmental conflict between the various policies bundled under the general heading of 'immigration policy' is extensive. It is an objective fact of political and administrative life, and is widely recognised by almost all actors involved in immigration. The fundamental tension is that between deterring illegal or uncontrolled immigration, and treating in a humane and sensitive way those forced to seek access by irregular channels, or who are suspected of being clandestine immigrants. The remit of the Ministry of the Interior is public order and border security, and the Ministry is likely to believe that achieving these goals will be more difficult, the more that would-be immigrants see Italy as a relatively easy country to enter, and to stay within even if subsequently apprehended. Any measures which foster a perception that illegal immigrants are not summarily expelled, but rather allowed to stay temporarily in conditions of considerable liberty pending appeal, request for asylum, or amnesty, and thus to have a chance to make their escape to another EU member state, are unlikely to be welcomed by the Ministry. Border security and domestic public-order pose particular dilemmas for the Interior Ministry. It is in practice extremely difficult to repel really determined mass attempts to secure entry without risk of major loss of life, but the more often that major influxes are treated in a tolerant and humanitarian way, the greater the risk that others will be tempted to emulate those who have gone before. Equally, populist protest and social tensions generated by relations between immigrants and local communities are more likely, if Italian citizens themselves come to believe their country is an excessively easy country to enter.

There is little doubt that Italy *has* been a relatively easy country to enter. Several factors contribute to this. One is Italy's judicial system, and the entrenched concern for judicial correctness and the protection of civil rights. Another is the fact that a large part of the party spectrum shares a strong sense of social equality and commitment to social welfare that extends to immigrant communities and would-be immigrants. A third is the difficulty of drawing sharp lines of distinction between the lawful and the unlawful in the field of immigration. Major influxes from adjacent trouble-spots (Albania, Yugoslavia, Turkey), economic migration to a labour market in need of seasonal labour, and efforts at family reunification, all blur the lines between technically illegal, or at best semi-regularised emergency flows, and fully legal immigration, while the humanitarian plight of many of those involved generates a strong temptation to depart from formal rules. In so far as departments other than

Interior, (most notably Social Solidarity, Justice, and Health), are
the mouthpieces for the humanitarian dimension of immigration
policy, while Interior itself stands for domestic security, there is
therefore an in-built tension between these departments in the
immigration field, which is visible in all four case studies.

A similar tension exists between on one side pressures to treat
immigrants – even illegal ones – with compassion and on the other
Italy's commitments to its European Union partners under the
Schengen agreement on the other. Even if formal rules on immigration and asylum have converged under Schengen, the geographi-
cally-determined porosity of Italian coastal borders makes it difficult
for Italy to persuade its EU partners that its borders really are secure.
If Italian arrangements favouring clandestine immigration flows lead
to increased rates of transborder crossings into other EU member-
states, it is the Ministry of Foreign Affairs above all which has to take
responsibility, and which will be concerned with the impact on
Italy's standing, and on other intra-EU bilateral relations. In a less
stark way, there is a potential tension between the concerns of the
Ministry of Labour and of Foreign Affairs. The former is concerned
above all with the labour-market. Its objectives include the supply of
sufficient labour, especially seasonal labour, to fill jobs that Italians
do not fill. At the same time it seeks to ensure that such jobs are
filled on a regulated basis, rather than through the black market. The
Ministry of Foreign Affairs has to deal with the consequences of this
need in Italy's bilateral relations with supplier countries, and therefore it wants some guarantee that those given work permits have
jobs to go to, and receive decent treatment when they arrive.

The Growth of Core-executive Arbitration

From the preceding section it can be seen that the key contextual
features of the immigration sector are institutional divisions
between different agencies of government, with no really dominant
lead-department, complemented by marked divisions within the
party spectrum. These factors have made the emergence of a clear-
cut and cohesive coalition for reform especially difficult to manage
and have engendered two key responses from the government:

1. Increased efforts at core executive arbitration from the Presidency of the Council of Ministers involving the prime minister,
   the deputy prime minister, and the minister without portfolio in
   charge of the Department for Social Solidarity, (which is itself a
   department within the Presidency).
2. Overall framework legislation encompassing as many different
   aspects of immigration policy as possible, in order to generate both

a social and parliamentary consensus on the overall balance of policy, and a procedural framework in which the work of various government agencies can be coordinated in a predictable manner.

These two features clearly complement one another. Without core-executive involvement, and in the absence of a dominant lead department, the establishment of an interdepartmental consensus, or something approaching it, is unlikely. And without such a consensus it is a great deal more difficult to get the framework legislation that can then enshrine clear objectives, procedures, and departmental roles over an extended period of time. Such legislation also gives the government a degree of freedom to impose policy by delegated decree,[5] and if properly drafted, it provides a set of guidelines within which competing ministerial departments can be required to operate.[6] It also enables Parliament to exercise what its members see (rightly or wrongly) as overall supervision of the policies involved. Certainly, in a sector where emotive issues can be exploited for partisan ends, where the risks or xenophobia and civil disturbance are considerable, and where striking a balance between competing needs requires careful consideration, there is great advantage in ensuring that members of Parliament feel some strong sense of *ownership* of policy, even if the implementation of that policy may be subject to a considerable degree of executive discretion. Naturally there are also corresponding disadvantages in trying to fit everything into one legislative package – most notably the complexity of the agenda, and the potentially long wait before legislation emerges. The range of issues which have been included in the legislative agenda during the 1990s has included:

1. general visa and entry policy;
2. labour-market policy;
3. mechanisms to cope with sudden influxes;
4. asylum policy;
5. measures to monitor and keep track of applicants for asylum awaiting the results of their applications, or those found to be clandestine immigrants, who are notionally preparing to leave, or have been given notice to leave;
6. the social integration of immigrants;
7. family reunification;
8. relations with (non-EU) third countries;
9. relations with EU partners under Schengen;
10. voting and other civil rights' issues.

Finding simultaneous solutions to such a broad agenda proved extremely difficult until the parliamentary situation clarified after

1996. Even then some issues – most notably asylum – had to be treated separately.

The Antecedents of the 1998 Legislation

The Martelli Law

The first serious attempt to regulate immigration flows in postwar Italy was law no. 943, 30 December 1986, which dealt with foreign workers' rights and employment regulations, and sought to bring illegal entrants out into the mainstream labour market. It was a judicious combination of liberalism and efforts to tighten the law against clandestine entry. On the liberal side, it provided guarantees of parity of treatment with Italian nationals in the labour market to *legal* immigrants, including family unification, housing access, health care, etc. It devised a new mechanism for regulating the entry of foreign workers, and decoupled residence permits from employment status. On the coercive side, it provided for criminal sanctions against employers aiding illegal entry, or hiring illegal entrants at exploitative rates.

Enforcing this legislation, which contained within it a number of serious contradictions, proved difficult.[7] The provision for equal treatment of legal entrants in the labour market and in social services (Article 1) was in direct conflict with the provision in Article 5 by which foreign workers made unemployed were placed on different local labour-office hiring lists from those of Italian and EC workers. More seriously, various elements of Article 12, dealing with sanctions against abusive employers, and of Article 16 requiring illegal immigrants to regularise their status within three months, proved ineffective. It was estimated that the 107,000 who applied for regularisation under the 1986 provisions represented somewhere between one sixth and one tenth of the total number of illegal immigrants.[8] An illegally employed immigrant who made himself known to the authorities had a strong incentive to declare himself unemployed, and remain in black-market employment. To declare himself employed, as he was legally required to do, would endanger his job, since his employer was liable to back payment of social security, and would face hefty wage increases and inspection of his hiring practices. The new law also created an area of uncertainty about inspection and enforcement between the Ministry of Labour and the police.[9]

The difficulties of the 1986 legislation quickly prompted the search for new legislation. The previous law had been piloted through largely by the Ministry of Labour, in association with the

Ministry of the Interior, and its main institutional inheritance was a national consultative body – the *Consulta nazionale per i problemi dei lavoratori extracomunitari e delle loro famiglie* – which became a forum under the aegis of the Ministry of Labour for the monitoring and discussion of immigrant issues with representatives from national government departments, local government, the trade unions, the Italian Council for Refugees, and others. By 1989, however, the government concluded that a greater degree of central coordination was required, and the drafting process was placed in the hands of Deputy Prime Minister Claudio Martelli. A commission, drawing in representatives from all the interested departments involved in the issue, foreshadowed the approach to be adopted by the Ciampi and Prodi governments,[10] which was to be based around the principle of interdepartmental coordination under the guidance of the Presidency of the Council of Ministers. The commission was headed by the diplomatic Counsellor at the PCM, with head of the legislative office as secretary. There were three other officials from the PCM, a single representative from each of the Ministries of Labour, Foreign Affairs, and Interior, a representative of the CNEL, one from each of the three main trade-union confederations, and one from each of three principal charitable organisations dealing with immigrant welfare.[11] 1989/90 was therefore a watershed in the process by which immigration became a national cross-departmental political issue, no longer the preserve of the Ministry of Labour and the Ministry of the Interior. Henceforth, the Presidency of the Council of Ministers (deputy prime minister, Minister without Portfolio at the Department of Social Affairs, officials within the PCM) were to play a much higher-profile role acting as brokers and facilitators.

The main thrust of the new law involved regularisation of illegal immigrant status. Once again, a deadline was set for illegal immigrants to come forward to register, and the problems of the 1986 experience were addressed by relieving employers of the burden of back payment of social security and tax contributions. Under the new scheme, residence permits would be issued for two years, with the possibility of two-year or four-year extensions under certain conditions if during the two initial years certain thresholds of income and self-sufficiency had been achieved. Nearly a quarter of a million illegals came forward under the new legislation – generating considerable administrative difficulties in the processing of the applications – but in at least this sense the Martelli law was a considerable advance on the 1986 law. However, the new law still suffered from a number of drawbacks. The system for estimating labour market needs proved defective, as did the mechanisms for

social integration of immigrants at subnational level. Local authorities were given too little guidance, and far too little financial assistance, to cope with the problems posed by immigration. A number
of institutional reforms were put in place, both by the 1986 law[12]
and by the Martelli law, including a standing national commission
to monitor the law itself, but these agencies were soon seen as seriously inadequate in the face of the emergencies that Italy started to
face almost as soon as the Martelli law was approved.

Indeed, the greatest limitation of the Martelli law was that it was
conceived of as tidying up the problems of the past, and facing
future problems simply by counting on being able to restrict future
entry. The future was quickly to prove much more difficult than the
past, and with the crises first in the former Yugoslavia, and later in
Albania, it became clear that tougher controls were simply impractical without accompanying changes on a number of other fronts.
Given the increase in the numbers of displaced persons involved,
given the level of public sympathy towards them in their desperate
plight on first arrival, given the continuing absence of an EU-wide
system of coordination, and given the range of civil rights' guarantees available to immigrants, further reform was urgently called for.

The deteriorating parliamentary situation after 1992 made the
search for further legislative improvement extremely difficult, however, with governments naturally turning to short-term expedients,
introduced by decree law, and focusing on individual aspects of
policy – labour-market issues, housing, health, etc. The Berlusconi
government hardly had time to approach the issues at stake before
it was overtaken by internal strife, and indeed in the process failed
even to issue a decree (as it was required to do under the Martelli
law) laying before Parliament its estimates of the numbers of entry
visas and work permits to be issued to non-EC immigrants for the
following year (the estimate was finally drawn up in September
1995 – nine months into the year to which it applied!). The Dini
Government faced equally difficult circumstances – the 1996 estimates arriving in Parliament even later (December 1996). It also
resorted to the unapologetic use of decree laws – in particular
decree law no. 489, 18 November 1995, reiterated, in the absence
of parliamentary agreement on new legislation, no fewer than five
times without ever being converted into law.

Decree 489 and its successors were in fact an uncomfortable
compromise between the Department of Social Affairs' carrot (supported in Parliament by much of the PDs, the Catholics, and the left
in general, and outside by charitable associations, and the unions)
and the Ministry of the Interior's stick (supported in Parliament by
the right). A government bill for a more comprehensive framework

legislation report faced similar stalemate, and was never presented to Parliament. The result was an almost entirely 'administrative' approach to immigration. The decree laws contained vigorous new law-and-order mechanisms, including the use of the armed forces, but in practice the deployment of these measures was used sparingly, and to some degree as a political reassurance mechanism when social pressures began to build. The decree spelled out in detail the measures contained in Article 7 of the Martelli Law concerning repatriation. The main thrust was to speed up and simplify expulsion procedures, not only for those who constituted a security or public order threat, or had committed crimes, but also for those who had simply evaded frontier controls and lacked appropriate residence permits. The measures included, for the first time, the principle of confinement in reception centres for those awaiting deportation, (the centres themselves materialised only slowly) and much foreshortened judicial procedures.

The Contri Commission

Of the four governments which held office from 1992-96, the one which made the most serious effort to provide a new and comprehensive framework to bring together all dimensions of the problem in a single piece of framework legislation was that of Carlo Azeglio Ciampi. Like several other aspects of the Ciampi experience, the attempt proved long on distinguished academic and expert input, but decidedly short on basic political backing necessary to get the ideas turned into legislation. The Ciampi Government's approach built upon the lesson of the Martelli law that good coordination through the PCM was necessary both in drafting legislation that could be effective, and in coordinating the efforts of the various administrations involved. On this occasion, however, there was no input from a committed deputy prime minister, nor the political cohesion in the government which could persuade the various departments involved to compromise.

The task of preparing the legislation was assigned to Fernanda Contri, Minister without Portfolio at the Department for Social Affairs. The Contri Commission[13] certainly represented an ambitious attempt to get to grips with the problem. It assembled 28 experts – half from the various departments involved[14] and half from among outside experts, mainly sociologists, demographers, and lawyers. The report it eventually delivered to the prime minister on 14 April 1994 was an extraordinarily ambitious draft of a government bill running to 173 articles and 211 pages. Unfortunately, its impracticality was evident from the frank confession to the prime minister that on many issues there was open disagreement inside the commission between key departments.[15] Its report would therefore have been a dead letter even if, two weeks later, the 1994 general election had not changed the political situation dramatically by making the vehemently anti-immigrant Northern League the arbiter of the parliamentary situation for the following two years. In particular, there was vigorous opposition from the Ministries of the Interior, Labour, and Foreign Affairs for the central principle of a 'National Department for Immigration' (Article 158) which would take over and centralise a number of key functions in regard to policy planning in the sector. This departmental hostility was probably not helped by the decision to entrust the final drafting of the government bill to a restricted group of four members of the commission three of whom were academic lawyers, and the fourth from the PCM serving as secretary to the other three. There is little doubt that the bill was as a result seen as an effort to impose an abstract and impractical conception of administrative order on departments which believed their own practical understanding of the issues was greatly superior to that of the drafters.

Nevertheless, the experience of the Commission was not without its positive effects. Problems and principles were aired more openly and more honestly than before, and there was a recognition of a real dilemma: Italy needed its migrant labourers, but it had increasingly urgent obligations to its European partners that could not be postponed, and it could not cope with the periodic reality of massive and unforeseeable influxes of economic migrants without better border policing facilities, stronger legal powers for the courts and the police, better relations with the countries sending migrants, and in general a more orderly approach towards the flow of workers and others that were to be allowed to enter the country. Above all, it was increasingly conceded that the chaotic process of dealing with applications for residence and asylum by stateless and often paperless clandestine immigrants could not continue without some parliamentary backing for the principle of administrative detention while individuals awaited the outcome of their application. In so far as the Contri Commission was the first serious, albeit unsuccessful, effort to bring representatives of the key departments together to solve a problem collectively, it was at least a step forward.

The Turco Commission and the 1998 Legislation

The experience of immigration policy between 1991 and 1996 was unquestionably highly unsatisfactory. Very few of the many decree laws were converted into proper law; sanctions were employed in a highly unpredictable and sometimes arbitrary way; numerous 'sanatoria' risked undermining the authority and credibility of the law; basic civil rights' were at times put at severe risk; and Parliament was by-passed on frequent occasions.

At another level, however, the slow and frequently friction-ridden interaction between departments of government did probably lead eventually to a better understanding of where the balance between liberal and repressive measures ought to lie, and provided an unquestionably improved administrative atmosphere on which to build when the political circumstances changed following the general election of 1996. Five months after that election, the new Minister of Social Affairs (now technically 'Solidarity'), Livia Turco, convened a new commission to make a fresh attempt at drafting overall framework legislation. Lessons in the politics of drafting legislation had clearly been learned. The slimmed-down Turco Commission contained only two members who were not departmental officials from interested departments. It also abjured any attempt at ambitious new structures like the ill-fated Department for Immigration. It was more modest in its efforts to legislate in detail – its draft document ran to only thirty pages and forty-six articles. It set out more flexible procedures. It reported in only six weeks, and by February its draft was laid before the Council of Ministers. By September, it had reached Parliament, and with minor amendments passed through the Chamber of Deputies by the end of the year, and through the Senate seven weeks later. On 6 March 1998, six years after the first serious efforts to reform the Martelli law, the new provisions became law.[16]

Whatever view is taken of individual sections of the new immigration law, its passage has represented a significant achievement for the Prodi government. Finding any sort of balance between the conflicting pressures of civil rights' protection and social provision on the one side, and firm disincentives to clandestine entry on the other, had proved impossible through the 1990s. The solutions adopted may not be perfect, but they have at least won the all-important sanction of parliamentary approval and they have set out new and clearer procedures for implementation. The three key provisions of the new law cover the planning of entry flows, measures against illegal immigration and criminal exploitation of migration flows, and the social integration of new arrivals. A new system of quotas is to be put in place which establishes more accurately and with more administrative backup the numbers and countries of origin of seasonal workers, linked to the number of other types of immigrants (family reunification, asylum seekers, etc.) to be dealt with. Expulsion procedures are to be simplified, and the all-important principle of administrative detention for those who cannot be expelled immediately has been enshrined in law. Finally, a range of social measures, with better administrative coordination and more financial resources, covering health, education, assistance to minors, and to women, is to be established.

It is of course easy to be sceptical about the provisions of the new law. The law itself is only the beginning. It has to be implemented and made effective. There was early evidence that financial provision for it was not adequate.[17] More seriously, there were numerous administrative problems in implementing the annual quotas of residence permits established by decree under the new legislation, as the 15 December deadline approached by which time those with regular job contracts, fixed lodgings, and proof of their entry before 27 March 1998 had to register. Uncertainty prevailed over the criteria to be adopted by the authorities should those registering exceed the 38,000 quota for the year.[18] Uncertainty certainly prevailed amongst immigrants, as massive queues built up at the *questure*, and as large numbers of immigrants from elsewhere in Europe headed for the Italian border in the hope of registering as residents in Italy.

Meanwhile during 1998 the flow of clandestine immigrants showed little sign of abating, and political tensions between the central government and local authorities over the management of immigration continued to ebb and flow. November proved an especially difficult month. For all its successes in Albania, it was clear that the Italian government had not stabilised a regime capable of stemming the commerce in clandestine immigration through the Albanian route. The flow of Albanian citizens may have been stemmed, but that of other groups from elsewhere in the Balkans and beyond continued to generate concern, and the occasional maritime tragedy.[19] No-one expected the tighter control procedures contained in the new law to broadcast a message to would-be clandestine immigrants across the trouble-spots of Europe and the Middle East immediately, but the events of the autumn were a clear reminder of how the immigration problem was unlikely to be resolved rapidly, however orderly the legislative framework was. And as if to impress this fact deep into the Italian public consciousness, these events coincided with the delicate judicial and diplomatic crisis generated by the Oçalan affair. The potent site of Europe's Kurds (and in Germany, Europe's Turks) taking the ethnic and racial tensions of the Middle East onto the streets of Rome and other European capitals was a stark reminder that the new immigrants in western Europe were not necessarily as easily assimilable into their new societies as many of those who sought to welcome them might hope.[20]

The 'achievement' ascribed to the Prodi government is therefore so far largely a legislative one. But in the context of the controversy surrounding Italian immigration in the 1990s even a legislative success is important. It is certainly the *sine qua non* of a subsequent improvement in administrative performance. In this sense, it must be counted as significant evidence of an improvement in the capacity for coherent and purposive policy making at the centre.

The explanation of the successful passage of the government bill no doubt lies partly in factors going well beyond the Prodi government itself. The bar, by the Constitutional Court (*Sentenza n. 360, 24 ott.1996*), on the long-disputed practice of the reiteration of decree laws which have expired without being converted into law, no doubt concentrated the new government's attention as much as the objective need for new measures and the sanction of proper law, though while this has happened for immigration, it has not happened in several other areas. The approach of full Italian participation in the Schengen area agreement in spring 1998 no doubt also played a role. For reasons that go well beyond immigration itself, and touch on Italy's more general 'European' credentials, the new government felt it urgent to be able to demonstrate compliance with European norms and practices. And finally, as the preceding section of this case study has illustrated, the experience of Italian immigration policy in the 1990s in general, for all its short-termism, was in a sense an iterative process, by which the political system in its entirety – parties, pressure groups, public opinion, and the administrative system – gradually developed a clearer sense of what a consensus on immigration policy might look like, and what changes that would require.

Nevertheless, to build on these incentives to reform, the political circumstances also had to be appropriate, and the government needed the internal cohesion to exploit its opportunities. In this sense, the changed political circumstances following the election of the Prodi Government undoubtedly played the key role. Its majority in Parliament was far more united than at any time since the start of the decade. The distance between the two major parties of the majority, the PDS and PPI on this issue was modest (and on most issues the PPI adopted the more liberal positions) and *Rifondazione Comunista* and the Greens proved generally content to accept that a left-wing government would exercise greater restraint in the use of the new measures on detention than its predecessors. Moreover the arrival at the Ministry of the Interior, of a strong, well-respected and prestigious figure like Giorgio Napolitano, who had nothing to prove to his much younger and more junior PDS colleague Livia Turco, provided almost the ideal combination of political leadership for a compromise between Interior and Social

Solidarity. The former department was able to play a key role in persuading Parliament of the new government's liberal credentials, while Napolitano (and Dini) delivered the consent, albeit still somewhat sceptical, of the two key ministries that had prevented the success of the Contri Commission in 1994. Crucially, over the intervening period the proposal for a separate 'Department for Immigration' under the Presidency had been excised, and Interior, Foreign Affairs (and Labour) were guaranteed the sort of role they saw as necessary in the planning procedures for entry policy envisaged by the new law.

Conclusions

Immigration policy making in Italy provides a good test of the ability of the core executive to coordinate complex issues across a large number of affected departments. As a relatively 'new' issue area, it is not one in which a single department has established control over agenda-setting and the drafting of legislation. It is an issue area which has been highly politicised, and one that requires considerable flexibility on the part of the authorities in their response to changing situations. And it is an issue area that faithfully reflects the Italian aversion for centrally imposed, dirigiste solutions to policy problems.

This last feature has greatly affected the way in which the core executive, and especially the PCM, has sought to manage the problem. It has tried hard firstly to generate a broad social consensus on the way immigration issues should be handled, and it has encouraged participation of a wide range of actors beyond central government departments (Parliament, regional and municipal government, the CNEL, the voluntary sector, the trade unions). And it has allowed its structures and capacities (especially the Department of Social Solidarity, and its legislative drafting office) to become facilitating arenas for interdepartmental consultation, without bringing the political authority of the Prime Minister himself into play in order to impose solutions unilaterally.

It is clear that, in the early years of policy development, it was quite difficult to bring the relevant departments involved together into a meaningful and cooperative dialogue, and that this, together with the absence of a lead-department, increased the importance of finding a successful legislative formula which would assign clear roles, and clear procedures for interdepartmental cooperation, to all actors. In that search Parliament naturally became an important arena at least in the sense that nothing could be expected to pass through Parliament unless it had been carefully prepared both interdepartmentally and politically in advance of the parliamentary process. This explains the long delay between the 1990 legislation and that of 1998 which replaced it. Until the political circumstances of a fairly cohesive and stable government were created through the 1996 general election, it proved impossible, even on single aspects of immigration policy, let alone general framework legislation encompassing all aspects of policy, to persuade Parliament to translate decree-laws into proper law.

The major question mark that hangs over the immigration issue is whether the linkages that, fitfully and imperfectly, developed in the 1990s have been, or in the future can be, translated into a form of self-sustaining policy community at the level of ministerial cabinets, legal affairs departments of the ministries and the operational units further down the ministerial hierarchies that have grown up to deal with immigration during the 1990s. The process leading to the final text of the government bill presented to Parliament showed evidence that this was possible in the right political circumstances, when political leadership was relatively strong, and in relation to a legislative objective. It also has to be made to work at the administrative level, in order to generate a strong administrative policy-community that can overcome the sort of difficulties that emerge when political leadership is less cohesive, and that are perennially present in discontinuities generated by changes in the personnel of ministerial cabinets and in the personnel in the Presidency of the Council resulting from turnover in government. What this requires of course, is the development of habits of trust, knowledge of other departmental perspectives, and a sense of common purpose and cooperation across all departments. Such characteristics do not develop overnight, and probably do not develop naturally in an isolated area of policy, if they are not also being fostered by other structural features of the public service. The absence of career fluidity across departments, and discontinuities in policy networks generated by frequent changes in the personnel of ministerial cabinets and in the personnel of the PCM resulting from frequent changes of government would certainly tend to get in the way of such confidence-building measures.

Notes

1. The bibliography is extensive. For an introduction see U. Melotti, *L'immigrazione: una sfida per l'Europa*, Milano Molisv: 1992. For a very up to date survey of legislative and administrative aspects, see G. D'Auria, *Rivista Giuridica del Lavoro* XLVIII, 2, 1997: 141-72.

2. Leaving aside immigrants who have obtained Italian citizenship (especially
    those returning as second-generation emigrants from Latin America), there
    were estimated to be, by 1994, almost exactly one million resident in the coun-
    try, (U. Melotti, 'Problemi e prospettive dell'immigrazione extracomunitaria in
    Italia', Quaderni regionale XIV, January-March 1995: 83). Although this still
    implied a ratio of immigrants to native citizens less than half the average ratio
    for the EU as a whole the rapidity with which the phenomenon emerged posed
    a particularly difficult policy problem in the Italian context. Moreover, a far
    higher proportion than elsewhere in the EU were from outside the Union: from
    the poorer parts of Africa (especially Morocco (88,000 in a 1991 estimate),
    Tunisia (46,000) and Senegal (27,000)); Asia, especially the Philippines
    (40,000) and China (20,000); the former communist block (90,000); and Latin
    America (50,000). Within these figures, the level of illegal immigration was
    extremely high.
3. See M. Natale, 'L'immigrazione straniera in Italia', *Polis*, 1 April 1997: 16.
4. The Department of Social Affairs was established by decree in 1990 (DPCM, 13
    Febuary. 1990 no. 109 'Regolamento concernente istituzione e organizzazione
    del Dipartimento per gli Affair Sociali nell'ambito della Presidenza del Con-
    siglio dei Ministri'), and renamed Department of Social Solidarity in 1996. Ref-
    erences to the department in this paper are to its name at the time of the event
    in question.
5. 'Delegated decree' is not to be confused with 'decree law'. The former is the
    equivalent of delegated legislation used in most modern legislatures, requiring
    the government simply to report back to Parliament the measures it intends to
    enact in pursuance of the authority given to it by the legislature by the original
    statute. 'Decree law' is a (controversial) Italian procedure by which govern-
    ments may issue decrees with the force of law, but these must be converted
    into proper law within sixty days. In principle they should not be reiterated if
    the sixty-day deadline is not met, and the Constitutional Court finally banned
    such a practice in 1997, though not before the system had been systematically
    abused by governments over many years.
6. It should be noted that framework legislation and the more extensive use of the
    authorisation it frequently gives to the government to issue *leggi deleghi* (dele-
    gated legislation) has increased significantly in recent years. Other obvious
    examples are the *leggi Bassanini* on administrative reform, or the *legge comu-
    nitaria* for the implementation of EU legislation, or framework laws for pri-
    vatisation or for budgetary procedure. Though criticised in some quarters for
    the shift in the balance of power from Parliament to government that this ten-
    dency generates, the practice provides considerable advantages – especially in
    comparison to the past, when Italian legislation tended to be highly fragmented
    because the belief that Parliament should keep control of the detail of the leg-
    islative process ran up against the objective reality that the broader the scope
    of a bill, the more difficult it was to secure a majority for it.
7. For a survey see G. D'Auria, op. cit., esp. pp. 143-45.
8. See P. Onorato, 'Per un statuto dello straniero', *Democrazia e diritto*, Novem-
    ber-December 1989: 303-28.
9. R. Sestini, La disciplina degli stranieri in Europa, *Democrazia e diritto*, 6,
    November- December 1989: 329-50.
10. The procedure is described by Massimo Saraz, an official working in the PCM
    at the time, in the official proceedings of the 1990 National Immigration Con-
    ference. See Massimo Saraz, 'La nuova politica dell'immigrazione in Italia e la
    sua applicazione', in CNEL, *Atti della Conferenza nazionale dell'immigrazione*,
    Roma, 4-6 giugno 1990 Roma: Editalia, 1991.

11. The composition of the consultative committee is reported in CNEL, *Atti della Conferenza nazionale dell'immigrazione*, Roma, 4-6 giugno 1990, Roma: Editalia, 1991, p. 9.

12. The Ministry of Labour established a new internal department (*Servizio per i problemi dei lavatori extracomunitari*) and the Ministry of Foreign Affairs established a commission to review agreements with third countries on labour migration. At regional level, various consultative and participatory organs, including within them immigrant representatives, were established.

13. Decreto Ministro per gli Affari Sociali, 8 sett. 1993: *Commissione di Studio per una legge organica sulla condizione giuridica dello straniero in Italia.*

14. Ministries represented covered Interior (Farrace and Cazella), Foreign Affairs (Corrias), Labour (Quattrocchi), Colla (Justice), Amatucci (Education), Dell'Olio (health), Massicci (Treasury), and Conti (Industry). There were also three representatives from departments within the PCM (Bolaffi – Social Affairs), Nardini (Legislative Office) Dragonetti (Public Service Department), Carpani (Regional Affairs), and Di Lisio (Scientific Research).

15. *Disciplina della condizione giuridica dello straniero nella Repubblica italiana, schema di disegno di legge (prima bozza) testo provvisorio consegnato dal Min. per gli affari sociali al Presidente del Consiglio dei Ministri in data 14 aprile 1994.* The author is grateful to dott. Guido Bolaffi of the Dip. Affari Sociali for provision of this document.

16. Legge 6 marzo 1998, n. 40 'Disciplina dell'immigrazione e norme sulla condizione dello straniero', *Gazzetta Ufficiale*, n. 59, 12 marzo 1998, supplemento ordinario n. 40. Decreto Legislativo 25 luglio 1998, n. 286. The consolidated text of all immigration legislation was published later in the year as 'Testo unico delle disposizioni concernenti la disciplina dell'immigrazione e norme sulla condizione dello straniero', *Gazzetta Ufficiale* n. 191 del 18 agosto 1998 – Supplemento Ordinario n. 139.

17. See 'Immigrati, legge a rischio', *La Repubblica*, 10March 1998: 23.

18. See 'Immigrati, basta file disumane', *Corriere della Sera*, 7 November 1998: 13.

19. See 'Clandestini, assalto alle frontiere' *Corriere della Sera*, 16 November 1998: 11.

20. See F. Alberoni, 'Immigrazione, in Italia nasceranno comunità nuove e potenti' *Corriere della Sera*, 23 Nov. 1998: 1.

9

FINANCE BETWEEN MARKET AND POLITICS

Giacomo Vaciago

In 1998 – as in most recent years – there were significant changes in Italy's financial system. They were part of a broad international process through which the traditionally highly regulated monetary and financial sectors have been subject to constant pressures towards greater competitiveness. Every country, Italy included, has been subject both to the pressures of globalisation applied by the markets, and to those exerted by the countries with which they are competing, or into which they are seeking to integrate. In the Italian case such pressures have certainly been operating, and have been working on a system in need of radical modernisation. Italy has been one of those countries with a large proportion of its financial institutions operating under direct public control (bank ownership in particular), with some of the most stringent national supervision exercised by any central bank, and with the most restrictive regulatory framework.

In 1998, as in other recent years, it has been the european Community which has been the source of the greatest pressures towards liberalisation, and which has further reduced the margin of policy discretion available to the national authorities. There has also been further harmonisation of market activities and of trends towards fiscal neutrality. In some fields, there has been a good deal of success – especially in the operation of financial markets, which for reasons connected with the country's formidable public debt problems, have engaged the attention of the Italian authorities very systematically. Not by chance the same has applied to financial-market aspects of the introduction of the euro on 1 January 1999. However, progress has been much slower in two other areas where political interference, direct and/or indirect, has traditionally been greater – the reform of banking foundations, and of the so-called 'golden shares' which the state holds in privatised companies. The preference for the market is the preference for rules and institutions over politics. Achieving this is not easy, however, not least because even the best markets display imperfections: as the summer of 1998 clearly showed. The alternative is politics, the long-term capacities of which are rarely superior to those of markets. In 1998, as in earlier years, the innovatory impulses in Italy have concerned both areas: there has been much progress towards better-functioning markets, and some small steps towards less political interference.

The Consolidated Text on Financial Markets

The year began, symbolically as well as temporally, with the inauguration on 2 January of *Borsa Italiana SpA*, an event which marked the completion of the privatisation of all Italy's financial markets,[1] and which reversed the long-standing assumption that market supervision and market management were unquestionably public functions. The reform is intended expected to develop Italian financial markets towards greater integration and make them more competitive. The reform of market regulations which also came into effect on 2 January, to coincide with the new private Stock Exchange, was directed to the same ends. The changes, which in many respects bring Italian law into line with that of other countries, focused on behaviour and organisational rules, and both obligations and sanctions.

An innovation of even greater scope – which has prompted both the Bank of Italy and Consob to issue a large number of new regulations – was the enactment of the Consolidated Text of the Provisions on Financial Markets (*Testo unico delle disposizioni in materia di mercati finanziari*: d. legislativo 24 febbraio 1998, n. 58).[2] Consolidated Texts in Italy reorder and complete legislation that has accumulated over many years, but the Financial Market Text also highlighted some gaps still to be addressed and the contradictions (or overlaps) in the regulatory framework that remained. It was hoped that the example of the Consolidated Text of the Laws on Banking and Credit (*Testo unico delle leggi in materia bancaria e creditizia*: d. legislativo 1 settembre 1993, n. 385) – which the Bank of Italy republished[3] with the addition of subsequent legislation – would be repeated in the case of the rules disciplining financial intermediaries, markets and companies. Even if there were no european directives to provide a benchmark, numerous problems would still remain, especially on company law and corporate governance. The most thorough and systematic part of the new Consolidated Text – to which the two regulatory authorities, the Bank of Italy and Consob, have made the greatest contribution – concerns financial intermediaries and markets. The aim[4] was to amalgamate the entire range of activities connected with asset management into a single figure – the broker[5] (*gestore unico*) – along lines already established in most other countries, and to rationalise the supervision system. The latter in Italy has been divided between the Bank of Italy and Consob, though there are numerous overlaps of function. The basic distinguishing principle is the purpose served by each regulatory institution: Consob monitors the transparency and correctness of financial transactions, while the Bank of Italy oversees the financial stability of the intermediaries themselves.

The Consolidated Text thus completes the revision of the organic law on stock market intermediaries (the SIM law of 1991), implementation of which had been fiercely opposed by foreign firms, which were prevented from operating in Italy unless they had an approved subsidiary inside the country. Indeed, the law was rejected by the european Court of Justice on the ground that it breached principles set out in the Treaty of Rome. In the meantime, however, the EEC directive on investment services was issued in 1993, along with the EEC directive on capital requirements. With the conversion of these directives into Italian law (legislative decree of 23 July 1996, no. 415, also called 'euroSIM') the SIM law was brought into line. The legislative decree of 1996 was then transformed into the new Consolidated Text, which ensured compliance with the requirements of european integration and provided a response to the competitive pressures applied to financial intermediaries and companies by globalisation. In the Italian case, the two main needs were the self-regulation of businesses, on the one hand,[6] and measures to protect the interests of those businesses on the other. In the latter connection, such needs applied to companies listed on the Stock Exchange, though to a degree also to all companies above a certain size, and was related to the frequency, in Italy, of the abuse of dominant position.

The overall verdict on the Consolidated Text was therefore positive – approval coming from both the Bank of Italy and Consob – though a number of issues relating to company law were postponed until political circumstances were more favourable. Thus provision has been made to support minority shareholders, and to improve the operation of the market (against insider-dealing,[7] for example), but the important issues of the autonomy of management and the right to challenge of ownership arrangements are still to be addressed. These latter two aspects are of course complicated in Italy by the very large number of small businesses.

The generally favourable reception given to the new Consolidated Text – apart from Consob's criticisms of its insider-dealing provisions (perhaps because it is a well-established tradition in Italy?) – mainly focus on deregulation and the simplification of the legal framework, on the expanded roles allowed to financial intermediaries, and more generally on harmonisation with legal frameworks in other countries that enhanced opportunities for Italian financial markets to integrate into the wider international order. The progress made in these directions was rewarded by significant growth achieved by the market during 1998, despite the instabilities that have afflicted it.

Reform of Taxation on Financial Activities

On the same day (1 July 1998) that the Consolidated Text came into force, so too did the law reforming taxation on the income from financial instruments.[8] The tax burden was generally simplified and standardised, although, for various reasons and in various ways, priority was given to the growth of the financial market. In place of a system in which capital returns were taxed according to a range of criteria which depended on the financial instruments concerned (bank deposits, government securities, shares, derivatives, and so on), on the issuers, on the purchasers, and on the taxable type (coupons, capital gains), the reform introduced much simpler and more transparent arrangements, albeit with the constraints of yield parity, and of the pre-existing reduced rate for government securities. These constraints have led to the adoption of two rates: the ordinary one of 27 percent and the special lower rate of 12.5 percent for government securities and private bonds. It is likely that, when it is possible to remove these two constraints (when, that is, the public debt is no longer the problem that it has been in recent years, and when it is possible to forgo a proportion of tax revenue), the two rates will be 'harmonised' – the expression, not coincidentally, is used mainly at the european level – to a single rate (something like 20 percent would be a reasonable compromise). In the meantime, the reform has the merit of seeking to correct the previous distortions, which concerned three aspects in particular:

1. the relationship between *debt* and *owner's equity* in the financing of firms. The Italian fiscal tradition promoted the principle that 'well-off owners own poor businesses', since corporate assets were subject to more tax than family estate, and since corporate debts, but not family ones, were tax deductible. The

tax reform of 1998 reversed the situation, thereby encouraging business recapitalisation;

2. the relationships between *ownership* and *market*, encouraging listed companies as well as reducing costs and disincentives;

3. the relationship between *savers* and *professional brokers*. Here too, the traditional preference (fiscal rather than psychological!) of Italian savers for anonymity, so that they preferred to manage their assets themselves, has been reversed by the reform. Anonymity (and the connected simplification of savers' dealings with the tax authorities) was obtained by assigning their assets to administered or managed saving funds, but could not be achieved in the ordinary system (also known as *della dichiarazione* because the taxpayer is required to declare other sources of income on his or her tax returns).[9]

Apart from the quantitative aspects of this reallocation of the tax burden – whereby the taxing of capital gains 'finances' both tax-relief on Stock Exchange quotation, and the elimination of the tax on Stock Exchange contracts (the so-called 'contract note' from which foreign operators were already exempt) – it should be pointed out that this overhauling of the tax structure has success-fully pursued three interconnected goals. Firstly, the reform com-plements the Consolidated Text discussed above, and has therefore helped to fulfil objectives concerning both market development and corporate governance (the latter since the owner's equity stake counts for more, and so too does the quality of company balance sheets). Secondly, Italy is now moving towards a tax system more easily integrated with those of other countries and therefore con-ducive to Italy's participation both in the global financial system and in financial aspects of european integration. Thirdly, the reform has superseded the traditional approach to the relationship between tax and the Stock Exchange. Traditionally, the relationship between the two was viewed as a fit target for economic manage-ment, and was thus viewed in terms of incentives which were either temporary or were targeted on particular sectors. Permanent and *erga omnes* (universal) incentives avert suspicions like those voiced concerning the temporary tax concessions approved in 1994, when it was asked whether their purpose was not in fact to favour the companies owned by the then head of government!

Rules for the Introduction of the Euro

As late as the early months of 1997, Italy still had not complied with any of the five convergence parameters fixed for participation, on 1

January 1999, in the launching of the euro. It is not surprising that Italy's preparation for the introduction of the euro was delayed, compared with countries like the United Kingdom, which although it had decided not to join, at least for the time being, had ensured that its financial structure – and above all the City – would be ready.

When in the course of 1998 it became certain that Italy would join the euro, it became necessary to make up for lost time rapidly. On the basis of a special statutory instrument enacted in December 1997, two legislative decrees were issued: the first (10 March 1998, no. 43) adjusted the Bank of Italy rules to the requirements for participation in the european system of central banks and in the operation of a common monetary policy; the second (24 June 1998, no. 213) set out the measures necessary to undertake the changeover from the lira to the euro.

The operations involved in the changeover of Italy's financial system to the euro have been widely publicized.[10] Two other areas – the public administration and companies – have received much less attention though this is perhaps understandable, given the complexity and urgency of the tasks involved.

Of particular interest are the contents of the second decree, which regulates the procedures for conversion, with particular reference to: parameters of indexisation and the use of decimals in intermediate calculations; accounting and balance-sheets; and the redenomination and 'dematerialisation' of financial instruments. The decree also regulates necessary conversion activity in the public administration and provides for the automatic conversion into euros of all systems of penal and administrative fines.

All this was necessary as a result of decisions taken at the Madrid european Council in December 1995, and of subsequent regulations which devolved implementing decisions to the member-states as regards:

1. redenominating the public debt in euros;
2. also redenominating in euros elements of the public debt issued in the currency of another member-state, as well as the financial instruments of private issuers;
3. permitting the use of the euro in the negotiation, remuneration and liquidation of financial instruments;
4. permitting the use of the euro in regulating the exchange and settlement of payments.

The crucial aspects of the changeover as formalised by the euro Committee in its first publication, in June 1997, have been summarised in four 'essential propositions' regarding the four areas of action, as follows:

1. *Payments:* From 1 January 1999, the euro may be used for all payment and collection operations where coins and banknotes are not required, for both financial market operators and the general public.
2. *Markets:* From 1 January 1999 transactions in all monetary and financial markets will take place in euros.
3. *Instruments:* From 1 January 1999 all government securities will be denominated in euros. On the same date every form of transferable treasury certificate, bill or bond will be converted into euros. Non transferable government securities like Post Office saving certificates will be converted into euros on 1 January 2002. The conversion of other financial instruments will be staged. Programmed redomination will be facilitated by measures to reduce the cost of conversion to issuers.
4. *Statistics:* From 1 January 1999 all the financial operators required to submit reports to the authorities for supervisory and statistical purposes may use euros. The authorities will publish statistics in euros.

The introduction of the euro has changed so many features of the economies and economic policies of the european countries that examining it solely from the financial point of view would be overly simplistic.[11] However, this aspect is more important in Italy's case than in others, for the many reasons already mentioned, which help to explain not only Italy's desire to be involved in the launching of the euro, but also the euro's rapid and complete adoption on the financial markets in order to prevent distinctions between old and new issues which would penalise Italian securities. Accordingly, the conversion programme took pains to emphasise that the objective was to ensure a changeover from the lira to the euro that would 'safeguard the competitive situation of the system'[12]. This focused firstly on minimising the costs to issuers – whether the issuer was the Treasury or the private sector – in order to underwrite the efficiency and liquidity of the market; and secondly – ensuring that individual savers could obtain from good quality domestic financial services, and therefore ensuring that financial intermediaries from other countries were not given undue advantage.

The importance that the Treasury and the Bank of Italy, within their respective areas of competence, have attached to these objectives has made sure that the great deal of work performed in 1998 has been successful.

Reform of the Banking Foundations

Much less success, however, has been achieved in the last two areas to be examined, which are more closely tied to politics, in all its aspects (both more honourable and less so). This is certainly the case of the enabling law for reform of the banking foundations that arose when the publicly owned banks were divided (by the Amato-Carli law) between ownership – which was transferred to the foundations – and business, which was conducted by the bank operating under the foundation's control. The debate on the reform of the foundations, in the Chamber and the Senate, as well as in the country at large, lasted almost two years, at times growing extremely heated. The importance of the issue certainly cannot be overestimated.

At stake are assets estimated at L70,000 billion. The power attaching to the administration of such wealth and the management of its returns is obvious. Moreover, although the importance of the foundations has diminished as a result of privatisation, they still control a significant part of the Italian banking system. At the end of the 1980s, 70 percent of the system (in terms of intermediation funds) was run by the publicly owned banks. The privatisation in 1993 of the IRI and Treasury banks reduced this share to 60 percent. Thereafter, although there have been several divestitures, in many cases the foundations have remained part of the 'stable core' which steer and control the activities of the banks. They are in fact the majority shareholders, or the largest single shareholders, in four of the five leading Italian banking groups. Furthermore, they are now extending their presence to the 'stable nucleus' of large privatised companies, and also acquiring substantial shares of private companies. It is on these latter aspects that the debate has concentrated:

1. Should the foundations pursue solely aims of social utility – on which they should concentrate their resources – divesting themselves of their bank shareholdings?
2. Although they are not required to delegate administration of their portfolios to third parties, should not restrictions be nevertheless placed on their investments, or restraints on their profitability?

The more general issue behind these problems is that, although now transformed into private corporations, these foundations still comprise a stock of wealth which is public in nature and usually identified with the part of the country in which the original bank operated. Since their assets are public, the foundations are naturally conditioned by the local authorities, which appoint members to their boards. With some praiseworthy exceptions, these appointees are usually characterised more by their political allegiance than by their banking expertise. Given that this practice is to some extent unavoidable, critics of the 'reform' have called for measures to prevent politics (and the political parties) from influencing banking activities and privatisations through the foundations.

Between two extremes – those on the political right or left who defended the *status quo* on the one hand, and those who urged radical reform on the other – it has proved impossible to find a compromise – intellectually unpopular in a country invariably unable to manage institutional innovation, even using market incentives.[13] The best solution would probably have been a situation in which the foundations operated under private law, were devoted solely to non-profit activities, and were administered by professional bankers, whose sole objective was the maximisation of medium-period returns. It would then have been possible to establish a transitional period and to introduce regulations providing the incentives and sanctions necessary to achieve the situation desired within a realistic time frame. This would have satisfied those who resented the continuing interference of politics in the restructuring of Italian capitalism, as well as those who realistically accepted that the banking foundations had a stop-gap role to perform while the financial market grew, and the development of institutional investors like the pension funds found in other countries was awaited. With the hope of fully fledged public companies once again postponed, it proved equally impossible to introduce genuine foundations. The unsatisfactory nature of the compromise eventually reached was demonstrated in two aspects of policy on which there was a very large majority in both houses of Parliament:

1. The foundations may continue – on their own or (better) jointly – to control banks.
2. They may – besides pursuing aims of social utility – also 'promote economic development', which if not something already included within the scope of social utility (despite its permissively broad definition including: education, scientific research, culture, etc.) may only supplement what others (and the local authorities in particular, according to the legislation of the last ten years) should do.

The realism of those who still regard this reform as a step forward – the Bank of Italy, for example – is contradicted by a set of unresolved issues and by some manifest confusions. It is well known that the only reason why the long-drawn-out debate of the previous two years was so hastily concluded in the last days of 1998 was that a number of important exercises in bank restructuring undertaken in that year would have otherwise lost the tax benefits provided by the new law. But other uncertainties that arose at the end of that year show that confusion still reigned. Two examples will suffice. The law incorporated a proposal by the Bank of Italy that the foundations should be among the subjects entitled to share in its capital. This, however, was criticised by the left, on the ground that since the foundations possess banks supervised by the Bank of Italy, they should not also be co-owners of the Bank of Italy!

But after the Antitrust Authority had been extremely critical of some aspects of the new law, especially as regards the unfair competition that might derive from tax incentives extended to foundations which did not pursue social ends alone but also had shares in companies, banking or otherwise, the central bank too lapsed into confusion. The Bank of Italy complained that the Antitrust Authority had intervened in matters that were not within its competence, given that it was not the authority that was guarantor of competition and the market but the Bank of Italy itself. Law 287/90, in fact, gave the Bank powers to combat arrangements restricting free competition and abuse of dominant position *vis-à-vis* … banking companies and credit institutions!

As these examples confirm, then, reform of the banking foundations has been postponed to some time in the future.[14]

The Consolidated Text on Privatisation

To some extent, the proposal to reform the law on privatisation has suffered the same fate. Indeed, only when Italy was referred to the european Court of Justice by the EU Commission in mid-December 1998, did the Italian Council of Ministers approve, for onward transmission to Parliament, the bill which had been drafted by the Treasury in July allowing for the removal of the Treasury's own 'special powers.'[15] These were retained under Article 2 of law no. 474/1994 where privatisation affected specific sectors (defence, public services, telecommunications, transport). As with discrimination against foreign financial intermediaries lacking local subsidiaries operating in Italy, so in the case of 'golden shares', more general reform would enable Italy to comply with the prescriptions of Brussels. But only in the cases of market organisation and in adjustments to its banking system has Italy respected EU rules.

The planned Consolidated Text deals with 'provisions on the divestiture and management of shares in publicly owned companies'. The government's aim – even more than in the cases of other Consolidated Texts – was not only to revise and co-ordinate existing procedures, but also to rework them into a better conceived and more permanent framework than in the past. Previously many publicly owned assets had been sold off through the device of decree laws some of which (having expired after the statutory sixty days expired) had had to be reiterated several times. In practice this meant that each divestiture came about by distinct mechanisms, and with its own specific rules. This may have had political advantages, but it is not compatible with predictable regulations and efficient financial markets. As the preface to the Consolidated Text emphasises, what counts is to have 'predictable and flexible regulations'. The basic goal of the rules governing the divestiture of public assets (and any intermediate stages to that end) should be that the state ceases to be an entrepreneur, and limits itself to the role of regulator. Collective goals should then no longer be achieved through public ownership but through a system of rules which produces the public good represented by efficient markets.[16] It is this general principle that has determined the procedures adopted to decide and implement divestitures, and also to exercise – transparently and with an appropriate code of conduct – the rights of the shareholder, 'in order to enhance the value of participations, the efficiency of the markets, and the development of productive activities' (Article 2). The public and political debate on the draft version of this Consolidated Text has not yet begun, but it is already possible to foresee the points of controversy that will arise.

Discussion here is restricted to the two issues that at the moment seem most important. At the state level, a still unresolved problem is the relationship between ministries. Since the Minster of State-Controlled Enterprises was abolished in 1993, and shareholder rights were transferred to the Treasury Minister, the problem has repeatedly arisen of the relationships of the publicly owned companies with the ministers responsible for the sectors in which they operate. The Cavazzuti Committee, which has drawn up the new bill, understandably gives continuing priority to the Treasury: but it is unclear whether this priority will survive the bill's parliamentary passage. The second problem concerns local public services, which in recent years have been targeted by various legislative texts, without, however, any of the reforms proposed passing into law. The Consolidated Text on privatisation is intended to establish a substantially uniform regulatory framework for the sale of state shareholdings and the 'non-state public activities'. If there are to be differences in treatment, these will have to be justified by the differences, particularly the economic differences across the specific sectors. Yet this question too, as valid for the non-state 'administrations' as it is critical in relation to the state, has yet to be resolved by Parliament. The experience of the political debate on the banking foundations gives an idea of what will happen to divestiture by local authorities as the matter passes through Parliament (the signs are already evident, in fact). After all, the provisions of law 142 of 1990 regarding the management forms to be adopted for public services defined as having 'economic and business importance' has not yet been fully implemented. It will therefore be difficult to impose transformation into joint-stock companies as the obligatory step prior to the transfer, partial or total, of shareholdings in the companies that run local public services. Yet delays in this area will be paid for later: the backwardness of the sector – which certainly cannot be remedied by prolonging muncipal ownership – will render it vulnerable to competitors from other european countries. Delaying modernisation will mean, in fact, having encouraged colonisation.

Conclusions

The reforms accomplished or begun in 1998 are all highly significant. They are part of the adjustment of the Italian financial system to the requirements of european integration, which is in its turn part of a process of financial globalisation. Despite the many difficulties witnessed during the year, that process is not likely to be stopped.

Success for Italy depends on whether, in a reasonable timescale, it will be able to deal with its principal anomalies:[17]

1. the restricted growth of its capital market and therefore the dominance of banks over other financial institutions;
2. and yet despite this dominance, the absence of stable long-term relations between banks and businesses that typify systems geared to the banking system.

Italy's has long been a capitalism 'of the few', because the 'few' have controlled both the largest private enterprises and the largest public ones. It has proved impossible to transform into strengths the two features that give the country's economic system its greatest competitive capacity and act as its principal sheet anchor: on the one hand, the incredible vitality of a myriad of small firms, on the other, a high propensity to save. Yet some things have changed in recent years: bank mergers, the growth of private banking, and the development of the Stock Exchange are three areas in which much has been done. There are still delays in other sectors – typically privatisation and bank ownership – and in these cases the little that has been achieved contrasts with the great deal left to be done – especially regarding local public services and the banking foundations. The latter are still what Renzo Costi[18] has described as standing midway between holdings and charitable institutions – 'charitable holdings', one might say.

Translated by Adrian Belton

Notes

1. See 'Rapporto IRS sul mercato azionario, 1998', *Il Sole 24 Ore*, Milan, 1998, pp. 168-73. This report argues that it would have been preferable – compared with what actually happened – for ownership of *Borsa Spa* to have been less concentrated in the hands of a small number of banking groups. Instead ownership should have been more diffused, with all components well represented, and with a significant presence of foreign institutions.

2. The provisions of the Consolidated Text came into force as and when the enabling regulations were issued in the period 1 July-31 December 1998. For a comment by the Bank of Italy, see P. Ciocca, 'Testo unico della disciplina in materia di intermediazione finanziaria', *Bollettino Economico*, February 1998. For a comment by Consob, with critical remarks, see Consob, *Relazione per l'anno 1997*, Rome, 1998, pp. 41-45.

3. See Banca d'Italia, *Testo unico delle leggi in materia bancaria e creditizia*, Rome, 1997.

4. See on this IRS, op. cit., pp. 174-82.

5. In recent years, so-called 'managed saving' has acquired great importance in Italy as well. The share of 'managed' family financial activities rose from 10 to 33 percent in the period 1990-97, and according to estimates it grew even further in 1998. On the other hand, the average share of 'managed' family savings in the more developed countries is more than 40 percent. This size of this stock of wealth explains the interest aroused by the Italian market in foreign operators.

6. More in general, there has been a complete downgrading of public powers. Functions have been transferred to the Treasury which previously required legislative intervention, and tasks have been transferred to the Bank of Italy (or Consob) which were previously the responsibility of the Treasury. See 'La disciplina degli intermediari emanata dalla Banca d'Italia in attuazione del Testo unico delle disposizioni in materia di intermediazione finanziaria', *Bollettino Economico*, October 1998, pp. 12*-16*.

7. Consob has been most critical of the legislation as reformed by the Consolidated Text, calling for 'the deterrent capacity of the rules, and therefore rapidity and clarity (esemplarità) in their application' and pointing out that the fight against insider trading has been largely unsuccessful. Ibid., pp. 45 and 191-2.

8. In fact, the fiscal 'novelties' of 1998 were much broader: the law reforming taxation on business income came into force, with the introduction of IRAP (*Imposta regionale sulle attività produttive* or regional tax on productive activity) and DIT (Dual Income Tax); tax benefits were introduced for companies quoted on Italian – regulated markets; and taxation on contracts for the transfer of shares and securities has been reformed. These various reforms are intended to foster the growth of the Italian financial markets by eliminating or reducing fiscal discriminations that might damage them (*where* operations are performed) or Italian intermediaries (*who* may perform these operations). On these various aspects see Irs, op. cit. pp. 99-100, 124-25, 182-85, 223-55, 311-23.

9. Overall, the reform seeks to preserve fiscal neutrality among the various options available to savers. Hence, for example, the equaliser (*equalizzatore*) mechanism designed to offset taxation on managed savings (earned income is taxable) with taxation under the other two systems ('della dichiarazione' and administered savings: for both the realised income is taxable and there is a time delay in the levy which reduces it in effective terms). However, the advantages of 'channelling' savings in the form of administered savings are still evident, and even more so those of managed savings. See M. F. Ambrosanio, La riforma della tassazione dei redditi delle attività finanziarie: riflessi sugli intermediari, *Quaderno* 158, Assbb – Milan Università Cattolica: 1998.

10. What follows is taken from: Ministero del Tesoro, *Schema Nazionale di Piazza*, (3rd ed.), Rome, May 1998. The euro Committee was organized into three Subcommittees responsible for the areas 'Public Administration'; 'Finance' (monetary and financial system, including insurance); 'Business' (system of industrial, commercial, crafts and agricultural firms). The regulations set out by the two legislative decrees (nos. 43 and 213) were scheduled to come into force on 1 January 1999.

11. See on this the two essays by L. Filippa, 'Gli effetti dell'Unione economica e monetaria sulla borsa italiana' and by F. Di Pasquali, 'Alcuni aspetti dell'impatto del passaggio all'euro per il mercato dei titoli obbligazionari privati', in IRS, op. cit., pp. 257-80 and 293-310.

12. Ibid., p. 3.

13. See on this the interview with Sabino Cassese, *Il Sole 24 Ore*, 28 April 1998, and for more positive judgement on the new law, the interview with Roberto Raton, *Il Sole 24 Ore*, 20 December 1998.

14. The entire affair of the public banks over the last ten years has been a story of partial reforms designed to pursue certain objectives, but implemented to pursue others, and then criticised for not pursuing a yet different range of objectives. When the Yamato Law was enacted it was already evident (and in the related white paper issued by the Bank of Italy) that the immediate goal was not to privatise the public banks but to emphasise that banks are businesses; to introduce greater competition; to increase the capitalisation of the public banks; and to ensure separation between banks and industry. I have written on these matters in an article published in *Il Sole 24 Ore*, 29 August 1995.

15. The 'golden share' Italian-style allows the Treasury to exercise rights of veto/approval, but also to appoint members of the board. The bill approved by the Council of Ministers states that: the law must be harmonized with EU regulations; many of these powers will simply be repealed; only special temporary powers will be envisaged.

16. This theory as briefly set out in the report attached to the bill is also present in other government measures, for example with reference to the decree law which deregulates the electricity market.

17. See P. Rossi and A. M. Tarantula Raunchy, 'Intermediari finanziari e sistema delle imprese: profili istituzionali ed evoluzione recente', *Rivista Internazionale di Scienze Sociali*, April-June 1998, 215-42. This study conducts useful analysis of the contribution by successive EEC directives to modernizing the Italian financial system. Comparison (table 1, p. 220) between the dates of the directives and their transposition shows a reduction in adjustment times. For critical analysis of the relationships between firms and the financial market see L. Caprio, 'Mercati finanziari e sistema delle imprese', *Rivista Internazionale di Scienze Sociali*, April-June 1998: 243-73.

18. See Cnel, *Gruppo di lavoro su Fondazioni Casse di Risparmio*, Rome, 1994, p. 12.

10

MALPENSA 2000

David Hine

Introduction

During 1997, a major conflict arose between the Italian govern-ment and the European Commission, and more specifically between the Ministry of Transport in Rome, and the Transport Directorate (DG VII) in Brussels. The dispute concerned the trans-fer of all scheduled passenger services other than the Milan-Rome shuttle from Linate, hitherto Milan's main airport, to Malpensa air-port, hitherto Linate's much smaller neighbour, but now expanded and modernised to serve as the major hub for northern Italy. The terms of the dispute can be stated very simply. They arose from the objections of the main European airlines to the alleged advantage given to Italy's flag-carrier, Alitalia, by the timing of and conditions for the transfer of services between the two airports, as determined by the Italian government. Tangential to this central issue, but complicating it, were other arguments concerning Italian interests affected by the airport development. These included Alitalia's domestic competitor, Air One, various Italian consumer groups, the trade unions, and representatives of Italian cities and regions unhappy about the switch of domestic Italian services to an airport that, until provided with better ground transportation systems, was a great deal less convenient for passengers than Linate. But the principal argument was over a complicated issue of EU law. Did the fact that the airport was being opened before ground trans-portation links were in place constitute discriminatory action by the Italian authorities in favour of the national flag carrier, Alitalia? The argument that it did, as we shall see, depended on the possibility that the switch of services would consign European airlines to an inconvenient airport from which they would have difficulty attracting passenger traffic to the transoceanic routes operating our of their home airports, while Alitalia could continue to feed transoceanic routes operating out of Rome-Fiumicino from Linate?

Like many other conflicts between national governments and the Commission over state-aids and competition policy, this one involved a high degree of brinkmanship. Once the Ministry of Transport had given notification of the date for opening the new terminal, there was a year for preparations to be made, schedules to be altered, ground services to be switched, and so on. This naturally involved major operational decisions with far-reaching implications for airlines, ground services, their employees, and travellers. Malpensa would, overnight, become the largest airport in northern Italy. Such changes needed careful planning and detailed consultation with numerous parties. Yet as the deadline approached, neither the Commission, nor the Italian government, appeared willing to back down from the positions each had adopted concerning the terms and timing of the transfer. Airlines, passengers, and ground-service providers were therefore left in a state of extreme uncertainty about the outcome until the last possible moment.

Indeed, during the autumn of 1998, the Italian government appeared to be heading for a direct challenge to the Commission's regulatory competence on a key point of competition policy. As in several other recent disputes – the closure of the Bagnoli steel-works, and the arguments over Italian milk quotas – Italy faced the embarrassing contradiction of being the government most committed to the extension of the powers of EU institutions, while simultaneously appearing to be unwilling to accept the full implications of transferring sovereignty in commercial matters to the EU level. In the end, a compromise was found, and the new terminal opened on time – though not without many initial teething troubles due at least in part to the last-minute nature of the decision-making procedure. The European Commission forced the Italian government to make major revisions to the terms of the transfer of traffic, and a much larger volume of traffic than originally intended remained at Linate for a transitional period.

The argument provided a timely reminder, in Italy's 'year of Europe', that, notwithstanding the remarkable success Italy had achieved in satisfying the convergence criteria for monetary union, it continued to face serious difficulties in coping with the demands of economic liberalisation, and with the rules and procedures of the internal market programme. At the specific level of the air transport sector, the affair threw into sharp relief the difficulties the Italian governments of the 1990s faced in reconciling the EU's increasingly assertive policy to liberalise passenger traffic with efforts to rectify many years of inadequate policy in relation to both airport development and the competitiveness of Alitalia, the country's major airline.

The Ambiguities of EU Air Transport Policy

Battles of will between national governments and the Commission are frequent in competition policy, not least because the precise meaning of the law relating to competition is complex and most commercial situations to which it has to be applied contain many uncertainties. Deciding what is an anti-competitive or discriminatory practice frequently appears, to outsiders, to be a subjective matter. Moreover, when acting in its quasi-judicial role as regulator and enforcer, the Commission never finds it easy to sustain credibility in its authority or neutrality. The Commissioners themselves often either play – or appear to commentators to play – the role of brokers between their own national governments and the Commission. The Commission is often suspected of seeking to expand its sphere of policy competence and authority by asserting its will over national governments in ways which from a legal point of view leave room for some doubt. This institutional self-interest in the outcome of proceedings that establish breaches of the law relating to state-aids and competition can also undermine confidence in the Commission's impartiality. Yet at the same time, precisely because of the scarce resources of which it disposes, and because of the difficulty it has in enforcing its will in a time frame sufficiently short to be meaningful in commercial terms, the Commission has to be willing to compromise. National governments know this, and they themselves are also at times disposed to test their policies to the limit in the hope that they can extract a deal from the Commission that exceeds what the letter of the law suggests they are entitled to.

Italy was certainly not the first member state to come to this conclusion. In fact, its main misfortune in 1998 was that it was trying to rectify its failure to do so more aggressively in earlier years, when the Commission's transport policy had been much less developed. In fact, it was only in the latter half of the 1980s that air-transport policy really developed any momentum at the European level. Until then, notwithstanding a clear treaty-base for a common transport policy (art. 84.2), and notwithstanding a number of detailed provisions of competition policy preventing discrimination,[1] very little progress had been made. The traditional system of bilateral agreements, regulated by a number of wider multinational accords, established at the end of the Second World War, continued to dominate the industry. There was, obviously, a greater deal of international cooperation in such an international industry, but almost all of it was through intergovernmental agencies such as the International Civil Aviation Organisation, and within Europe specifically ECAC (the European Civil Aviation Conference) and Eurocontrol (the European Organisation for the Safety of Air Navigation). States controlled air transport because they retained full sovereignty over their national airspace, and they therefore pursued policies built almost exclusively on a definition of national interest determined by the prestige of national flag-carrier airlines, by employment in the airline sector, and by the commercial needs of the aircraft construction industry. The European approach to air transport regulation was therefore, in the words of one observer, a policy of 'protectionism, collusion, and anti-competitive practice.'[2]

The main factors which changed this situation were the liberalisation of air transport regulation in the US in the 1970s and early 1980s, the liberalising philosophy of the EC's own internal market programme in the mid-1980s. and the landmark judgement by the European Court of Justice in 1986, which established that the EC's competition provisions should apply to the air transport industry.[3] The result, the following year, was the first of three packages of liberalisation which have gradually opened up the sector to a considerably higher degree of competition. The third of these – agreed in 1992 – was in many respects the most far-reaching in relation to price competition and access to markets, giving airlines far greater freedom to set their own fares, and establishing a common EU regime for access to markets. In relation to the anti-competitive practices which were the main issue in the Malpensa case, however, the basic breakthrough was already achieved in the first package, which allowed the EC's competition rules to apply to air transport, though adding the general proviso applying to many areas of state aids: namely that the Commission had the discretion to grant exemptions in certain specific instances (for example regional development aid). This, and the 1990 Merger Regulation, greatly changed the environment in which national governments and national airlines operated. Mergers were henceforth subject to Commission approval, and governments were required to notify the Commission of plans to provide state assistance to airlines whether directly, or through the granting of licences and concessions. Where grants, loans, or guarantees were made, they had to be given on market terms, and with a reasonable expectation of an effective commercial return. Where operating concessions were granted, they had to be non discriminatory, and in 1993 the Council of Ministers approved a regulation establishing a code of conduct requiring that the allocation of airport landing slots be allocated on a non-discriminatory basis.[4]

In the 1990s, therefore, the Commission began to look very carefully at various forms of state assistance to national airlines, frequently approving proposed measures only in return for modifications, or for assurances about the need for no future aid packages. By 1994 it was expressing the view that state support should be phased out entirely by 1997, and though this was clearly unrealistic, and has not been achieved, the very fact that the Commission could express such an aspiration indicates how far the intellectual climate has changed in relation to air transport in the 1990s.

For the Prodi government, the first really serious test of the impact of this new policy came in 1997. The government was concerned about the consequences for Alitalia of the liberalisation of air transport. Competition on both the domestic front (Air One and Meridiana) and from new low-cost foreign airlines, was eroding Alitalia's position. It faced key decisions over its future marketing strategy (how far to develop its own low-cost feeder airline, Alitalia Team), its route network, its alliances, and the modernisation of its fleet. And it had to do so with some of the highest paid and most militant pilots and cabin staff in Europe. Privatisation had been the official government strategy for Alitalia for several years, but earlier attempts to put the company on a sound financial footing in preparation for the flotation of the 86.4 percent held by IRI, had foundered on opposition at the political and trade-union levels. The managing director (*Amministratore delegato*) Roberto Schisano, who was removed in 1995, and Renato Riverso, who resigned as President in March 1966, had both been unsuccessful in getting agreement to a restructuring plan preparatory to full privatisation. Undeterred, the Prodi government, and the new *managing director* Domenico Cempella, announced in the spring of 1997 a new three-phase financial restructuring package for the company, involving the injection of L2.750 billions by its parent company IRI. By now, however, negotiations were complicated not only by domestic politics and the trade unions, but also by the increasing assertiveness of the Transport Directorate in Brussels.

The directorate, which had recently attracted heavy criticism for its leniency over approval of state aid packages to Iberia and Air France, was determined to lay down exacting conditions in relation to the Alitalia package, and ruled that the cash injection was not

justifiable on straight commercial grounds, and therefore constituted state aid. Several weeks of difficult negotiations were
required in the summer of 1997 between Claudio Burlando, Minister of Transport, and the EU's Transport Commissioner, Neil Kinnock, before agreement was reached. The conditions laid down by
the Commission included:

1. substantial cuts in personnel;
2. limitations on Alitalia's pricing policy to ensure that it did not
   use the subsidy to undercut its competitors;
3. strict capacity limits during the period of the restructuring package;
4. a bar on the purchase of stakes in other airlines;
5. more transparent accounting methods;
6. a commitment by the Italian government not to provide any further assistance to the company, and to limit itself to the role of
   a 'normal' shareholder;
7. regular reporting and monitoring procedures to enable the Commission to judge whether its conditions had been observed,
   including the key provision that the 1998 and 1999 tranches would
   only be authorised following receipt of a satisfactory report.

Some of these externally imposed conditions were probably not
entirely unwelcome to the Italian government. The European *vincolo esterno* can at times be a helpful discipline on matters of
labour costs and staffing in the public sector. The last two conditions, however, (no further state aids, and regular monitoring) contained considerable potential difficulties, and were likely to make
the Commission more than usually vigilant about any future assistance the Italian government might seem to be offering Alitalia.

Nevertheless, it was by no means clear that, having been a tough
enforcer of competition rules in the spring, the Commission would
become an even tougher one over the much less clear-cut case it
was to face in relation to Malpensa in the autumn. Certainly, had
the terms of the Burlando decree moving air traffic from Linate to
Malpensa been issued in earlier decades, or possibly even earlier in
the 1990s, they would have generated a good deal less controversy.
European governments have a long history of the manipulation of
routes in ways that have given national flag carriers advantages
over their competitors. The French government has continued to do
so into the late 1990s in relation to its two Parisienne airports of
Orly and Roissy/Charles de Gaulle, (though its efforts have never
been on the dramatic scale seen in relation to the switch from
Linate to Malpensa, and indeed it too has encountered difficulties

with the Commission). Moreover, the policy of creating a regional hub airport in northern Italy was by any criteria a desirable step, and indeed one supported by the European Union itself in that EU financial support for it was granted in 1994, when it was included in the EU's new programme of transnational transport and communication networks. It was not therefore unreasonable of the Italian government to expect to be able to bring the airport into operation as soon as possible. Alitalia was supposed to be put on a sound commercial basis for privatisation and to bring the airport into full operation would give the company the opportunity to develop a far better base in northern Italy than it had hitherto enjoyed at Linate.

The Italian government therefore had at least some reasons to hope that, notwithstanding the tougher framework against state aids in air transport which had developed in the 1990s, it would not encounter difficulties over Malpensa. Competition law in this area was very unclear, and the Commission itself had previously backed away from conflicts with other EU governments. In any case, the hub-airport principle was squarely in line with EU thinking. On the other hand, the Transport Directorate within the Commission was growing bolder by the year, and by the start of 1998 had an agenda of unfinished business with the Italian government which was set to complicate matters considerably.

Malpensa 2000

The development of Malpensa airport has a long history. It was opened in 1948, and hopes were raised that it would become a major international airport serving northern Italy. However, located 53 km. from the Milan city centre, it was always much less accessible than Linate, only 10 km. from the centre. Linate became the major airport, and as ground transportation in the Milan hinterland became more congested, Linate's locational advantage grew. By 1997 Malpensa's passenger volume was still only 3.9 million, whereas Linate's was fourteen million. The latter had by then become grossly overcrowded (its safe and comfortable capacity was only eight million) and experts had long advocated turning Malpensa into the main international airport. Indeed, the first studies for this go back to the mid-1960s, but it was only in 1986 that plans were finally approved, and financing made available. In 1990, work began on the Malpensa 2000 terminal, and in 1994, the project became one of the fourteen principal projects to be supported under the EU's trans-European networks programme.

By the 1990s, the key concept in air transport planning, and one of the key factors determining the success of commercial airlines, was the existence of 'hub and spokes' networks by which smaller regional airports fed major hubs, the volume of traffic between which became the major commercial battleground for European airlines. Access to a regional network feeding into a major international hub which itself was no subject to any serious capacity limits, came to be seen as a *sine qua non* for a successful international airline of any size. Italy's problem was that it had such a hub in Rome's Fiumicino airport, but Fiumicino was not optimally located from either an Italian or a European point of view. It was important to have a northern hub as well, but Linate was too overcrowded to perform such a role, and capacity for expansion nonexistent. This placed Alitalia at a severe disadvantage in comparison with other European airlines, and clearly created a serious drainage of passenger volume to other European hubs, and therefore to other carriers, especially for Italians flying to North America and the Far East. For an airline already burdened with serious handicaps (low levels of investment, poor staff morale, and intense union militancy, etc.) Milan's airport problem needed a radical solution. The Italian government therefore finally decided in 1994 that Malpensa should become northern Italy's main airport, and in 1996, with the Malpensa 2000 terminal nearing completion, though with ground infrastructure links still some way away from completion, the Transport Ministry took the radical step of approving, in principle, the eventual transfer of *all* commercial flights other than the lucrative Milan-Rome shuttle, dominated, naturally enough, by Alitalia, to Malpensa.

As long as nothing was fixed in relation to the phasing in of this transfer, these decisions remained relatively uncontroversial, at least from the point of view of EU competition policy, though several user groups among both airlines and passengers were already worried about the switch from a city centre airport to one so far from the city. All this changed on 25 October 1997, when Transport Minister Claudio Burlando issued the controversial decree requiring that all services other than those generating at least two million passengers per year (in effect only the Milan-Rome shuttle) would move to Malpensa within one year, i.e. on 25 October 1998.

At most levels, the decree was a logical step. If Malpensa was to develop quickly into a real hub, it made no sense to feed either domestic or European domestic lines into a northern airport from which there were no connections, and force onward passengers to travel by ground transport across the city and 53 km. out to the northwest. The argument did not apply to flights between Milan and Rome, since Rome's Fiumicino was a hub airport in itself. But most other services flying into Milan carried both passengers terminating their journeys there, and others connecting to extra-European services. Southern cities protested that passengers terminating at Milan now faced a considerable disadvantage compared with passengers coming from Rome, but the authorities argued that this was temporary, was counterbalanced by the advantages for those making connections at Malpensa, and that anyway, given Linate's capacity, it made little sense to close the airport down to scheduled services entirely.

The real problem lay in the transferring of flights to Malpensa before the new ground transportation systems were ready. Passengers for all destinations other than Rome would have to make their way out to Malpensa: a journey of well over an hour at peak times given the poor quality of the overcrowded A8 motorway serving Malpensa, and given the lack of a fast rail-link. The A8 was to have a new emergency lane which would improve its capacity and free it from endemic jams caused by breakdowns and accidents, and a new fast rail-link was in progress, but the former would not be ready for at least two years after Malpensa opened, and the latter, under construction by *Ferrovie Nord*, would not be operative until May 1999 at the earliest.

Airlines and passengers thus faced not only the predictable teething difficulties of transferring such a huge volume of traffic from one airport to another, but also at least two years' difficulties in ground communications with the airport. Most significantly of all, the decision appeared to competitors to give Alitalia a major advantage in terms of connections from Linate to the Rome hub, compared with those from Malpensa to hubs in other EU member states; connections to Alitalia's major hub in Rome via Linate were now much more convenient than those to competitors' major hubs elsewhere in Europe via Malpensa.

Negotiations Between Burlando and Kinnock

The Burlando decree provided all parties – airlines, service providers, and the European Commission – with a year to prepare for the transfer to Malpensa. On the face of it, the notice was adequate, since airlines had known about the switch in principle for some years, and the only reason for not defining the date more precisely had been that until it was clear that works at the airport would be complete, it was unwise to set a fixed date. In fact by no means everything would be complete by October 1998. In addition to ground transportation links to Milan, the monorail system connecting the new 2000 terminal with the older one would not be completed until 2002. What airlines immediately complained

about, however, was that they were expected to move all their services to Malpensa before ground transportation was in place.

Two days after the decree was issued, representatives of the
nine main EU airlines affected by the decision met with representatives of the Transport Ministry to protest against the plan and
demand that a proportion of their services should continue to use
the Linate link, in order to connect with their hubs elsewhere in
the EU. The ministry showed no inclination to modify the terms of
the decree, however. It emphasised that the transfer of traffic had
been the subject of extensive consultation with the European Commission, which had judged it to conform with the vital EC regulation on access (Regulation 2408/92).[5] The following day the nine
companies announced their resolve to appeal to both the Competition and Transport Directorates of the European Commission, and
to bring a case before the Court of Justice.

The months that followed saw the wheels of commercial litigation at EU level gradually enmeshed, though it was only in February that the airline companies were ready to file their complaint
with the Commission, and only the following June, when it began
to emerge that the Commission was taking the complaint seriously,
that negotiations began in earnest. The Italian authorities were
understandably unwilling to make any clear offers of compromise
in advance of the Commission's decisions, though they expressed
some irritation that the procedures were taking so long. Until they
knew what view the Commission would take, there was no reason
to reveal any fall-back positions they might have, particularly since
such fall-back possibilities had significant domestic political consequences. In essence, however, there were four such possibilities:

1. to close Linate entirely, and move all flights to Malpensa from
   day one;
2. to prevent through check-ins from Linate to connecting Alitalia
   flights from Rome-Fiumicino (the so-called 'volo senza valigia'
   option, which would address directly the claim that Alitalia
   would benefit commercially from staying at Linate, by draining
   off north-Italian feeder-passengers from its competitors);
3. to switch the Milan-Rome shuttle to Rome-Ciampino, which
   would have the same deterrent effect in making the shuttle less
   desirable as a feeder to Rome-Fiumicino;
4. to delay the full transfer of airline traffic from Linate to Malpensa
   until the completion of the ground transportation systems.

However, it was only in early September, six weeks before the
opening date, that the Commission's opinion was finally ratified

and communicated formally to the Italian government. Having established its view of the commercial facts as it understood them, the Transport Directorate had first to put the matter to the consultative management committee (effectively representatives of national governments) and then to the full college of Commissioners. What proved especially galling to the Italian government was that there was little understanding of its case at any of the three final stages. The Transport Directorate appeared determined to establish its right to judge on a matter of discriminatory action by national authorities. The consultative committee, which met on 17 August, appeared to split largely along lines of national interest, only the Italian and Dutch representatives (the Dutch airline KLM having an outline cooperation agreement with Alitalia) voting against the Transport Directorate's opinion.[6] And finally in the Commission, where it was hoped that a summer of lobbying would persuade other members of the Commission to challenge Neil Kinnock, there was solid support for the Transport Directorate.

The meeting of the college of Commissioners on 9 September finally confirmed that the Italian government would be operating in defiance of EU law if it went ahead with its decision to open the Malpensa 2000 terminal and transfer all services other than the Milan-Rome shuttle to Malpensa. In response, the Italian government asked the Commission to delay formal communication of this for one week, while it tried to find a compromise solution. A possible solution lay in the transferral of the Milan-Rome shuttle to Rome-Ciampino, thereby closing off the possibility of Alitalia's using the shuttle to feed its Fiumicino services. However, on 15 September, a meeting of all the main Italian actors convened by prime minister Romano Prodi ran up against the formidable obstacle of the mayor of Rome, Francesco Rutelli, and the Rome city council. They were vehemently opposed to a switch to Ciampino which they argued would damage Rome and its principal airport. Harsh words were exchanged between Roberto Formigoni, President of the Lombardy Regional Council, and Rutelli, but with the city of Rome against a switch of this type (which would in any case have been expensive and disruptive), the Ciampino option disappeared as quickly as it had been raised.[7] On 16 September, a further fruitless meeting was held between Burlando and Kinnock, the Commission by now visibly irritated that complex solutions aired by the Italian authorities, which required increasingly rapid study and response by the Transport Directorate, and were vanishing into thin air even before they were formally tabled.[8] On the prospect of a head-on confrontation between the Italian government and the Commission, shares in the small proportion of Alitalia's shares quoted on the Milan stock market fell by 4.3 percent: an ominous sign for Alitalia's eventual privatisation.

The meeting of the Transport Ministers' Council on 1 October seemed to offer some possibility of a last-minute compromise, but this too came and went without assistance to the Italian position.[9] By the last days of September, in any case, it was becoming clear that the only solution was for the Italian government to accept what – from its point of view – was the decidedly suboptimal solution of a phased transfer of services from Linate to Malpensa. This would undoubtedly slow down the development of Malpensa as a hub airport for Alitalia, though it would at least avoid outright Italian defiance of EU law. The initial positions between Rome and Brussels over this formula were very divergent – the former offering the possibility that 20 percent of flights would stay at Linate, the latter demanding a figure closer to 40 percent. There was also a good deal of detailed argument about how the services would be allocated, what proportion of them would be to the hub airports of Alitalia's competitors, and whether the parameters were to be defined by the number of flights, or by carrying capacity.

As negotiations proceeded, moreover, the issue got caught up with the emerging government crisis in Rome, making it more difficult for the government to manage the issue as a news story and to keep the Italian side united. The discordant note being struck by southern mayors, and by Alitalia's domestic Italian competitors, and the critical articles appearing in the press over Italian handling of the case, particularly in relation to the last-minute nature of negotiations, all worked to limit the government's freedom of manoeuvre. Moreover, having effectively conceded the case for retaining at least a proportion of services to other European capitals for a temporary period, there was a strong argument for issuing an amended decree giving effect to this, even if it did not satisfy the Commission fully. Doing so would put the Italian government on far stronger ground against the Commission in any subsequent litigation in the European Court of Justice, and might even deter the Commission from taking action altogether. Unilateral modification to the decree would not end the dispute altogether, but would at this stage be better than the full defiance implied by pressing ahead on the basis of the original 1997 decree. 5 or 6 October had at one stage been thought of as the last possible moment for issuing an amended decree, but on 8 October, with a political crisis in full swing, and a vote of confidence on the Prodi government due within twenty-four hours, the decree had still not appeared, nor had any deal had been finalised with the Commission. Burlando was still at that date reported to be ready to issue a new decree unilaterally. It would have met a good part of the Commission's demands, but would not have done so completely, and would therefore still lay the Italian government open to prosecution.[10] At the same time the Transport Ministry was preparing its legal counteroffensive against the Commission, claiming before the European Court of Justice that the Commission had exceeded its powers by its decision of 9 September.

In reality, however, time had finally run out for the Italian government. Romano Prodi, hitherto more hawkish than Burlando himself, judged that the political risks of confrontation were too great, and held the latter back from a final break.[11] Instead, with the reported help of the two Italian members of the Commission, Mario Monti and Emma Bonnino, further discussions were held with Neil Kinnock. On Wednesday 14 October, eleven days before the scheduled opening, a deal was finally approved by Brussels, and the long-awaited modified decree was issued in Rome. The terms of the decree allowed for a two-year transitional period, until completion of both the road and rail- links between Malpensa and the city centre, during which 34 percent of the flight departures of the previous year would be permitted to remain at Linate, though no new destinations could be added during that period. Airlines would have complete freedom to decide which services within the 34 percent would stay at Linate and which would go elsewhere.[12]

The new terminal thus duly opened on time, though there were understandable teething troubles. Some of these were no doubt caused by the last-minute uncertainties of the dispute with Brussels, but others were the natural difficulties of moving large numbers of flights between airports (Hong Kong and Oslo both faced similar levels of chaos in their opening days). Alitalia and the Italian government expressed themselves disappointed that, with such a large proportion of flights remaining at Linate, the benefits to the company of a new north-Italian hub airport would not come in fully until 2001, when all flights other than the Rome shuttle would be transferred to Malpensa. There was considerable relief in political circles that a bruising and damaging legal confrontation with the Commission had been avoided. Many passengers remained grateful for a postponement of the day when they had to make the 53 km. journey into the centre of the city to a time when communications had been modernised. Passengers from southern Italy were not so fortunate, and litigation was quickly though unconvincingly initiated in the Italian administrative courts to seek rectification of the perceived injustice. All in all, with the airport opening on time, honour had just about been saved on both sides, though there was little doubt that the Italian government had been forced to back down from a position which it had believed to have been entirely justified in legal and constitutional terms.

Conclusion

By bringing the Malpensa affair to a mutually acceptable conclusion before the official opening of the new terminal, the Italian authorities and the Commission spared themselves the indignity of open litigation in the Italian courts and the European Court of Justice over the Commission's power to intervene in detail over airport usage at national level. The merits of the Commission's powers to intervene, which were widely questioned in Italy,[13] have not therefore been tested in open court, and they cannot be resolved in this chapter. The strongest argument in the Italian government's armoury was undoubtedly that it was extremely difficult to judge the extent, if any, of the discrimination involved in allowing Alitalia to use Linate for the Rome-Milan shuttle, while moving all other services to Malpensa. Exactly how many passengers would have used non-Italian feeder services to non-Italian airports, for onward connections, instead of flying from Linate to Fiumicino, to connect with Alitalia onward services, clearly depended on a range of variables. These included scheduling, pricing, and the speed with which Malpensa itself was able to develop as a hub offering services which would make feeder-leg services unnecessary.

There can be no doubt that the underlying cause of the legal dispute was Italy's failure to manage the opening of the airport more effectively, however. There would have been no case at all for claiming discrimination if ground transportation services had been in place from the opening in October 1998. By failing in this respect, the Italian government could be said to have placed itself at legal and political risk. But in this sense the fault lay with the Italian political system more than with the Prodi government. The Prodi government inherited the lack of a decent hub airport in Italy's most populous and prosperous region, it inherited a much-overdue project to rectify that lack, and it inherited the business difficulties of Alitalia. All three were the consequences of the policy failures of earlier governments. It also inherited the timetable for the building of the road and rail- link with the city, together with all the legal, technical, and planning problems involved.[14] Faced with the timing problem, the Italian government did what any European government would do. It decided to open the airport without delay, and give northern Italy a hub airport capable of competing with those long since established elsewhere in the EU.

In so doing, it would also put Alitalia in a better position to compete commercially without further state support, by giving it a hub airport close to a large population. Even a two-year delay in bringing these results about would be commercially damaging for Alitalia. Until the company was privatised, it could not realistically expect to get to grips with its difficult problems of over-manning and low productivity, yet it could not be privatised until it could offer prospective investors a clear business plan for the future. Given that the chief failure of Italian air transport policy over the years had been the failure to give its national flag-carrier the support other governments had given theirs, the Italian government could reasonably consider that it was justified in opening the airport fully in October 1998.

The principal criticism that can be levelled at the Prodi government, therefore, is that it failed to handle its *political* relationships with the European Union well, and that as a result it suffered extensive delays in coming to a settlement, and projected the impression of intransigence, lack of preparation, and improvisation. Even this criticism has to be considered carefully, however. If Italy lacks influence in EU decision-making this is mainly the consequence of its alleged passivity in the preparatory phase of the legislative process, especially in working parties, consultative committees, and the Council of Ministers. Here the technical deficiencies of the Italian public administration, and the poor coordination of Italian political objectives have probably been to blame. But there is less evidence that, despite some periodic exasperation with Italy for delays in implementing EU law, or for breaking it, that there is systematic discrimination against Italy on the part of the Commission. Personal relations between Claudio Burlando and Neil Kinnock were obviously severely strained by the issue, but there is no obvious evidence that this was other than the natural consequence of the complexity of the issue and the approaching deadline.

It is in fact much more plausible to argue that the Prodi government simply encountered bad luck in the timing of the incident. The government came up against a Transport Directorate which had been enjoying a rising status in Brussels, as transport policy became more important within the EU as a whole. Member states were at last beginning to show a willingness to accept more far-reaching levels of liberalisation of public transport services than in the past. Indeed, with the development of the trans-European networks programme, the Commission was beginning to develop an appetite for a role in transport planning that far exceeded anything that had gone before. From its role as competition regulator, it was seeking to move on to the role of strategic policy leader, intervening in infrastructure provision and even developing views of corporate mergers and consolidation in the airline industry to enable Europe to face transatlantic competition. The Transport Directorate had the great majority of member states (and their national flag-carriers) behind it on the Malpensa issue, and could pose not only as the guardian of legality, but as the guardian of the convenience of consumer. Even if the legal standing of its case was untested, therefore, the Transport Directorate was in a good position to take on the Italian government. In the last stages of the dispute, moreover, it faced a government in deep political difficulties. Against tougher and more united governments, the Commission had often chosen to retreat. In this case, with more urgent political battles to fight at home, and with the Alitalia share-price to worry about, it was the Prodi government which appears to have judged it expedient to climb down.

But while the Prodi government had bad luck in facing an assertive Commission at a moment of domestic political weakness, there are clearly lessons of a more general nature to be gleaned from the affair. The first is that the liberalisation of public services in Europe has had the paradoxical consequence of increasing the legal and political complexity of the decision-taking process. Governments that do not take adequate account of this are likely, as the Italian government found, to be embarrassed by some apparently minor aspect of policy that they have not dealt with adequately. Above all, liberalisation has increased the number of regulators with a stake in decisions. At the European level there is the Commission and the Court of Justice. At national level, regulatory authorities have sprung up, alongside supervisory ministries, while administrative courts have also become involved, especially in the provision of local public services, but also increasingly at national level as well. (The recent involvement of the TAR in the case of Professor Di Bella's anti-cancer treatment was a dramatic illustration of the unexpected consequences of this.) And while one might expect that with liberalisation, the law relating to public services should become less complex – and indeed eventually almost disappear – in fact it may instead become more complex, as both national governments and the European Union try to legislate to prevent private monopolies substituting the previous public ones. It is possible in due course that the legal uncertainties produced by the overlapping jurisdictions of European, national, and local tiers of authority will disappear, but this is by no means guaranteed. The national champion mentality is unlikely to disappear at national government level as long as there are national-flag carriers like Alitalia. Even the privatised flag-carriers like British Airways continue to enjoy a significant degree of political support from national governments, and this support includes encouraging the Commission to involve itself in legal proceedings whenever there is the suspicion of state support or discrimination.

Faced with these complexities, the lesson for governments is vigilance, and clear-sighted and effective policy-making. Rules and their policy implications need to be properly understood by all actors in the political system, both nationally and locally, if outcomes like that in the Malpensa case are to be avoided. But governments also need to be effective managers of the public presentation of policy issues, and this is perhaps the second important lesson of the Malpensa affair. Every EU state has its peculiarities in dealing with the EU. In the British case, for example, a recurrent problem is that, having been politically isolated on so many occasions, the UK press has a natural tendency to focus on situations where policy isolation seems to bear a serious cost for the United Kingdom. Yet precisely because public opinion is suspicious of integration initiatives, UK governments are frequently unable to reverse this by building alliances and pushing forward their own agenda. UK governments are criticised if they are isolated, and criticised for the consequences of making friends. In the Italian case, the problem operates in the same way, though starting from different assumptions. There is a tendency in Italian public opinion to be highly supportive of the European Union and integration initiatives, and to regard European governance as in at least some respects superior to Italian governance. The consequence is sometimes that, when Italy is not fairly treated by Brussels, it is difficult to mobilise public opinion behind the government in Rome. This is partly because the government itself is frequently distracted by domestic political problems, as in the case of the Prodi government in the autumn of 1998, but also because the government has some difficulty in presenting a strong case to the Italian public, that will win unequivocal domestic support, and give the government the confidence to carry its disagreement with the EU to a conclusion.

Notes

1. In the Treaty of Rome the following articles were in principle capable of prohibiting many of the practices by which governments supported their national airlines: Article 7 (prevention of discrimination between EC nationals), art. 85 (outlawing restrictive practices) Article 86 (abuse of dominant market position), Articles 90-94 (discrimination in favour of public enterprise).
2. Kassim, H. 'Air transport' in Menon, A., and Kassim, H., *The European Union and National Industrial Policy, London*, Routledge, 1996, p. 114.

3. Ibid. p. 114.
4. Council of Ministers, Regulation 95/93, *Official Journal*, L 14, 22 January 1993.
5. 'Braccio di ferro su Malpensa' *La Stampa*, 28 October 1998, p. 23.
6. 'Malpensa 2000, primo no europeo', *Il Sole 24 Ore*, 18 August 1998.
7. 'Ultimo mosse per Malpensa' *Il Sole 24 Ore*, 15 September 1998.
8. 'Malpensa, naufraga la trattiva' *Il Sole 24 Ore*, 16 September 1998.
9. 'Malpensa, nuova fumata nera' *Il Sole 24 Ore*, 2 October 1998.
10. 'Malpensa, Prodi in campo' *Il Sole 24 Ore*, 8 October 1998.
11. 'Malpensa, Prodi in campo' *Il Sole 24 Ore*, 8 October 1998.
12. The decree was published in *Il Sole 24 Ore*, 15 October 1998.
13. See, in particular, Maurizion Maresca, 'Ma sullo scalo milanese Bruxelles non ha poteri: si tratta di una scelta di politica dei trasporti di competenza esclusiva di uno Stato membro', *Il Sole 24 Ore*, 12 August 1998.
14. Such projects are notoriously difficult to coordinate, as the history of the high-speed rail link between London and the Channel Tunnel – which will still not be in operation a full decade after the opening of the tunnel (and of the French high-speed link with Paris) – clearly demonstrates.

DOCUMENTARY APPENDIX

Compiled by Marzia Zannini

The documentary appendix to this edition of *Italian Politics* follows the pattern of earlier volumes in the series, providing important supplementary information on the events analysed in the individual chapters.

The tables cover economic, political, and social aspects of the complex and changing profile of Italian society, and reveal interrelationships between these various aspects.

The appendix follows previous practice in its first two sections. The first section (tables A1-A7) covers population, the labour force, crime, and public finances. The second section (tables B1-B8) covers electoral behaviour, including the results of the provincial and municipal elections held in June, and those held in November. The section includes data on voter turnout, and votes for party lists. It also covers the regional elections held in Trentino-Alto Adige, Fruili-Venezia Giulia, and Valle d'Aosta.

The third section (tables C1-C4) deals with institutional behaviour. It lists the composition of the D'Alema government which took office in October 1998, together with the composition of the parliamentary groups. It also provides a summary of changes in party-group affiliations in the legislature from the election of 21 April 1996 until 31 December 1998.

Table A1 *Resident Population by Age Group and Sex (in Thousands[a])*

	0-14	15-64	65 and Over	Total Population
		Age Group		
	Both Sexes			
1988	10,218	39,293	7,887	57,398
1989	9,924	39,467	8,112	57,503
1990	9,620	39,620	8,335	57,575
1991	8,993	38,991	8,773	56,757
1992	8,856	39,110	8,995	56,961
1993	8,725	39,210	9,203	57,138
1994	8,620	39,247	9,401	57,268
1995	8,678	39,090	8,872	56,640
1996	8,517	39,171	9,645	57,333
1997	8,443	39,178	9,840	57,461
	Males Only			
1988	5,245	19,482	3,162	27,889
1989	5,096	19,586	3,255	27,937
1990	4,941	19,678	3,349	27,968
1991	4,600	19,373	3,575	27,548
1992	4,534	19,450	3,671	27,655
1993	4,468	19,508	3,762	27,738
1994	4,415	19,528	3,848	27,791
1995	4,465	19,460	3,634	27,559
1996	4,364	19,498	3,956	27,818
1997	4,328	19,522	4,044	27,894

[a] Rounded figures.

Sources: Istat, *Annuario statistico italiano* (Rome, 1986-1997). 1997 data are taken from Istat, *Bollettino mensile di statistica* (Roma, marzo 1998).

Table A2 *Present Population by Position on the Labour Market (in Thousands)*

| | Labor Force | | | | | | Seeking Job | | |
| | Employed | | | | | | | | |
	Agriculture	Industry	Other	Total	Unemployed	Seeking First Job	Other Seeking Job	Total
				Both Sexes				
1988	2,058	6,788	12,256	21,102	537	1,412	937	23,988
1989	1,946	6,753	12,305	21,004	507	1,405	954	23,870
1990	1,863	6,940	12,593	21,396	483	1,357	912	24,148
1991	1,823	6,916	12,853	21,592	469	1,285	898	24,244
1992	1,749	6,851	12,859	21,459	551	1,370	878	24,258
1993	1,669	6,725	12,073	20,467	845	1,005	485	22,802
1994	1,574	6,587	11,959	20,120	983	1,048	529	22,680
1995	1,490	6,494	12,025	20,009	1,005	1,150	570	22,734
1996	1,402	6,475	12,211	20,088	1,011	1,204	548	22,851
1997	1,370	6,449	12,268	20,087	1,031	1,225	548	22,891
				Males Only				
1988	1,345	5,155	7,489	13,989	305	687	248	15,229
1989	1,261	5,103	7,487	13,851	286	676	257	15,070
1990	1,197	5,233	7,586	14,016	264	667	246	15,193
1991	1,165	5,259	7,678	14,102	256	645	241	15,244
1992	1,105	5,214	7,626	13,945	297	692	238	15,172

continued overleaf

Table A2 *continued*

1993	1,045	5,145	7,141	13,331	490	518	90	14,429
1994	999	5,022	7,036	13,057	593	552	105	14,307
1995	956	4,934	7,043	12,933	597	599	115	14,244
1996	915	4,912	7,073	12,900	594	630	112	14,236
1997	903	4,874	7,080	12,857	607	633	108	14,205

Note: In 1993 new definitions of 'labour force' and 'people seeking a job' were introduced. Since then these groups include people who are at least fifteen years (whereas the prior definitions applied to fourteen-year-olds as well). In addition, individuals who lose their job for reasons other than dismissal (resignation or end of temporary employment) are now excluded from 'others seeking job'.

Source: Istat, *Compendio statistico italiano 1997* (Rome, 1997). 1997 data are taken from Istat, *Forze di lavoro* (Rome, 1998).

Table A3 *Labour Conflicts: Number and Impact of Contractual and Non-Contractual (i.e. Political) Disputes*

	Conflicts	Thousands of Participants	Thousands of Hours Lost
Contractual Disputes			
1988	1,767	1,609	17,086
1989	1,295	2,108	21,001
1990	1,094	1,634	36,269
1991	784	750	11,573
1992	895	621	5,605
1993	1,047	848	8,796
1994	858	745	7,651
1995	545	445	6,365
1996	904	1,689	13,510
1997	923	737	8,299
Non-Contractual Disputes			
1988	2	1,103	6,120
1989	2	2,344	10,052
1990	–	–	–
1991	7	2,202	9,322
1992	8	2,557	13,905
1993	7	3,536	15,084
1994	3	1,868	15,967
1995	–	–	–
1996	–	–	–
1997	3	19	149

Notes: The figures for participants and numbers of hours lost are in thousands. 'Non-contractual conflicts' concerns political economic measures, social reform, and national and international political events.
Source: Istat, *Compendio statistico italiano 1997* (Rome, 1997). 1997 data are taken from Istat, *Bollettino mensile di statistica* (Rome, March 1998),

Table A4 *Births and Marriages*

	Births		Marriages			
	Total Births	% Variation	Total Marriages	% Variation	Religious Marriages	% Variation
1988	569,698	+3.29	318,296	+3.93	266,534	+1.79
1989	560,688	−1.58	321,272	+0.93	267,617	+0.41
1990	569,255	+1.53	319,711	−0.48	266,084	−0.57
1991	562,787	−1.14	312,061	−2.39	257,555	−3.20
1992	575,216	+2.21	312,348	+0.09	255,355	−0.85
1993	549,484	−4.47	302,230	−3.24	248,111	−2.84
1994	533,050	−2.99	285,112	−5.66	230,573	−7.07
1995	521,345	−5.12	283,025	−0.73	227,209	−1.46
1996	525,640	+0.82	272,049	−3.88	216,671	−4.64
1997	528,901	+0.62	273,111	+0.39	216,265	−0.19

Source: Istat, *Annuario statistico italiano*, (Rome, 1988-1997). 1997 data are taken from Istat, *Bollettino mensile di statistica* (Rome, March 1998).

Table A5 *Classification of Officially Recorded Crimes*

	Against Persons	Against Family or Morality	Against Property	Against Economy or Public Trust	Against the State	Other	Total
1987	138,272	14,826	1,507,040	394,360	47,093	103,395	2,204,986
1988	136,685	14,228	1,529,876	416,387	46,158	90,597	2,233,931
1989	125,769	13,073	1,573,805	422,166	41,968	97,314	2,274,095
1990	103,039	7,363	1,575,016	223,740	21,550	67,366	1,998,074
1991	121,881	10,256	2,255,918	326,584	35,590	66,834	2,817,063
1992	202,149	11,552	2,032,579	378,331	43,297	72,983	2,740,891
1993	183,072	12,694	1,980,831	373,155	54,034	76,182	2,679,968
1994	194,007	13,702	2,059,869	387,791	59,417	77,956	2,792,742
1995	199,744	14,566	2,228,538	347,560	64,934	82,738	2,938,080
1996	245,004	10,736	2,238,523	332,385	63,271	84,123	2,974,042

Note: For 1990 and subsequent years, the data are no longer fully comparable with those for earlier years. For criminal accusations against a person already subjected to investigations, the new Code of Criminal Procedure (Article 405) identifies the start of judicial action as the moment at which the person is formally charged with a crime. Unlike previous years, then, the statistics no longer include cases closed without trial for lack of evidence or other causes. In comparing 1990 and 1991 data, it should be kept in mind that orga-nizational difficulties linked to the implementation of the new Code have caused delays in judicial action and in the transmittal of infor-mation to Istat. Thus, for more classifications above, the Istat data register decreases in 1990 and then increases in 1991.

Source: Istat, *Annuario statistico italiano* (Rome, 1997); 1997 figures not yet available.

Table A6 *Gross Domestic Product (in Market Prices) and Consumer Price Index: Yearly Values and Percentage Variations over Previous Year*

	Gross Domestic Product (Billions of Lire)				Consumer Price (Index 1995 = 100)
	Current Prices	% Variation	1990 Prices	% Variation	Index % Variation
1988	1,090,023	+ 10.91	1,246,966	+ 3.87	+ 4.9
1989	1,191,961	+ 9.35	1,282,905	+ 2.88	+ 6.3
1990	1,310,659	+ 9.96	1,310,659	+ 2.16	+ 6.5
1991	1,427,571	+ 8.92	1,325,582	+ 1.14	+ 6.3
1992	1,502,493	+ 5.25	1,333,072	+ 0.56	+ 5.3
1993	1,550,296	+ 3.18	1,317,668	– 1.16	+ 4.6
1994	1,638,666	+ 5.70	1,346,267	+ 2.17	+ 4.1
1995	1,772,254	+ 8.15	1,385,860	+ 2.94	+ 5.2
1996	1,872,635	+ 5.66	1,395,018	+ 0.66	+ 4.0
1997	1,950,680	+ 4.17	1,416,055	+ 1.51	+ 2.0

Source: Banca d'Italia, *Relazione annuale* (Rome, 1998)

Table A7 *National Debt and Annual Budgetary Deficit, in Absolute Terms and as a Percentage of the Gross Domestic Product*

	National Debt			Budget Deficit		
	Billions of Lire	% Variation	% of GDP	Billions of Lire	% Variation	% of GDP
1988	1,011,780	+ 13.58	92.82	124,986	− 2.53	+ 11.2
1989	1,141,836	+ 12.85	95.79	119,466	− 4.42	+ 10.4
1990	1,284,895	+ 12.53	98.03	122,471	+ 2.52	+ 11.4
1991	1,449,980	+ 12.85	101.57	118,620	− 3.14	+ 10.6
1992	1,634,371	+ 12.72	108.78	107,189	− 9.64	+ 10.2
1993	1,815,840	+ 11.10	117.13	133,684	+ 24.72	+ 9.9
1994	1,984,067	+ 9.26	121.08	126,199	− 5.60	+ 9.0
1995	2,129,307	+ 7.32	120.15	146,592	+ 16.16	+ 7.0
1996	2,267,368	+ 6.48	121.08	119,896	− 18.21	+ 6.4
1997	2,316,016	+ 2.15	118.73	14,714	+ 12.27	+ 0.75

Source: Banca d'Italia, *Relazione annuale* (Rome, 1998).

Table B1 Electoral Participation: Municipal Elections, 24 May and 29 November 1998

	First Round, 24 May											Second Round, 7 June							
	Entitled to Vote	Voters	Valid Votes	Invalid Votes	Mayor Votes Only	Votes for Lists	Blank Ballots	% of Non Voters	% of Invalid Votes	% of Mayor Votes Only	% of Votes for Lists	Voters	Valid Votes	Invalid Votes	Blank Ballots	% of Additional Abstentionism	% of Abstentionism	% of Valid Votes	% of Invalid Votes
Asti	62,854	47,497	44,084	3,413	4,416	39,668	1,154	24.43	7.86	10.02	89.98	39,553	37,994	1,559	476	12.64	37.07	96.06	3.94
Cuneo	45,956	35,993	33,870	2,123	3,285	30,585	499	21.68	5.90	9.70	90.30	27,481	26,369	1,112	378	18.52	40.20	95.95	4.05
Como	73,964	52,284	49,249	3,035	8,011	41,238	951	29.31	5.80	16.27	83.73	38,135	36,396	1,739	526	19.13	48.44	95.44	4.56
Rovigo	44,005	34,399	32,129	2,270	3,757	28,372	1,110	21.83	6.60	11.69	88.31								
Verona	216,014	159,848	151,390	8,458	22,615	128,775	3,147	26.00	5.29	14.94	85.06	113,842	110,757	3,085	996	21.30	47.30	97.29	2.71
Savona	57,570	44,053	41,119	2,934	4,595	36,524	948	23.48	6.66	11.17	88.82								
Parma	144,767	108,784	104,345	4,439	20,987	83,358	1,566	24.86	4.08	20.11	79.89	92,769	89,780	2,989	1,039	11.06	35.92	96.78	3.22
Piacenza	86,334	68,349	64,499	3,850	6,386	58,113	1,585	20.83	5.63	9.90	90.10	57,495	55,591	1,904	632	12.57	33.40	96.69	3.31
Lucca	75,574	52,081	48,233	3,848	7,566	40,667	1,246	31.09	7.39	15.69	84.31	41,435	39,848	1,587	494	14.09	45.17	96.17	3.83
Pistoia	76,163	53,120	49,417	3,703	6,686	42,731	1,601	30.25	6.97	13.53	86.47								
Frosinone	40,114	33,883	32,116	1,767	2,385	29,731	483	15.53	5.21	7.43	92.57	27,650	26,879	771	222	15.54	31.07	97.21	2.79
Rieti	37,815	31,968	30,486	1,482	2,813	27,673	361	15.46	4.63	9.23	90.77								
L'Aquila	59,225	48,372	46,177	2,195	3,858	42,319	592	18.32	4.54	8.35	91.64	43,146	42,061	1,085	340	8.82	27.15	97.48	2.51
Isernia	18,027	14,227	13,516	711	539	12,977	443	21.08	4.99	3.99	96.01	11,997	11,581	416	130	12.37	33.45	96.53	3.48
Lecce	79,260	63,903	60,915	2,988	4,842	56,073	772	19.37	4.67	7.95	92.05								
Matera	45,884	38,891	37,199	1,692	1,000	36,199	571	15.24	4.35	2.69	97.31	33,385	32,340	1,045	225	12.00	27.24	96.87	3.13
Enna	27,636	20,664	19,191	1,473	1,064	18,127	150	25.23	7.13	5.54	94.45	18,084	17,194	890	127	9.34	34.56	95.08	4.92
Messina	207,120	161,975	145,327	16,648	10,081	135,246	6,581	21.80	10.28	6.94	93.06								

First Round, 29 November

	Entitled to Vote	Voters	Valid Votes	Invalid Votes	Mayor Votes Only	Votes for Lists	Blank Ballots	% of Non Voters	% of Invalid Votes	% of Mayor Votes Only	% of Votes for Lists
Ragusa	58,663	45,310	40,771	4,539	5,546	35,225	1,611	22.76	10.02	13.60	86.40
Siracusa	103,101	78,336	69,713	8,623	6,446	63,267	2,098	24.02	11.01	9.25	90.75
Trapani	60,020	45,001	40,200	4,801	3,097	37,103	1,197	25.02	10.67	7.70	92.30
Cagliari	152,934	108,753	102,785	5,968	17,751	85,034	1,624	28.89	5.49	17.27	82.73
Oristano	27,136	21,619	20,583	1,036	1,112	19,471	153	20.33	4.79	5.40	94.60
Gorizia	33,102	24,925	23,503	1,422	3,200	20,303	546	24.70	5.70	13.62	86.38
Udine	83,441	57,719	54,469	3,250	7,857	46,612	1,054	30.80	5.60	14.42	85.57
Brescia	161,358	124,360	118,760	5,600	23,389	95,371	2,104	22.93	4.50	19.69	80.31
Sondrio	19,391	14,929	14,410	519	1,954	12,456	112	23.01	3.48	13.56	86.44
Treviso	71,562	53,602	51,930	1,672	9,964	41,966	525	25.10	3.12	19.19	80.81
Vicenza	91,216	66,747	63,324	3,423	10,533	52,791	1,294	26.83	5.13	16.63	83.37
Massa	58,538	45,327	42,301	3,026	3,335	38,966	959	22.57	6.68	7.89	92.12
Pisa	80,506	57,210	54,150	3,060	5,638	48,512	1,025	28.94	5.35	10.41	89.59
Pescara	108,359	83,722	80,387	3,335	9,255	71,132	1,145	22.74	3.98	11.51	88.49

Second Round, 13 December

	Voters	Valid Votes	Invalid Votes	Blank Ballots	% of Abstentionism	% of Additional Abstentionism	% Valid Votes	% Invalid Votes
Ragusa	38,320	37,033	1,287	384	34.68	11.92	96.64	3.36
Siracusa	50,603	48,416	2,187	649	50.92	26.90	95.68	4.32
Trapani	36,427	35,070	1,357	1,357	39.31	14.28	96.27	3.72
Oristano	15,742	15,325	417	142	41.99	21.66	97.35	2.65
Gorizia	17,780	17,206	574	185	46.3	21.6	96.8	3.2
Udine	43,409	41,533	1,876	658	48.00	17.10	95.70	4.30
Brescia	97,884	94,908	2,976	1,082	39.34	16.41	96.96	3.04
Sondrio	12,389	12,045	344	104	36.11	13.10	97.22	2.78
Treviso	45,634	44,663	971	348	36.23	11.13	97.87	2.13
Vicenza	54,019	52,504	1,515	511	40.78	13.95	97.19	2.80
Pisa	46,775	45,336	1,439	495	41.90	12.96	96.92	3.08

Note: 'Additional abstentionism' is obtained by subtracting the percentage of first round non-voters from the percentage of second round non-voters.

Source: Calculated from data provided by Ministero dell'Interno-Direzione centrale per i servizi elettorali.

Table B2 Municipal Elections, 24 May and 29 November 1998: List Votes (Percentage of Votes Cast)

	Number of Mayor Candidates	Number of Lists	Number of Parties	Number of Civic Lists	DS	CI	RC	PPI	Verdi	RI	Socialists mixed	Lega	FI	AN	CCD	CDU	CDR per TUDR	MS-FT	Other Lists	Civic Lists and Others
Asti	5	11	9	2	16.35	...	8.10	7.44					2	...	13.87	27.92	11.05	6.92	...	...
3								2												
...	1.63	3.50																		
Cuneo	9	17	6	11	.	...		1		5	4		9	1.76	12.29					51.61
1				**9**																
7		**3**						0			4		2 4.59						19.24	
Como	5	11	7	4	...	...	5.59	...	...		1.75	20.61	19.96	12.14	...	...	...	1.77	19.24	18.95
Rovigo	4	11	11	0	15.42	...	5.00	8.86	3.34	0.92	13.80	12.90	...	...	...	...	...			
1			**4**					.				6					0 9.76 11.36			...
...	4.03	...																		
Verona	10	19	14	5	12.13	...	4.06	7.93	...	...		...	11.67	3.11	17.09	21.60	8.46	5.24	2.94	...
2								**6**					81.43	2.49	8.85					
0								**3**												
Savona	6	16	12	4	29.31	...	8.71	3.82	1.38	2.64	3.98	3.60	13.54	3.45	...	6.68	...	...	12.69	10.20
Parma	7	13	10	3	16.57	...	12.38	3.68	2.72	0.98	4.07	6.63	13.97	...	...	...	...	...	...	...
7						**4**				**7** ...										
Piacenza	5	9	7	2	20.71	...	7.30	9.01	2.74	...	...	13.27	...	...	...	...	...	...	41.27	5.70
Lucca	7	15	8	7	7.29	...	4.86	7.16	4.93	...	...	...	15.51	17.22	6.15	...	...	1.01	...	35.88
Pistoia	6	9	8	1	33.20	...	12.87	7.21	5.11	...	5.29	2.64	25.29	...	...	4.76	...	...	...	3.62

Election of 29·November

	Number of	Number	Number of	Number	Number of												CDR	Civic Lists
Frosinone	6	15	12	3	11.86	…	2.07	6.68	3.008	…	…	…	…	…	…	…	…	4.55
13.10	…	13.15	13.16	4.95	9.70	…	1.19	2.61	10.39	1.23	12.41	5.83	15.50	26.43	9.41	…	3.35	…
Rieti	6	11	10	1	14.29	…	5.88	9.89	…	…	…	15.04	7.69	9.43	3.66	…	…	…
L'Aquila	3	11	11	0	19.83	…	5.47	11.52	…	…	…	…	…	…	…	…	…	2.49
4							**2**								**6**			
3					**9**		**6.**					15.04	…	…	7.91	…	…	**9**
Isernia	7	11	6	5	…	…	4.92	10.00	…	…	15.04	…	7.69	9.43	…	…	…	43.45
Lecce	4	18	13	5	15.86	…	2.37	10.00	2.52	1.57	3.39	4.45	8.77	…	11.36	1.79	2.51	15.16
Matera	4	12	10	2	21.02	…	3.55	12.91	4.91	6.04	1.91	11.01	16.84	13.92	…	…	0.60	…
8.45	7.81	9.07	…	…	…	16.55	1.67	…	…	…	…	…	…	…	…	…	…	**7**
Enna	4	11	8	3	26.27	…	1.67	18.42	…	5.19	…	10.27	10.23	7.17	…	…	…	…
6					**1**	14.59	**9.**											
Messina	5	16	14	2	9.56	…	1.35	10.09	…	2.67	8.74	17.22	11.14	9.71	8.58	10.58	8.74	0.80
Ragusa	6	13	10	3	16.10	…	6.78	13.67	2.91	2.66	…	11.89	10.69	6.39	9.34	6.34	…	13.23
Siracusa	6	16	13	3	9.79	…	2.50	10.24	2.37	8.23	3.34	14.93	9.01	2.82	4.82	10.20	7.33	13.71
Trapani	3	13	12	1	8.64	…	2.67	6.24	1.03	5.30	9.24	15.77	7.02	17.52	8.00	…	16.86	1.70
Cagliari	5	17	12	5	11.16	…	3.97	5.90	2.47	…	…	…	…	…	…	…	…	6.05
2							**2**								**2**	5.76	29.45	
1.19	5.13	…	…	13.31	…	…	4.10	…	…	…	…	…	…	…	…	…	…	13.38
Oristano	5	13	10	3	10.50	…	4.10	13.49	1.45	6.22	4.17	11.86	12.09	8.30	8.30	10.69	…	17.12
Gorizia	6	10	8	2	…	…	4.60	…	4.17	…	…	31.63	9.05	6.51	6.51	5.39	24.70	5.61

Table B3 *Municipal Elections, 24 May and 29 November 1998*

	Candidates	Lists Supporting Candidate[a]	% of First Round Votes	% of Second Round run-off Votes	First Round Votes	Second Round run-off Votes	First Round % Votes for Lists	First Round Votes for Lists	Mayoral Votes Only
Asti	Florio Luigi	AN, CCD-CDU-*Altri*, FI (p. pens.)	44.79	59.24	19,747	22,508	45.89	18,203	1,544
	Fassone Antonio	DS, RC, PPI-RI, *Verdi*-Others	35.70	40.76	15,740	15,486	35.12	13,931	1,809
	Bonino Guido	*Lega* Nord, Civic List	15.33		6,757		14.75	5,85	907
	Reggio Giuseppe	Part.Pens.	2.47		1,089		2.61	1,037	52
	Cantarelli Germano	PRI-Others	1.70		751		1.63	647	104
	Total		100.00	100.00	44,084	37,994	100.00	39,668	4,416
Cuneo	Rostagno Elio	DS-*Altri*, PPI-*Altri*, SDI, Cuneo Eco-Soc, Centro	41.35	59.82	14,004	15,775	41.21	12,604	1,400
	Bonino Guido	AN, FI-*Altri*, Un. Dem. Bonino (*Cuneo, Grande Cuneo, Cuneo Progresso*)	17.90	40.18	6,062	10,594	18.56	5,678	384
	Dutto Claudio	*Lega* Nord, Cuneo Indipend.	15.02		5,087		14.27	4,364	723
	Menardi Giuseppe	Grande Cuneo, Cuneo Progresso	8.52		2,885		7.26	2,219	666
	Brondolo Remo	Cuneo	5.43		1,838		6.29	1,925	-87
	Rosso Mario	Rinascita Di Cuneo	4.14		1,402		4.52	1,383	19
	Baravalle Roberto	Impegno Per Cuneo	3.34		1,130		3.52	1,077	53
	Streri Stefano	Cuneo Giust. Lib.Dem.	2.42		818		2.51	769	49
	Bertone Marco	Con.Giov. Cuneese	1.90		644		1.85	566	78
	Total		100.00	100.00	33,870	26,369	100.00	30,585	3,285

Elections of 24 May and second-round run-off of 7 June

City	Candidate	%	%	Votes	Votes	Parties	%	Votes	Votes
Como	Botta Alberto	42.46	58.26	20,913	21,204	AN, FI, Centro	40.77	16,811	4,102
	Terragni Emilio	29.02	41.74	14,290	15,192	*Ulivo*, RC, SDI, Paco (*Civic List*)	30.63	12,631	1,659
	Mascetti Alberto	22.09		10,880		*Lega Nord*, PIU	21.49	8,860	2,020
	Campisani Salvatore	4.55		2,240		Civic List	5.35	2,206	34
	Bussetti Silvano	1.88		926		MS-FT	1.77	730	196
	Total	100.00	100.00	49,249	36,396	Total	100.00	41,238	8,011
Rovigo	Baratella Fabio	52.91		16,999		DS, RC, PPI, RI, *Verdi*, SDI, Nordest	51.37	14,575	2,424
	Bernardi Annamaria	23.66		7,603		AN, FI-Others	24.37	6,913	690
	Ruggero Maurizio	11.99		3,852		*Lega Nord*	12.90	3,660	192
	Avezzó Paolo	11.44		3,675		CCD	11.36	3,224	451
	Total	100.00		32,129		Total	100.00	28,372	3,757
Verona	Sironi Michela	40.30	58.39	61,014	64,670	AN, CCD, CDU, FI	38.23	49,228	11,786
	Brugnoli Giuseppe	30.55	41.61	46,254	46,087	DS, RC, PPI, *Verdi*-Altri, SDI, Citta Che Vogliamo (*Unione Nord Est, civica, Forza Verona, Progetto Verona*)			
	Girondini Francesco	15.92		24,096		*Lega Nord*	31.02	39,948	6,306
	Brunelli Tito	3.67		5,557		Progetto Verona	17.09	22,008	2,088
	Guerra Massimo	3.01		4,561		RI, *Lega Aut. Ven.*	3.77	4,851	706
	Ottaviani Achille	2.32		3,517		Unione Nord Est	3.30	4,247	314
	Mantovani Sergio	1.92		2,912		Civic List	2.49	3,212	305
	Bellazzi Luigi	1.40		2,125		MS-FT	1.70	2,191	721
	Bettini Giuliano	0.51		765		Forza Verona	1.43	1,844	281
	Bevilacqua Giovanni	0.39		589		CDR-Others	0.58	751	14
	Total	100.00	100.00	151,390	110,757	Total	0.38	495	94
							100.00	128,775	22,615

continued

Table B3 *continued*

Candidates	% of First Round Votes	% of Second Round run-off Votes	First Round Votes	Second Round run-off Votes	Lists Supporting Candidate[a]	First Round % Votes for Lists	First Round Votes for Lists	Mayoral Votes Only
Savona								
Ruggeri Carlo	52.73		21,683		DS, RC, PPI, *Verdi*, PRI,	54.53	19,916	1,767
					Savona Europa, SDI, Savona Viva			
Gervasio Francesco	37.08		15,246		CDU, FI, Linea, Per Savona	34.84	12,726	2,520
Arazzi Gabriella	3.52		1,449		*Lega Nord*	3.60	1,315	134
Buzio Mauro	3.29		1,352		AN	3.45	1,260	92
Tuvä Rosario	2.28		937		RI	2.64	966	-29
Ghione Ugo	1.10		452		Rota Saonae	0.93	341	111
Total	100.00		41,119		Total	100.00	36,524	4,595
Parma								
Ubaldi Elvio	31.10	57.23	32,453	51,382	FI-CCD, *Civiltà Parmigiana*	27.48	22,903	9,550
Lavagetto Stefano	30.50	42.77	31,826	38,398	DS, RC, PPI, PRI-RI, SDI	35.18	29,323	2,503
Tommasini Mario	18.90		19,717		*Verdi*, Mario Tommasini	16.13	13,443	6,274
Moine Massimo	6.58		6,864		AN-UDC	7.47	6,229	635
Pedrelli Mariano	5.74		5,990		*Lega Nord*	6.63	5,527	463
Lottici Renata	4.85		5,063		Insieme Per Parma	4.62	3,847	1,216
Magnani Claudio	2.33		2,432		Socialista	2.50	2,086	346
Total	100.00	100.00	104,345	89,780	Total	100.00	83,358	20,987
Piacenza								
Politi Ultimino	41.21	48.90	26,582	27,185	DS, RC, PPI-RI-Others,	39.76	23,106	3,476
					Verdi (Pri-pens.-soc.)			
Guidotti Gianguido	35.71	51.10	23,032	28,406	*Polo Per Le Libertà (Civic List, p.pens.)*	37.95	22,056	976

Location	Candidate	%	Votes	Runoff votes	Runoff %	List	%	Votes	Pref.
	Polledri Massimo	16.35	10,545			*Lega* Nord, Civic List	15.62	9,079	1,466
	Soprani Giorgio	3.41	2,198			P.Pens.	3.35	1,945	253
	Pareti Stefano	3.32	2,142			PRI-L.Pens.-Soc.	3.32	1,927	215
	Total	100.00	64,499	55,591		Total	100.00	58,113	6,386
Lucca	Fazzi Pietro	39.07	18,846	21,839		AN, CCD, FI, Cen Des (Civic List) (*Per Lucca*)	39.62	16,113	2,733
	Rossetti Antonio	27.68	13,350	18,009		DC, RC, PPI, Rete-*Verdi*, Cen Sin, Ambiente E Futuro	27.92	11,356	1,994
	Lazzarini Giulio	23.28	11,228			Civic List	21.94	8,923	2,305
	Bedini Gilberto	6.44	3,104			Per Lucca	7.05	2,868	236
	Giuntoli Francesco	1.78	858			Comunisti	1.77	719	139
	Bacci Frediano	1.06	509			MS-FT	1.01	410	99
	Mazzerelli Alessandro	0.70	338			Mov. Aut. Tosc.	0.68	278	60
	Total	100.00	48,233	39,848		Total	100.00	40,667	7,566
Pistoia	Scarpetti Lido	54.42	26,891			DS, PPI-RI, *Verdi*, SDI-PRI-UD	50.81	21,713	5,178
	Semplici Umberto	23.11	11,420			Cen Des (Contr.Uff.)	25.29	10,806	614
	Frosetti Floriano	11.86	5,862			RC	12.87	5,499	363
	Bonafede Eugenio	4.33	2,140			CDU	4.77	2,036	104
	Lorenzi franco	3.66	1,809			Civic List	3.63	1,549	260
	Gai Vezio	2.62	1,295			*Lega* Nord	2.64	1,128	167
	Total	100.00	49,417			Total	100.00	42,731	6,686
Frosinone	Marzi Domenico	38.33	12,310	14,717	54.75	DS, PPI, *Verdi*, SDI, All.Fros.	39.08	11,619	691
	Perlini Italico	31.55	10,131	12,162	45.25	AN, CCD, FI	31.26	9,295	836
	Piacentini Adriano	18.52	5,947			CDU-CDR Per L'UDR, Segni-PRI-P.Lib., Unione Fros., Civica	18.26	5,429	518

continued

Table B3 *continued*

Candidates	% of First Round Votes	% of Second Round run-off Votes	First Round Votes	Second Round run-off Votes	Lists Supporting Candidate[a]	First Round % Votes for Lists	First Round Votes for Lists	Mayoral Votes Only
Ottaviani Nicola	8.06		2,590		RI-Others	8.13	2,418	172
Notarcola Francesco	2.24		719		RC	2.07	615	104
Villa Franco	1.30		419		MS-FT	1.19	355	64
Total	100.00	100.00	32,116	26,879	Total	100.00	29,731	2,385
Rieti								
Cicchetti Antonio	62.18		18,956		AN, CCD, FI, Civic List	55.87	15,462	3,494
Festuccia Adalberto	13.80		4,206		DS	14.29	3,954	252
Bigliocchi Paolo	13.48		4,108		CDU-CDR, PPI, SDI	19.38	5,363	-1,255
Dionisi Angelo	6.73		2,051		RC	5.88	1,628	423
Valeri Mauro	2.72		829		PRI	3.35	926	-97
Mancini Claudio	1.10		336		RI	1.23	340	-4
Total	100.00		30,486		Total	100.00	27,673	2,813
L'Aquila								
Tempesta Biagio	48.52	56.42	22,403	23,730	AN, CDU, CCD-Others, FI	44.56	18,857	3,546
Centi Carmine	43.04	43.58	19,873	18,331	DS, RC, PPI, RI-Altri, *Verdi*, SDI-Others	47.53	20,116	-243
Lombardi Enzo	8.45		3,901		CDR Per L'UDR	7.91	3,346	555
Total	100.00	100.00	46,177	42,061	Total	100.00	42,319	3,858
Isernia								
Colalillo Vincenzo	37.27	42.96	5,038	4,975	CDU-CDR, Centro, Dem.Crist.	45.33	5,883	-845
Caterina Giuseppe	35.84	57.04	4,844	6,606	Ulivo, RC (*La Bilancia, Noi per la Città*)	29.46	3,823	1,021
Colasanti Alda	14.34		1,938		AN, FI-CCD	13.22	1,715	223

City	Candidate	%	Votes	Ballot %	Ballot Votes	List	%	Votes	Diff
	Di Ronza Nicola	4.41	596			La Bilancia	4.28	555	41
	D'Achille Maria Teresa	3.83	517			Noi Per La Città	3.74	485	32
	Mancini Giovancarmine	3.01	407			MS-FT	2.51	326	81
	Di Placido Nicola	1.30	176			Civic List	1.46	190	-14
	Total	100.00	13,516		11,581	Total	100.00	12,977	539
Lecce	Poli Bortone Adriana	54.01	32,899			AN, CCD, CDR, FI, Un.Rep.Udr, Segni, Marine E Primo Piano, Lg. Cittad. E Ambiente, Patto per Il Centro	56.11	31,463	1,436
	Salvemini Stefano	43.78	26,666			DS, RC, PPI, *Verdi*, SDI, Riformisti Salvemini, Città Insieme	41.72	23,394	3,272
	Fiore Ottorino	1.45	883			RI	1.57	880	3
	Sperduto Francesco	0.77	467			MS-FT	0.60	336	131
	Total	100.00	60,915			Total	100.00	56,073	4,842
Matera	Minieri Angelo	48.07	17,883	52.85	17,091	DS, RC, PPI, RI, *Verdi*	48.43	17,530	353
	Acito Francesco	41.90	15,587	47.15	15,249	AN, CCD, CDU, FI-UDC, Nuovogiorno Matera	43.47	15,735	-148
	Bagnale Salvatore	7.29	2,713			Matera Attiva	6.20	2,244	469
	Di Giacomo Pasquale	2.73	1,016			SDI	1.91	690	326
	Total	100.00	37,199	100.00	32,340	Total	100.00	36,199	1,000
Enna	Petralia Giuseppe	42.28	8,114	47.08	8,095	DS, PPI, RI, Enna Che Vogliamo	54.46	9,872	-1,758
	Alvano Antonino	32.44	6,226	52.92	9,099	AN, FI-CCD, Proserpina, Civic List	30.51	5,530	696
	Faraci Claudio	22.26	4,272			CDR-It.Fed-Altri, Soc-CDR Per L'UDR	13.37	2,423	1,849
	Fragalà Giuseppe	3.02	579			RC	1.67	302	277
	Total	100.00	19,191	100.00	17,194	Total	100.00	18,127	1,064

continued

Table B3 *continued*

	Candidates	% of First Round Votes	% of Second Round run-off Votes	First Round Votes	Second Round run-off Votes	Lists Supporting Candidate[a]	First Round % Votes for Lists	First Round Votes for Lists	Mayoral Votes Only
Messina	Leonardi Salvatore	53.24		77,369		AN, CCD, CDU, CDR, FI, Socialista	61.51	83,195	-5,826
	Providenti Francesco	42.08		61,149		DS, RC, PPI, SDI, Pensionati, Cen Sin (Contr.Uff.), Civic List	34.57	46,754	14,395
	Mollica Massimo	3.10		4,507		RI	2.67	3,611	896
	Ragusa Antonino	1.08		1,564		MS-FT	0.81	1,102	462
	Tringali Giuseppe	0.51		738		Noi Siciliani	0.43	584	154
	Total	100.00		145,327		Total	100.00	135,246	10,081
Ragusa	Arezzo Domenico	28.72	53.57	11,710	19,840	AN, CCD, FI (*CDU, CDR, Ragusa Soprattutto*)	28.97	10,204	1,506
	Chessari Giorgio	27.26	46.43	11,113	17,193	DS, RC, *Rete-Verdi (PPI, Uniti per Ragusa)*	25.79	9,086	2,027
	Antoci Giovanni	22.96		9,361		PPI, Uniti Per Ragusa, Ragusa Popolare	21.84	7,693	1,668
	Bocchieri Salvatore	12.65		5,158		CDU, CDR	15.68	5,525	-367
	Schembri Angelo	6.61		2,695		Ragusa Soprattutto	5.06	1,781	914
	Cascone Giorgio	1.80		734		SDI	2.66	936	-202
	Total	100.00	100.00	40,771	37,033	Total	100.00	35,225	5,546
Siracusa	Bellucci Angelo	27.15	41.73	18,926	20,203	AN, CCD, FI, Cen Des (Civic List) (*CDU, CDR*)	29.47	18,642	284

Dell'Arte Vincenzo	24.51	58.27	17,090	28,213	DS, RC, PPI, *Verdi*, SDI (*RI, Rete, SDI, fed.com.noi sic., lista Franco Greco*)	28.25	17,874	-784
Fatuzzo Marco	22.72		15,837		RI, Rete-Others, Fed.Com.Noi Sic.	18.98	12,010	3,827
Greco Franco	12.93		9,014		Lista Franco Greco	7.58	4,799	4,215
Salvo Aldo	12.01		8,370		CDU, CDR	15.02	9,500	-1,130
Iaconello Renato	0.68		476		MS-FT	0.70	442	34
Total	100.00	100.00	69,713	48,416	Total	100.00	63,267	6,446
Trapani Buscaino Mario	46.46	49.21	18,676	17,257	DS, RC, PPI, RI, SDI, Rete-*Verdi*, UD, Dem.Riform.	50.14	18,605	71
Laudicina Antonio	42.14	50.79	16,941	17,813	AN, CCD, FI (*Socialista, CDU-CDR per UDR*)	40.31	14,956	1,985
Gianno Leonardo	11.40		4,583		CDU-CDR Per UDR, Socialista	9.55	3,542	1,041
Total	100.00	100.00	40,200	35,070	Total	100.00	37,103	3,097
Cagliari Delogu Mariano	56.76		58,336		AN, CCD, FI	48.89	41,570	16,766
Carboni Boy Rita	27.69		28,463		DS, RC, PPI, RI, *Verdi*, F.Dem.Soc.It., Costit. Sardista	31.68	26,938	1,525
Grauso Nicola	14.47		14,878		PS D'Az., Socialista, CDU, CDR, Civic List	18.42	15,660	-782
Benone Giampaolo	0.55		563		Sardigna Natzione	0.60	509	54
Melis Marco	0.53		545		Forza Sardegna	0.42	357	188
Total	100.00		102,785		Total	100.00	85,034	17,751
Oristano Ortu Piero	41.83	65.42	8,609	10,026	CDR, CDU, RI, SDI, PS.D'Az., Centro Lib.Dem.	42.88	8,350	259
Scarpa Mariano	27.34	34.58	5,628	5,299	DS, RC, PPI	28.10	5,471	157

continued

Table B3 *continued*

Candidates	% of First Round Votes	% of Second Round run-off Votes	First Round Votes	Second Round run-off Votes	Lists Supporting Candidate[a]	First Round % Votes for Lists	First Round Votes for Lists	Mayoral Votes Only
Salis Giovanni	24.59		5,062		AN, FI	23.95	4,663	399
Cugusi Domenico	4.65		958		Cen Des (Civic List)	3.62	705	253
Atzori Andrea	1.58		326		*Verdi*	1.45	282	44
Total	100.00	100.00	20,583	15,325	Total	100.00	19,471	1,112
Gorizia								
Valenti Gaetano	48.33	61.69	11,358	10,615	AN, CDU per Gorizia, FI	47.19	9,581	1,777
Rupeni Ario	31.87	38.31	7,491	6,591	*Ulivo*, RC, Isontino per l'Europa	32.33	6,565	926
Formentini Michele	7.89		1,855		*Lega Nord*	8.36	1,697	158
Cosma Sergio	5.31		1,249		MS-FT	5.39	1,094	155
Bon Alessandro	4.25		999		*Verdi*	4.17	846	153
Marzaroli Vittorino	2.34		551		Obbiettivo Gorizia	2.56	520	31
Total	100.00	100.00	23,503	17,206	Total	100.00	20,303	3,200

Elections of 29 November and second-round run-off of 13 December

Candidates	% of First Round Votes	% of Second Round run-off Votes	First Round Votes	Second Round run-off Votes	Lists Supporting Candidate[a]	First Round % Votes for Lists	First Round Votes for Lists	Mayoral Votes Only
Udine								
Commessatti Pietro	27.57	39.42	15,015	16,374	FI-FDC, PPI, Autonomisti per Udine, Partito Liberale (AN, CCD)	29.99	13,981	1,034

	%	%				%		
Cecotti Sergio	23.18	60.58	12,624	25,159	*Lega Nord*, Per Cecotti, Un impegno per la città	19.96	9,306	3,318
Businello Giovanni Paolo	20.34		11,079		DS, SDI, Centro dei Valori, *Lega Friuli*	19.93	9,289	1,790
Di Prampero Maria Santa	17.11		9,320		AN, CCD	17.83	8,311	1,009
Gottardo Emilio	3.92		2,133		*Verdi*	4.14	1,931	202
Zucconi Paolo	3.58		1,948		MS-FT, Sos Italia	3.41	1,588	360
Kersevan Alessandra	3.47		1,888		RC	3.76	1,752	136
Belviso Marco	0.85		462		Under35	0.97	454	8
Total	100.00	100.00	54,469	41,533	Total	100.00	46,612	7,857
Brescia								
Corsini Paolo	41.77	53.13	49,606	50,422	DS, PPI, RI, SDI, *Verdi*, PRI, Cen.Sin (Civic List)	40.78	38,895	10,711
Dalla Bona Giovanni	32.92	46.87	39,098	44,486	AN, FI-CCD. Socialista, C.Libera, Pens.Cas.	33.28	31,738	7,360
Galli Cesare	19.75		23,453		*Lega Nord*, Cattolici Padani, Pensionati Padani, Lista Referendum	19.39	18,495	4,958
Lombardi Lamberto	3.00		3,560		RC	3.66	3,488	72
Gei Giovanni	1.11		1,314		UDR-fed.lib.	1.30	1,241	73
Cavagna Livio F. E.	0.94		1,118		Part.Onestà	1.05	1,006	112
Manzoni Alessandro	0.51		611		Italia Unita	0.53	508	103
Total	100.00	100.00	118,760	94,908	Total	100.00	95,371	23,389
Sondrio								
Molteni Alcide	43.25	55.92	6,232	6,735	RC, PPI-Civic List, Sondrio Democratica	41.83	5,210	1,022
Venosta Francesco	26.56	44.08	3,828	5,310	Libertà Federalismo, Civic List	26.88	3,348	480
Pini Diego	11.80		1,700		AN, CCD, FI	12.62	1,572	128
Molteni Danilo	10.40		1,499		*Lega Nord*	10.41	1,297	202

continued

Table B3 *continued*

Candidates	% of First Round Votes	% of Second Round run-off Votes	First Round Votes	Second Round run-off Votes	Lists Supporting Candidate[a]	First Round % Votes for Lists	First Round Votes for Lists	Mayoral Votes Only
Tremonti Pietro Luigi	4.40		634		MS-FT-Others	4.06	506	128
Zanesi Carlo	3.59		517		SDI	4.20	523	-6
Total	100.00	100.00	14,410	12,045	Total	100.00	12,456	1,954
Treviso Gentilini Giancarlo	42.78	59.46	22,216	26,557	*Lega* Nord-Liga Veneta	41.62	17,466	4,750
Luciani Domenico	31.34	40.54	16,275	18,106	DS-*Verdi*, PPI-RI, *Italia dei Valori*, Sinistra, Cen sin. (Civic List)	31.37	13,166	3,109
Bresolin Ferruccio	25.88		13,439		AN, FI, Centro, Civic List, Veneto Nord Est	27.01	11,334	2,105
Total	100.00	100.00	51,930	44,663	Total	100.00	41,966	9,964
Vicenza Hullweck Enrico	35.73	56.48	22,624	29,655	AN, CCD, FI, UDR, Nuovo Progetto	34.58	18,254	4,370
Sala Giorgio	33.08	43.52	20,945	22,849	DS, PPI, SDI, *Verdi*, Nord Est	32.99	17,416	3,529
Carta Veller Margherita	13.96		8,841		*Lega* Nord-Liga Veneta, Catt.Pad-Lav.Pad., Civic List	13.64	7,203	1,638
Beggiato Ettore	6.85		4,340		Liga Veneta Repubblica	7.59	4,006	334
Beggiato Giorgio	3.22		2,037		Buongoverno Vicenza	3.36	1,776	261
Germano Claudino Raniero	2.30		1,457		RC	2.56	1,353	104
Giometto Dilvano	2.10		1,329		Unione Nord Est	2.22	1,173	156
Rebesani Fulvio	2.02		1,281		Sinistra Democratica	2.27	1,196	85
Piccolo Renzo	0.74		470		Unione	0.78	414	56
Total	100.00	100.00	63,324	52,504	Total	100.00	52,791	10,533

		%	Votes	%	Votes		%	Votes	
Massa	Pucci Roberto	68.07	28,795			DS, CI, PPI, SDI, *Verdi, PRI*	69.49	27,077	1,718
	Lazzoni Andrea	21.09	8,923			AN, CCD, FI	20.35	7,931	992
	Quadrelli Sauro	7.37	3,117			RC	6.96	2,712	405
	Azzolina Gaetano	1.72	727			Ass.Prov. Pertini	1.65	644	83
	Silvestri Nicola	1.00	425			Azione Sociale	0.86	337	88
	Capulzini Cremonini A.A.	0.74	314			Lega Nord	0.68	265	49
	Total	100.00	42,301			Total	100.00	38,966	3,335
Pescara	Pace Carlo	51.26	41,206			AN, CCD, FI, Cattolici Dem., Dem. Crist., Pescara Futura	50.05	35,604	5,602
	Melilla Generoso detto Gianni	46.20	37,139			DS, RC, CI, PPI, RI-UDR, SDI, *Verdi*-altri, Nuova Pescara	47.13	33,526	3,613
	D'Andreamatteo Piergiuseppe	1.45	1,169			Il Timone	1.89	1,341	-172
	Provenzano Pasquale	1.09	873			Fronte Nazionale	0.93	661	212
	Total	100.00	80,387			Total	100.00	71,132	9,255
Pisa	Fontanelli Paolo	48.31	26,158	56.63	25,672	DS, CI, PPI, SDI, *Verdi*, Sinistra, Lista Persone	50.81	24,650	1,508
	Dringoli Carlo Alberto	34.42	18,639	43.37	19,664	AN, CCD, FI	32.05	15,546	3,093
	Cortopassi Sergio	7.80	4,225			Civic List	7.48	3,627	598
	Bini Maurizio	7.45	4,034			RC	7.60	3,689	345
	Ajello Benvenuti Maria Paola	1.11	603			MS-FT	1.17	569	34
	Romagnoli Franco	0.91	491			*Lega Nord*	0.89	431	60
	Total	100.00	54,150	100.00	45,336	Total	100.00	48,512	5,638

[a] The lists in italics have supported the candidate only at second round

Source: Calculated from data provided by Ministero dell'Interno-Direzione centrale per i servizi elettorali.

Table B4 *Electoral Participation: Provincial Elections, 24 May and 29 November 1998*

Elections of 24 May

	Entitled to Vote	First Round Voters	% First Round Voters	First Round Invalid Votes	% First Round Invalid Votes	First Round Valid Votes	% First Round Valid Votes	First Round Blank Ballots	% Blank Ballots/ Invalid Votes	Valid Votes for Lists	% Valid Votes for Lists	President Votes Only	% President Votes Only
Treviso	662,584	413,328	62.38	39,948	9.66	373,380	90.34	11,174	27.97	373,380	100.00	…	…
Ancona	384,248	246,587	64.17	31,301	12.69	215,286	87.31	12,928	41.30	215,286	100.00	…	…
Reggio Calabria	515,562	307,662	59.68	25,246	8.21	282,416	91.79	7,552	29.91	282,416	100.00	…	…
Agrigento	463,799	269,121	58.03	35,870	13.33	233,251	86.67	14,067	32.05	225,031	96.48	8,220	3.52
Caltanisetta	276,571	167,066	60.41	24,071	14.41	142,995	85.59	8,680	36.62	133,270	93.20	9,725	6.80
Catania	897,926	595,794	66.35	78,203	13.10	517,591	86.90	24,612	31.25	476,262	92.10	41,329	7.90
Enna	189,622	111,913	59.02	13,495	12.06	98,418	87.94	4,975	46.24	93,588	95.09	4,830	4.91
Messina	576,724	432,319	74.96	55,780	12.90	376,539	87.10	21,343	38.26	355,055	94.29	21,484	5.71
Palermo	1,068,202	623,654	58.38	88,497	14.19	535,157	85.81	26,175	28.65	499,761	93.39	35,396	6.61
Ragusa	245,310	177,489	72.35	24,091	13.57	153,398	86.43	10,203	42.35	133,412	86.97	19,986	13.03
Siracusa	349,951	235,881	67.40	32,512	13.78	203,369	86.22	12,893	29.05	190,120	93.49	13,249	6.51
Trapani	375,217	267,178	71.21	37,861	14.17	229,317	85.83	15,320	42.32	212,944	92.86	16,373	7.14

Elections of 29 November

	Entitled to Vote	First Round Voters	% First Round Voters	First Round Invalid Votes	% First Round Invalid Votes	First Round Valid Votes	% First Round Valid Votes	First Round Blank Ballots	% Blank Ballots/ Invalid Votes	Valid Votes for Lists	% Valid Votes for Lists	President Votes Only	% President Votes Only
Roma	3,231,337	1,843,785	57.06	154,231	8.36	1,689,554	91.64	37,477	24.40	1,689,554	100	...	...
Massa-Carrara	178,938	111,399	62.26	15,298	13.73	96,101	86.28	5,761	37.66	96,101	100	...	...
Benevento	270,717	181,824	67.16	12,995	7.15	168,829	92.85	4,760	36.63	168,829	100	...	...
Foggia	581,563	353,368	60.76	36,337	10.28	317,031	89.72	11,738	32.57	317,031	100	...	...

Source: Calculated from data provided by Ministero dell'Interno-Direzione centrale per i servizi elettorali.

Table B5 *Provincial Elections, 24 May and 29 November 1998. Candidates competition*

		Elections of 24 May and second-round run-off of 7 June						
Candidates	% of First Round Votes	% of Second Round run-off Votes	First Round Votes	Second Round Votes	Lists Supporting Candidate	Votes for Lists	% Votes for Lists	President Votes Only
Treviso								
Luca Zaia	41.4	60.0	154,687	139,161	*Lega* nord	154,687	100.0	-
Ivano Sartor	24.1	40.0	90,089	92,888	DS,PPI (pop), *Verdi*, Rif. com., RI (SDI)	90,089	100.0	-
Francesco Benazzi	16.8		62,542		AN, FI-CCD	62,542	100.0	-
Gianni Maddalon	8.7		32,444		Nordest	32,444	100.0	-
Carla Puppinato	7.2		26,900		CDU	26,900	100.0	-
Ruggero Zanatta	1.8		6,718		SDI	6,718	100.0	-
Total	100.0	100.0	373,380	232,049	Total	373,380	100.0	-
Ancona								
Enzo Giancarli	66.2		142,499		DS, PPI (pop), *Verdi*, Rif. com., RI, PRI, SDI	142,499	100.0	-
Franco Dolcini	30.0		64,543		FI, AN, CDU-Others	64,543	100.0	-
Nunzio Proto	2.1		4,530		CCD	4,530	100.0	-
Gabriele Virone	1.7		3,714		Mov. soc. tric.	3,714	100.0	-
Total	100.0		215,286		Total	215,286	100.0	-
Reggio Calabria								
Cosimo Calabrì	50.3		142,083		DS, PPI (pop), *Verdi*, Rif. com., RI, PRI, SDI	142,083	100.0	-
Umberto Pirilli	35.6		100,432		FI, AN, CCD, CDU	100,432	100.0	-

Province / Candidate	%	Votes	%	Votes	Coalition / Party	Votes	%	Votes
	Saverio Zavettieri	4.7	13,303			Socialista	13,303	100.0	–
	Giovambattista Bentivoglio	4.5	12,656			CDR	12,656	100.0	–
	Aurelio Chizzoniti	2.9	8,145			Patto Segni	8,145	100.0	–
	Domenico Barbitta	1.1	3,122			Mov. soc. tric.	3,122	100.0	–
	Francesco Caridi	0.5	1,374			All. euromedit.	1,374	100.0	–
	Pasquale Serino	0.4	1,301			Patto crist. esteso	1,301	100.0	–
	Total	100.0	282,416			Total	282,416	100.0	–
Agrigento	Vincenzo Fontana	50.8	118,588			AN, FI, CDU, CDR, Soc-Patto Segni-altri	116,956	98.62	1,632
	Stefano Vivacqua	44.8	104,449			DS, PPI (pop), Rif. com., RI, SDI, La Rete-Verdi	99,378	95.14	5,071
	Giuseppe Arnone	3.1	7,170			CCD	7,104	99.08	66
	Pellegrino Leo	1.3	3,044			Dem.c.f.com.noi sic.	1,593	52.33	1,451
	Total	100.0	233,251			Total	225,031	96.48	8,220
Caltanisetta	Filippo Collura	47.8	68,392	62.4	65,295	DS, PPI (pop), La Rete-Verdi, RI-UD, SDI	64,421	94.19	3,971
	Vincenzo Rampulla	27.7	39,640	37.6	39,389	CCD, FI, AN	37,144	93.70	2,496
	Michele Vizzini	14.5	20,788			Centro, CDU-CDR	19,585	94.21	1,203
	Luciano Vullo	9.0	12,806			Rif. com.	10,998	85.88	1,808
	Luca Bonanno	1.0	1,369			Dem. c.f. com. noi sic.	1,122	81.96	247
	Total	100.0	142,995	100.0	104,684	Total	133,270	93.20	9,725
Catania	Nello Musumeci	60.2	311,543			CCD, FI, AN, CDU, CDR	271,994	87.31	39,549
	Saro Pettinato	38.0	196,543			DS, PPI (pop), Rif. com., RI, SDI, La Rete-Verdi-Others, con Bianco, Socialista	196,188	99.82	355

continued

Table B5 *continued*

Candidates	% of First Round Votes	% of Second Round run-off Votes	First Round Votes	Second Round Votes	Lists Supporting Candidate	Votes for Lists	% Votes for Lists	President Votes Only
Francesco Condorelli	1.1		5,582		Mov. soc. tric.	5,242	93.91	340
Giuseppe Campo	0.4		2,269		Un giov. sud, Sud in mov.	1,499	66.06	770
Filippo Morana	0.3		1,654		Noi sic-FNS	1,339	80.96	315
Total	100.0		517,591		Total	476,262	92.02	41,329
Enna								
Michele Galvagno	56.3		55,408		DS, PPI (pop), RI, La Rete-Mov. dem.	54,538	98.43	870
Gaetano Lo Manto	32.7		32,198		FI-CCD, Soc.-CDU-CDR, AN	30,327	94.19	1,871
Gaetano Virlinzi	5.2		5,089		Rif. com.	4,298	84.46	791
Giuseppe Alfeo	2.9		2,851		SDI	2,824	99.05	27
Michele Crisafulli	2.4		2,358		Noi sic-FNS	1,374	58.27	984
Armando Piano del Balzo	0.5		514		Lista locale	227	44.16	287
Total	100.0		98,418		Total	93,588	95.09	4,830
Messina								
Giuseppe Buzzanca	67.1		252,777		Socialista, CCD, FI, AN, CDU, CDR	243,295	96.25	9,482
Mario Bolognari	30.7		115,583		DC, PPI (pop), Rif. com., cen-sin SDI, Pensionati	105,162	90.98	10,421
Giuseppe Scalisi	1.5		5,713		Mov. soc. tric.	5,249	91.88	464
Teresa Canepa	0.7		2,466		Noi siciliani-FNS	1,349	54.70	1,117
Total	100.0		376,539		Total	355,055	94.29	21,484
Palermo								
Francesco Musotto	55.3		296,045		Centro, CCD, FI, AN, CDU	285,669	96.50	10,376

Province	Candidate	%	Votes	%	Votes	Parties	Votes	%	Diff
	Pietro Puccio	43.1	230,852			DS, PPI (pop), Rif. com., RI, Verdi-Others, La Rete-Mov.dem., UDF, SDI	209,569	90.78	21,283
	Giuseppe Sciani	1.6	8,260			Noi siciliani-FNS	4,523	54.76	3,737
	Total	100.0	535,157			Total	499,761	93.39	35,396
Ragusa	Giovanni Mauro	56.6	86,833			CCD, FI, AN, CDU-CDR	69,903	80.50	16,930
	Rosario Cintolo	41.4	63,555			DS, PPI-UD-Others, Rif. com., RI, La Rete-*Verdi*, PPI (pop), SDI	61,672	97.04	1,883
	Giorgio Sortino	2.0	3,010			Noi siciliani-FNS	1,837	61.03	1,173
	Total	100.0	153,398			Total	133,412	86.97	19,986
Siracusa	Bruno Marziano	41.7	84,902	61.6	82637	DS, Rif. com., PPI (pop.), Fed.dei *verdi*, SDI (La Rete-altri, Fed. com. noi sic.)	77,368	91.13	7,534
	Mario Cavallaro	29.1	59,099	38.4	51588	CCD, FI, AN (CDU, CDR)	54,377	92.01	4,722
	Carmelo Fileti	15.3	31,136			CDU, CDR	31,398	100.84	-262
	Riccardo Gionfrido	13.9	28,232			RI, La Rete-Others, Fed. com. noi sic.	26,977	95.55	1,255
	Total	100.0	203,369	100.0	134225	Total	190,120	93.49	13,249
Trapani	Giulia Adamo	52.7	120,714			CCD, FI, AN, CDU-CDR	117,689	97.49	3,025
	Francesca Messana	41.2	94,568			DS, Rif. com., RI-Others, La Rete-*Verdi*, PPI (pop), SDI	92,021	97.31	2,547
	Giuseppe Bologna	4.7	10,858			lista locale	2,611	24.05	8,247
	Francesco Stalteri	1.4	3,177			lg. Sicilia federale	623	19.61	2,554
	Total	100.0	229,317			Total	212,944	92.86	16,373

continued

Table B5 *continued*

Candidates		% of First Round Votes	% of Second Round run-off Votes	First Round Votes	Second Round Votes	Lists Supporting Candidate	Votes for Lists	% Votes for Lists	President Votes Only
			Elections of 29 November and Second Round of 13 December						
Roma	Silvano Moffa	44.7	51.1	754,601	686,232	Socialista, FI, AN, CCD, Pens. Uv	754,601	100.0	-
	Pasqualina Napoletano	48.6	48.9	820,717	656,907	DS, PPI, *Verdi*, CI, Rif. com., SDI, RI, Lib. UD.PRI	820,717	100.0	-
	Giorgio Fanfani	2.2		37,577		UDR	37,577	100.0	-
	Carlo Alberto Ciocci	0.8		13,780		Dem. crist.	13,780	100.0	-
	Adriano Tilgher	1.5		24,869		Fronte nazionale	24,869	100.0	-
	Marco Duspiva	1.5		25,062		Mov. soc. tric.	25,062	100.0	-
	Fulvio De Vita	0.2		4,117		Part. umanista	4,117	100.0	-
	Umberto Silvestri	0.5		8,831		Lista Robin Hood	8,831	100.0	-
	Total	100.0	100.0	1,689,554	1,343,139	Total	1,689,554	100.0	-
Massa-Carrara	Franco Gussoni	61.0		58,605		DS, PPI, *Verdi*, CI, SDI, PRI	58,605	100.0	-
	Pier Luigi Bordigoni	25.3		24,267		FI, AN, CCD	24,267	100.0	-
	Paolo Zammori	11.6		11,188		Rif. com.	11,188	100.0	-
	Luana Bruschi	2.1		2,041		*Lega* nord	2,041	100.0	-
	Total	100.0		96,101		Total	96,101	100.0	-

Benevento	Carmine Nardone	DS, PPI, RI,SDI, UDR, Un. dem. per Mastella	102,493	60.7	102,493	100.0	–
	Ernesto Mazzoni	FI, AN, CCD	54,387	32.2	54,387	100.0	–
	Raimondo Mazzarelli	Fed. dei *Verdi*	7,792	4.6	7,792	100.0	–
	Antonio Broccoli	Rif. Com.	4,157	2.5	4,157	100.0	–
	Total		168,829	100.0	168,829	100.0	–
Foggia	Antonio Pellegrino	DS, PPI, *Verdi*, CI, Rif. com., SDI, RI	161,955	51.1	161,955	100.0	–
	Alberto Cicolella	FI, AN, CCD	122,028	38.5	122,028	100.0	–
	Giuseppe Zingrillo	UDR	20,459	6.5	20,459	100.0	–
	Giovanni Marciello	Nuova dem. crist.	9,254	2.9	9,254	100.0	–
	Antonio Nargiso	Mov. soc. tric.	3,335	1.0	3,335	100.0	–
	Total		317,031	100.0	317,031	100.0	–

Source: Calculated from data provided by Ministero dell'Interno-Direzione centrale per i servizi elettorali.

Table B6 *Valle d'Aosta Regional Elections, 31 May 1998*

Lists	Valid Votes	% of Valid Votes
Rif. com.	3,760	4.80
Per la Valle d'Aosta con l'*Ulivo*	5,323	6.80
Gauche Valdotaine-DS-PSE	6,455	8.25
Lega nord-Val d'Aohta libra	2,653	3.39
FI	5,088	6.50
Ensamble Zusammen	425	0.54
UV	33,311	42.57
Independantistes valdotains	828	1.06
Fed. auton. CCD-CDU	7,561	9.67
Un. walser valdostani-Uwv-Wa	569	0.73
AN	2,237	2.86
Autonomist	10,044	12.84
Total	78,254	100.00
Entitled to Vote	101,392	
Voters	83,074	81.93
Valid Votes	78,254	94.20
Invalid Votes	4,820	5.80
Blank Ballots	1,627	33.76

Source: Calculated from data provided by Ministero dell'Interno-Direzione centrale per i Servizi elettorali.

Table B7 *Friuli Venezia Giulia Regional Elections, 14 June 1998*

Lists	Valid Votes	% of Valid Votes
FI-CCD-FC	136,013	20.69
Lega nord	114,156	17.36
DS	100,783	15.33
AN	87,752	13.35
C. pop. rif.	72,387	11.01
Rif. com.	44,485	6.77
F. *Verdi*	32,392	4.93
UF	24,030	3.65
Pafvg	18,915	2.88
Laf	10,677	1.62
Fronte Giul.	6,719	1.02
Sos it.	5,211	0.79
Fiamma	3,977	0.60
Total	657,497	100.00
Entitled to Vote	108,4119	
Voters	702,459	64.80
Valid Votes	657,497	93.60
Invalid Votes	44,962	6.40
Blank Ballots	14,806	32.93

Source: Calculated from data provided by Ministero dell'Interno-Direzione centrale per i Servizi elettorali.

Table B8 *Trentino Alto Adige Regional Elections, 22 November 1998*

Lists	Valid Votes	% of Valid Votes
DS	38,108	6.48
Rif. com.	4,127	0.70
PPI (pop)	8,252	1.40
RI	6,187	1.05
Rif. com.-*Verdi*	11,166	1.90
Cen-sin (contr.uff.)	10,518	1.79
Lega nord	27,548	4.68
AN	17,118	2.91
FI-CCD	33,317	5.66
Verdi alternativi	19,696	3.35
Patt	35,266	6.00
SVP	171,829	29.21
Union fur Sud tirol	16,612	2.82
MS tricolore-Unital	6,241	1.06
AN-liberali	29,288	4.98
Die Freiheitlichen	7,533	1.28
Ladins-DPS	11,032	1.88
FI-CCD-Civica	11,352	1.93
Centro-UDA	5,338	0.91
AI-Far	10,730	1.82
Civica Margherita	62,669	10.65
Centro-UPD	29,595	5.03
Trentino domani	14,680	2.50
Total	588,202	100.00
Entitled to Vote	754,071	
Voters	621,859	82.47
Valid Votes	588,202	94.59
Invalid Votes	33,649	5.41
Blank Ballots	10,155	30.18

Source: Calculated from data provided by Ministero dell'Interno-Direzione centrale per i Servizi elettorali.

Table C1 *Ministers in Massimo D'Alema Government (21 October 1998)*

Minister	Party	Ministry	Number of undersecretaries
Massimo D'Alema	DS	Prime Minister	4
Sergio Mattarella	PPI	Deputy Prime Minister	
Laura Balbo	Greens	Equal Opportunities	
Angelo Piazza	SDI	Public Administration	
Katia Bellillo	PDCI	Regional Affairs	
Livia Turco	DS	Family and Social Affairs	
Gian Guido Folloni	UDR	Relations with Parliament	
Amato Giuliano		Institutional Reforms	
Enrico Letta	PPI	Comunitarian Affairs	
Lamberto Dini	RI	Foreign Affairs	4
Rosa Iervolino Russo	PPI	Interior	5
Oliviero Diliberto	PDCI	Justice	4
Vincenzo Visco	DS	Finance	2
Carlo Azeglio Ciampi		Treasury	6
Carlo Scognamiglio Pasini	UDR	Defence	4
Luigi Berlinguer	DS	Education	4
Enrico Micheli	PPI	Public Works and Urban Areas	3
Salvatore Cardinale	UDR	Posts and Telecomunications	˙2
Pier Luigi Bersani	DS	Industry	2
Antonio Bassolino	DS	Labour	4
Piero Fassino	DS	Foreign Trade	1
Rosaria Bindi (Rosy)	PPI	Health	2
Giovanna Melandri	Ds	Culture	2
Edoardo Ronchi (Edo)	Greens	Environment	1
Ortensio Zecchino	PPI	University and Research	2
Paolo De Castro		Agriculture	2
Tiziano Treu	Ri	Transport	2

Source: http://www.palazzochigi.it

Table C2 *Parliamentary Group in 1998*

Chamber of Deputies Parliamentary Group	President	Number of Members	Senate Parliamentary Group	President	No. of Members
Alleanza nazionale	Giuseppe Tatarella	91	Alleanza nazionale	Giulio Maceratini	41
Comunista	Tullio Grimaldi	21	Comunista	Luigi Marino	6
Democratici di sinistra	Fabio Mussi	166	Democratici di sinistra	Cesare Salvi	105
Forza Italia	Beppe Pisanu	110	Forza Italia	Enrico La Loggia	40
Lega nord per l'ind. della pad.	Domenico Comino	55	Lega nord per la Padania indipendente	Luciano Gasperini	24
Pop.democrat.-L'*Ulivo*	Antonello Soro	66	Partito popolare italiano	Leopoldo Elia	31
			CCD	Francesco D'Onofrio	12
UDR	Roberto Manzione	27	UDR	Roberto Napoli	20
			Greens - l'*Ulivo*	Maurizio Pieroni	14
Mixed	Mauro Paissan	75	Mixed	Mario Rigo	25
Rinnovamento italiano	Paolo Manca	19	Rinnovamento italiano and Indipendenti	Ombretta Carulli Fumagalli	7

Source: http://www.parlamento.it

Table C3 *Changes in Parliamentary Groups during XIII Legislature*

Chamber of Deputies	No. of Members at the Beginning of Legislature	No. of Members at 31/12/98
Alleanza nazionale	92	91
CCD	30	–
Dem. Sin.- l'*Ulivo*	172	166
Forza Italia	123	110
Gruppo comunista	–	21
Lega nord-Ind. Pad	59	55
Misto	26	75
Pop. Dem.-*Ulivo*	67	66
Rif. com. – Progr	35	–
Rin. Italiano	26	19
UDR	–	27
Total	630	630

Senate	No. of Members at the Beginning of Legislature	No. of Members at 31/12/98
Alleanza nazionale	43	41
CCD	15	12
Dem. Sin.- l'*Ulivo*	99	105
Forza Italia	49	40
Gruppo comunista	–	6
Lega nord - per la Padania indipendente	27	24
Misto	15	25
Partito Popolare Italiano	31	31
Rifondazione comunista	11	–
Rin. Italiano and Indipendenti	11	7
CDU	10	–
UDR	–	20
Greens - l'*Ulivo*	14	14
Total	325	325

Source: http://www.parlamento.it

Table C4 Deputies and Senators who Changed Parliamentary Group during the XIII Legislature

No. of deputies changing party group	Deputies	Initial parliamentary group	Intermediate stages				Group as at 31/12/98	
			Date	Group	Date	Group	Date	Group
1	Bastianoni	CCD-CDU					3/2/97	RI
1	Pivetti	Lega	17/9/96	Mixed			9/2/98	RI
1	Errigo	FI					14/1/98	RI
1	Li calzi	FI					3/2/97	RI
1	Negri	FI					3/3/98	RI
1	Saraca	FI					17/3/98	RI
11	Mastella and Others (1)	CCD-CDU					9/3/98	UDR
9	Buttiglione and Others (2)	CCD-CDU	3/2/97	Mixed-CDU			9/3/98	UDR
2	Scirea, Danese	FI					9/3/97	UDR
1	Acierno	FI	18/6/97	Mixed			4/3/98	UDR
1	Angeloni,	AN	18/3/97	CCD			9/3/98	UDR
1	Miraglia Del Giudice	AN	3/3/97	CCD			9/3/98	UDR
1	Savelli	FI	24/11/97	Mixed			9/3/98	UDR
2	Bicocchi, Masi	RI	21/12/96	Mixed			9/10/98	UDR
1	Rebuffa	FI					10/11/98	UDR
1	Del Barone	FI	9/9/97	CCD-CDU	9/3/98	UDR	23/10/98	Mixed
1	Parenti	FI	21/4/98	Mixed	15/6/98	Udr	23/10/98	Mixed

N	Name	Group	Date	Group	Date	Group	Date	Final
8	Casini and Others (3)	CCD-CDU					15/4/98	Mixed-CCD
1	Liotta	FI	29/1/98	RI			19/10/98	Mixed-CCD
1	Marinacci	CCD-CDU	3/2/97	Mixed-CDU	11/3/98	UDR	23/10/98	Mixed-CCD
1	Manca	Ri	29/1/97	RI			19/12/98	Mixed-FLDR
2	La Malfa, Sbarbati	Mixed		RI			19/12/98	Mixed-FLDR
1	Orlando	DS	29/1/97				16/12/98	Mixed-LDV
3	Sica, Veltri, Di Capua	DS					16/12/98	Mixed-LDV
1	Cambursano	PD					16/12/98	Mixed-LDV
1	Schietroma	DS					12/5/98	Mixed-SDI
9	Boselli and Others (4)	RI					21/12/96	Mixed
14	Bertinotti and Others (5)	RC					9/10/98	Mixed
1	Saraceni	DS					22/10/98	Mixed
1	Malavenda	RC					15/5/96	Mixed
1	Gambato	*Lega*					30/9/98	Mixed
1	Grugnetti	*Lega*					6/10/98	Mixed
1	Signorini	*Lega*					29/9/98	Mixed
1	Bordon	PD					23/10/98	Mixed
1	Lento	DS					9/10/98	Comunista
1	Savarese	FI					15/5/97	AN
1	Scozzari	Mixed-rete					16/12/98	PD
1	Benvenuto	PD					9/3/98	DS

continued

Table C4 *continued*

No. of deputies changing party group	Deputies	Initial parliamentary group	Date	Group	Date	Group	Date	Group
1	Guarino	RI					19/12/96	PD
1	Mussolini	AN	13/11/96	Mixed			9/12/98	AN
91	TOTAL							

(1) Mastella, Cardinale, Cimadoro, De franciscis, Di nardo, Fabris, Fronzuti, Manzione, Nocera, Pagano, Scoca.

(2) Buttiglione, Carrara, Grillo, Ostilio, Panetta, Sanza, Tassone, Teresio Delfino, Volontà.

(3) Baccini, Casini, D'alia, Follini, Galati, Giovanardi, Lucchese, Peretti.

(4) Boselli, Albertini, Brancati, Ceremigna, Crema, Fumagalli, Leone Delfino, Pozza Tasca, Villetti.

(5) Bertinotti, Boghetta, Bonato, Lenti, Valpiana, Cangemi, De cesaris, Giordano, Malentacchi, Mantovani, Nardini, Pisapia, Rossi, Vendola.

No. of senators changing party group	Senators	Initial parliamentary group	Intermediate stages				Group as at 31/12/98	
			Date	Group	Date	Group	Date	Group
1	Reccia	AN					20/7/98	FI
1	Siliquini	CCD					3/6/97	AN
1	Costa	CDU	25/3/98	UDR	21/4/98	CCD	28/7/98	FI
1	Callegaro	CDU					18/2/98	CCD
1	Campus	FI					20/5/96	AN
1	Cossiga	Mixed					25/3/98	UDR
10	Folloni and Others (1)	CCD	11/3/98	CDU-CDR			25/3/98	UDR
1	Cortelloni	FI	27/2/97	Mixed	6/10/97	RI and ind.	13/10/98	UDR
1	Di Benedetto	FI	1/8/97	Mixed	6/10/97	RI and ind.	13/10/98	UDR
2	Meluzzi and Scognamiglio	FI	10/3/98	Mixed			25/3/98	UDR
1	Martelli	AN	11/3/98	Mixed			25/3/98	UDR
1	Lauria	FI	19/2/98	RI and ind.			18/9/98	UDR
1	Filograna	FI					3/12/98	UDR
1	Misserville	AN					25/3/98	UDR
1	Jacchia	*Lega*	4/5/98	Mixed			23/10/98	UDR
1	Dentamaro	CDU	11/3/98	CDU-CDR	25/3/98	UDR	21/4/98	CCD
1	Zanoletti	CDU			25/3/98	UDR	21/4/98	CCD
1	Ronconi	CDU			25/3/98	UDR	22/10/98	CCD

continued

Table C4 continued

No. of senators changing party group	Senators	Initial parliamentary group	Date	Group	Date	Group	Date	Group
2	Besso and Iuliano	RI	11/2/97	Mixed			3/12/98	DS
2	De Carolis and Duva	Mixed					24/2/98	DS
1	Salvato	RC	14/10/98	Comunista			28/10/98	DS
1	Carcarino	RC	14/10/98	Comunista	5/11/98	Mixed	3/12/98	DS
4	Bruni, D'Urso, Fiorilli, Ossicini	RI	11/2/97	Mixed			6/10/97	RI and ind.
2	Manis and Mundi	FI					6/10/97	RI and ind.
1	Fumagalli Carulli	CCD					6/10/97	RI and ind.
1	Giorgianni	RI	11/2/97	Mixed	6/10/97	RI and ind.	14/10/98	Mixed
1	Mazzuca Poggiolini	RI	11/2/97	Mixed	6/10/97	RI and ind.	18/12/98	Mixed
3	Del turco, Manieri, Marini C.	RI	11/2/97	Mixed			11/2/97	Mixed
1	Milio	FI					27/1/97	Mixed
1	Vertone Grimaldi	FI					22/4/98	Mixed
2	Manfroi and Serena	Lega					9/10/98	Mixed
3	Co', Crippa, Russo Spena	RC					20/10/98	Mixed
1	Porcari	AN	23/12/97	CDU	12/3/98	Mixed (2)	27/10/98	Mixed
54	TOTAL							

(1) Folloni, Cirami, Loiero, Minardo, Napoli, Nava, Cimmino, Firrarello, Gubert, Camo
(2) After: CDU-CDR (25 March 1998) – UDR (23 September 1998).

ABOUT THE EDITORS AND CONTRIBUTORS

David Hine is Fellow at the Christ Church College of Oxford. He has directed many international research groups on the organisation of national executives. Among his publications: *Governing Italy: the Politics of Bargained Pluralism*, Oxford: Oxford University Press–Clarendon Press, 1993; David Hine and Hussein Kassim (editors) *Beyond the Market: the EU and National Social Policy*, London, Routledge, 1998.

Salvatore Vassallo is Lecturer in Political Science at the University of Bologna where he teaches Comparative Public Policy. Among his publications: *Il governo di partito in Italia (1943-1993)*, Bologna: Il Mulino, 1994; (with Sergio Fabbrini), *Il governo. Gli esecutivi delle democrazie contemporanee*, Roma-Bari: Laterza, 1999.

Sergio Fabbrini is Professor of Political Science at the University of Trento.

David Felsen is a doctoral student in Politics at the University of Oxford.

Mark Gilbert is a Lecturer on Italian History and Government, and Political Theory, at the Department of European Studies and Modern Language, University of Bath.

Oreste Massari is Professor of Political Science at the University of Palermo.

Renato Mannheimer is Professor of Methodology of social sciences at the University of Genova.

Simon Parker is a lecturer in Politics at the University of York (U.K.) where he teaches Italian Politics and Comparative European Politics.

Gianfranco Pasquino is Professor of Political Science at the University of Bologna.

Emanuela Poli is an official at the Communication Authority (Autorità per le garanzie nelle comunicazioni).

Giacomo Sani is Professor of Political Science at the University of Pavia.

Marco Tarchi is Professor of Political development at the University of Firenze.

Giacomo Vaciago is Professor of Economic Policy at the 'Cattolica' University of Milano.

Marzia Zannini participates in research activities at the Istituto Cattaneo in Bologna.

INDEX